ACKNOWLEDGEMENT

We wish to thank the following people who
were helpful in the completion of this book:

ANN FEARS CRAWFORD, Ph.D.
Consulting Editor

Stephanie Amster   Don Haughey   John Smithers
Hans Beacham   Frank Puente Harris   Marilyn Stewart, Ph.D.
Bob Burden   Louise Hudgins   Lisa Lundgren Watson
Elaine Burden   Sue Mayer   Iris Williams
Laurie Condrasky   Emma Lea Mayton   Fred Woody
Katherine Reid

Book design by: Jean O. Bollinger
Art Research: Contemporary Art Services, Ltd., New York
ISBN: 0-87443-101-8   Printed in United States of America.

W.S. Benson & Company, Inc., P.O. Box 1866, Austin, Texas 78767.

4 5 6 7 8 9   97 96 95 94

INSIDE
Art

CULTURE • HISTORY • EXPRESSION

BOOK ONE

Rebecca Brooks, Ph.D.
Professor of Art Education
The University of Texas at Austin

W.S. Benson and Company, Inc., Austin, Texas

TABLE OF CONTENTS

Art is everywhere. The creative ideas of artists influence the design of objects and the environment of today's world, from the chair you sit on to the towering sculpture outside the local bank.

Understanding and evaluating means. . .

- being aware of the important role visual art and artists have played in past cultures, and will continue to play in present and future societies.
- learning to value and appreciate the art and artists of cultures different from your own.
- learning how to look at and talk about art. To explore its uses and meanings, and judge its quality and importance.
- learning how to communicate through visual art. Sharing with others personal ideas, feelings, and moods, as well as the joy and satisfaction that comes through creative expression.
- becoming sensitive to the beauty and richness of the natural environment.
- learning to appreciate the diversity of life and the creative inspiration Nature provides.
- learning to value and appreciate your own art, and that of others.
- knowing that visual art is something everyone can share and enjoy.

Part One

UNDERSTANDING AND EVALUATING VISUAL ART

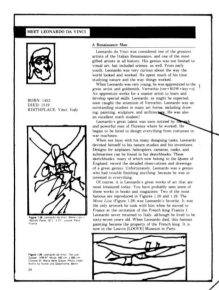

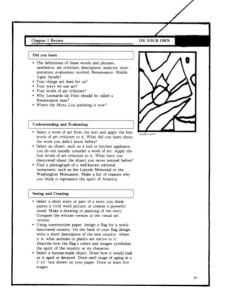

How to Use *Inside Art*

This book has been arranged so that you can use it easily. It is divided into 5 units and 20 chapters.

Units cover big blocks of related information, such as the art elements and design principles. Each unit is made up of chapters.

Chapter Organization

Each chapter begins with WORDWATCH. This is a list of important vocabulary words to watch out for as you read. These words will be shown in bold type and defined for you. They can also be found in the Glossary at the end of the book. Most have a pronunciation guide next to them in brackets.

Many visuals are included throughout each chapter. These are photographs of natural and humanmade environments and artworks created by professional and student artists. You will also find drawings and diagrams to help you see something special or practice something new.

At the end of each chapter you will find two sections called MEET THE ARTIST and ON YOUR OWN.

MEET THE ARTIST presents more information about an artist featured in the chapter. The page will show additional samples of the artist's works.

ON YOUR OWN gives you a chance to review and use some of the information you have read about in each chapter.

Several different kinds of activities let you explore art-making and art-thinking.

Symbols

As you read *Inside Art,* you will come across the following symbols next to a part of the text.

This is a safety warning. When you see this symbol, it means that the art material, tool, or process you are reading about, needs to be used with caution. Even materials that can stain your clothes will have this symbol next to them. When you see the symbol, read the text carefully. You will be instructed how to use the material or tool properly and safely.

When you see this symbol, you should be ready for some thinking! It indicates a question in the text that needs an answer. You can answer these questions in your own mind, since they are asked to make you think about art. Most of the questions have no right or wrong answers! It's your opinion that counts. And remember, everyone has an opinion.

The advertisement may seem silly, but every word is true. The study of visual art *is* exciting. It is filled with amazing places to visit, people to meet, and things to do. As you read this book, look at the artworks, and learn new ways to create art, you will take part in the adventure that is the study of visual art.

INSIDE ART is about **visual art**. The word **visual** means sight. We can define visual art as artworks created to be seen. There are other art forms, such as music, dance, and drama. These are called **performing arts**. To be enjoyed, they must be performed by artists for an audience.

Painting, sculpture, and drawing are all forms of visual art. These are the visual arts most people know. There are other visual art forms, such as ceramics, weaving, photography, and film. The materials used to create these forms are called art **media**. The singular form of media is **medium**. For example, a pencil drawing is an art form created in the medium of pencil.

When someone asks you about art, you probably think about making art, such as creating a drawing or painting. But learning about the visual arts includes more than making art. *INSIDE ART* is not only about ways of making art, but also about ways of thinking about art. Some of these ways of thinking about art may be new to you. You will be asked to look at art in new ways and to describe what you see. You will look for clues and connections in other artworks, make decisions, and express opinions. And, of course, you will have plenty to say, because everyone has an opinion!

The study of the visual arts is like a wonderful adventure story, full of exciting things to do, interesting people to meet, and fascinating mysteries to solve. What makes the study of art so very special is that you can be a part of it. You can make your own art, and say things through images about your feelings and life that no one else can say. The feelings and emotions expressed by artists through the visual arts are unique. No two artists ever really say the same thing, even though they may use the same subjects, ideas, and materials. Each artwork you make is as special and individual as you are. So, let the adventure begin!

Unit I
INTRODUCING VISUAL ART

COMING SOON TO A CLASSROOM NEAR **YOU!**

ART

- Never in the history of humankind has there been such a story!
- Over 25,000 years in the making!
- Come face to face with pharoahs, emperors, and creatures from imagination!
- Explore the desert in search of forgotten temples and gold treasures!
- Gaze from the heights of Macchu Pichu, lost city of the Incas.
- Learn the secrets of frottage, decalcomania!
- Meet artists, soldiers, sculptors.

Opposite Page. Frederick Remington. *The Scout.* 1890. Oil on Canvas, 18½" x 27". Photo courtesy: The Rockwell Museum, Corning, N.Y. Photograph by Nick Williams.

Figure 1.1. Marianne Brandt. *Teapot.* 1924. Nickel, silver and ebony, 7″ high. Collection, Museum of Modern Art, New York. The Phyllis B. Lambert Fund.

top left. **Figure 1.2.** Jan Vermeer. *Woman Holding A Balance.* c. 1664. Oil on canvas, 16¾″ x 15″. National Gallery of Art, Washington, D.C., Widener Collection.
top right. **Figure 1.5.** Theodore Roszak. *Spectre of Kitty Hawk.* 1946-47. Welded and hammered steel brazed with bronze and brass, 40¼″ x 18″ x 15″. Collection, The Museum of Modern Art, New York. Purchase.
middle. **Figure 1.3.** Duncan Phyfe. *Sofa.* Mahogany, H. 29⅝″. The Metropolitan Museum of Art, Gift of C. Ruxton Love, 1959.
bottom. **Figure 1.4.** Frank Lloyd Wright. *Robie House.* Frank Lloyd Wright Foundation.

Chapter 1

WHAT IS ART?

WHAT IS ART?

Look at the pictures on the opposite page (Figures 1.1-1.5). Can you pick out the artworks? How many would you call art? Did your classmates select the same ones?

People have trouble deciding what art is. One reason for this is that visual art can take many different forms—painting, sculpture, or architecture. And we haven't even mentioned photographs, cars, and furniture. Some examples of these are considered to be works of art too.

For some people, beauty is a measure of what art is. If a painting, car, or chair is thought to be beautiful, it may be called a work of art. In fact, the original definition of art was that of an object or an expression that was beautiful or **aesthetic** [es•THET•ik] in purpose. The study of **aesthetics** is the study of what is beautiful and why things are beautiful.

But people like different things. And they certainly do not always agree on what is beautiful. It is, therefore, unlikely that we can ever come up with a definition of art that satisfies everyone. There are as many definitions of art as individuals who look at art and who make art.

Our ideas about what is art are also influenced by both the time and culture in which we live. For example, an object considered a work of art today might not have been called art in Christopher Columbus's time. Many everyday objects, such as cooking utensils used in the past, were not considered works of art by their makers or owners. However, today these simple tools are collected and valued as works of art.

But does everyone have to agree on what art is? One of the interesting things about art is that you can talk about it. As a class, or with your friends or family, you can debate about what art is and the forms it can take. In these discussions, you are playing the role of art critic.

You have probably heard about movie critics. These are individuals hired by magazines, newspapers, or television networks to give opinions about movies. When you listen or read what they have to say about a current film you have seen, you may not always agree with their opinions. Because you have seen the film, however, you have an opinion about it. It is the same with art. Art critics give their opinion about works of art and the artists who create them. Sometimes you will agree with their opinions. Sometimes not. For now, start thinking about why *you* picked certain items and not others from the

> **WORDWATCH**
> aesthetics
> art criticism
> description
> analysis
> interpretation
> evaluation
> symbol
> Renaissance
> Middle Ages
> facade

Figure 1.6. Albert Bierstadt. *Indian Canoe.* c. 1886. Oil on canvas, 21⅝″ x 30″. Archer M. Huntington Art Gallery, The University of Texas at Austin. Gift of C.R. Smith, 1976.

Figure 1.7. Space Launch. Photo Credit: NASA

opposite page. Keep these reasons in mind as you finish reading this chapter.

WHAT DOES ART DO FOR US?

While we may not always be able to agree about what art is, we can identify some of the most important things art does for us as human beings.

Art Communicates

When we create a work of art, we communicate with others. We use a language without words. The language of art is made up of visual images. When you think about it, this is a very good way to communicate. Regardless of what country you come from or what language you speak, you can receive a visual message from art. However, we may not always agree about what the message means.

Although works of art can express feelings and emotions that are common to us all, art can also be very personal. A work of art may speak differently to each of us. This is part of the reason art mystifies some people. They want a work of art, like written or spoken language, to say the same thing to everyone.

Art, however, can communicate some feelings and emotions even better than words. For instance, the beauty of a landscape (Figure 1.6) or the awesome sight of a space launch (Figure 1.7), often touches our emotions in ways that leave us speechless. When we want to share these feelings, we have the language of images to use. Making art allows us to share personal ideas, feelings, and emotions about the events of our life.

We live in a fast-moving world. It is a world presented to us through many different forms of technology, such as television, newspapers, magazines, and movies. These forms of communication use visual images.

All these images communicate. Some inform you about current events, some about safety, and others about what tastes best in your cereal bowl. While we might not consider all of these images to be art, they *do* communicate information about our world. Part of learning about visual art is learning how to use images to communicate.

Art Records The Past

Did you realize that most of what we know about ancient civilizations, forgotten lands, and heroes and heroines of the distant past is through works of art? People have made art for at least 25,000 years.

Figure 1.8

Figure 1.9

Figure 1.8. Roman Emperor Augustus from Primaporta, 2.04 meters. Collection Vatican Museum, Rome. Photo credit: Archiv fur Kunst und Geschichte, Berlin.

Figure 1.9. *Tutankhamon and His Queen-Tomb of Tutankhamun: Throne Detail Showing King with Queen.* Photo credit: Lee Boltin Picture Library, New York.

Figure 1.10. Primitive Dance Mask of Pende People, Africa. Courtesy The Museum of Natural History, Smithsonian Institution.

Figure 1.11. *Pair Statue of Mycerinus and His Queen from Giza.* Dynasty IV, 2599-1571 B.C. Slate Schist, 54" h. Harvard MFA Expedition. Courtesy Museum of Fine Arts, Boston.

When archaeologists dig among the ruins of some mysterious, ancient building, it is usually works of art that tell them who lived there, how they lived, what they ate from, and what they wore. Art is like a time machine with which we can see a Roman emperor, admire the fabulous treasures of an Egyptian pharaoh, or wonder about the magical power of a primitive mask (Figures 1.8-1.10).

Art is a thread that runs through the centuries, through all the cultures of the world, and binds them together. In the artworks of the past, we recognize many of the same feelings, fears, and joys that we still experience today. Look at the work by an unknown Egyptian sculptor (Figure 1.11). It is a royal portrait of a great Egyptian king or **pharaoh** [FAY•row] and his queen.

This stone portrait of a married couple is very different from the portraits we see today. The Egyptian figures seem stiff and formal. But even though 4,000 years separate us from them, can't you tell how the couple felt about each other? Through this work of art, we are somehow able to feel the affection they obviously had for each other. Can you describe how the sculptor has shown this?

Art connects us to the past and to different cultures in other ways as well. Look at the photograph of the Colosseum in Rome (Figure 1.12). This great building was completed over 1,900 years ago. Does its shape look familiar? What modern building does it remind you of? Did the Romans have a Superbowl?

Figure 1.10

Figure 1.11

Figure 1.12. *Colosseum.* Rome, Italy. Dedicated 80 A.D.

Figure 1.13. Leonardo da Vinci. *A Star of Bethlehem.* 1506-8. Red Chalk finished with pen and ink. 19.8 cm. x 16 cm. Windsor Castle Royal Library ©1990 Her Majesty Queen Elizabeth II.

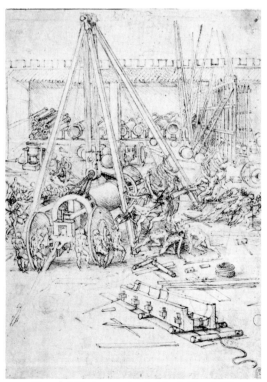

Figure 1.14. Leonardo da Vinci. *The Artillery Park.* c. 1490. Pen and ink on paper. Windsor Castle Royal Library ©1990 Her Majesty Queen Elizabeth II.

While the Colosseum was *not* built for football, it was designed to hold thousands of spectators. The architects of today's stadiums have made few changes in the basic shape of this ancient sports arena. As you read through this book, you will recognize other objects and structures from the past that seem very much like objects and structures of today. The art of the past has a powerful influence on the art and life of the present.

Art Helps Us Understand

Many people think that it is mainly the job of scientists to understand and explain the world. And this is certainly true. Through careful observation and experimentation, scientists discover new information about the physical universe. But artists help us understand also.

The great artist Leonardo Da Vinci [leo • NAR • do dah VEN • che] was also a great scientist. In fact, for Leonardo, science and art were of equal importance in understanding the world. When Leonardo made a drawing like the one pictured (Figure 1.13), he was looking and drawing with the eyes and hands of both an artist *and* a scientist.

Leonardo lived during a time known as the **Renaissance** [REN • i • sauns]. This period spanned the years 1450-1600 A.D. It was a busy and exciting time for science and exploration, as well.

The term *renaissance* means rebirth or reawakening. Surely, no artist of this time is a better representative than Leonardo. His restless mind invented the most fantastic machines—airplanes, helicopters, and submarines (Figure 1.14). During his lifetime, all these machines were destined to exist only in his wonderful drawings. For who in the world of five hundred years ago knew what to do with them!

Leonardo realized that while science allowed him to explain much of the physical workings of his world, art—drawing and painting in particular—helped him *see* in new ways. Art helped him give reality to his imagination. He could also understand and express the emotions and feelings that connected humankind to the world.

When Leonardo drew a landscape or sketched the delicate petals and leaves of a wildflower, he was drawing not only what he saw, but what he *felt*.

When you draw, paint, or sculpt from nature you look at the basic forms that make up the object. You also look at your subject with eyes that seek out details.

When you have to look so carefully at something, you learn new things about it.

Art lets you share some of this new information with others. You also share how you feel about what you are drawing, painting, or sculpting. Artists reveal new meanings.

Figure 1.15. *Great Wall of China.* Photo credit: Rosenthal Art Slides.

Art Maintains Our Humanity

Did you know that human beings are the only creatures on earth that create art? Making art and appreciating art are uniquely human activities.

Imagine for a moment that you are a visitor from space hovering in orbit above the earth. You look down on the oceans and continents for signs of intelligent life. The only clue you see is a long snake-like structure. This structure is one of the architectural marvels of the world. The only human-made object that can be seen from outer space is the Great Wall of China (Figure 1.15).

The creation of art is one of the first signs of the development of civilization. When human beings began to draw animals on the walls and ceilings of caves, and not just hunt them for food, human development had reached an important stage.

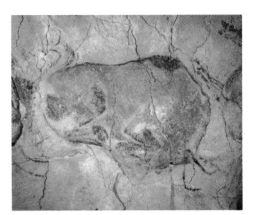

Figure 1.16. *Cave Painting-Bison.* c. 21,000-13,000 B.C. Altamira, Spain. Photo credit: Archiv Fur Kunst and Geschichte, Berlin.

Making drawings of the animals meant that humans placed themselves apart from other animals by creating visual images or **symbols**. A **symbol** is an image that stands in or substitutes for something else. The drawing of a bison (Figure 1.16) on the cave wall became a symbol or substitute for the real animal. The early artists/hunters could place the symbol of the bison where they wanted it. Through art, they believed they could control the bison's movements. They could imagine and draw a successful hunt.

Art gives our imaginations a form and a reality. Creating art not only makes human beings special among all living creatures, but it also gives us power to communicate, invent, and dream.

WAYS WE USE ART

Human beings use visual art for many purposes—for personal expression, for the preservation of cultural heritage, and as symbolic images of political and religious beliefs.

Personal Expression

Perhaps the most important use for visual art is personal expression. Think about the last time you saw, did, or thought something that you wanted to share with your family or friends. If it was something very exciting or scary, you probably told them about it in a breathless voice. You used words designed to help your listeners share the excitement or fear you felt. Words are wonderful tools to communicate a wide range of ideas and emotions.

However, they sometimes fail to create the exact mood or emotional setting that we experienced—the very thing that made the event so thrilling or frightening. As an example, read the short passage below. It is a description of what the police found when they entered the New York apartment of two elderly brothers in March, 1947. The story is true.

The Collyer brothers were both very old. They were recluses, hermits. According to neighbors, only one brother was ever seen, and he was seen only at night. He would comb the city sidewalks and streets for—anything. If he found an old bicycle or sewing machine, he would take it back to the apartment. He took every scrap of paper and junk he could find. He collected for years until the police were finally called.

The police found they couldn't get into the apartment because of the solid wall of decaying newspapers that greeted them at the door. The brothers

16

had dug tunnels through the mountains of paper just to move about. The police found *tons* of garbage. Much of it made into booby traps, so it would collapse on top of intruders!

There was everything. The jawbone of a horse, an entire car (in parts), thousands of cans, acres of paper, and even seventy- five pound concrete blocks. When the apartment was finally cleaned, over 140 tons of trash had to be removed!

This is a word description of a scene. Now, look at the work (Figure 1.17) by Ivan Albright. It is titled *Poor Room*. While it is not a painting of the Collyer brothers' room, its subject suggests the mood of the Collyer brothers' story. But notice how much more vivid the painting conveys the idea of old, aging objects. Of suffocating piles of garbage. Of collecting gone mad.

The very walls of the room seem pressed outward by the junk they contain. Is there anything in this incredible room untouched by the passage of time?

The many forms of visual art let us share impressions and emotions that are beyond words. By changing the color of the sky in a landscape, an artist can tell us not just about the weather, but how it *felt* to be under that sky. A sculptor can dig deep grooves into the surface of a block of stone or let us share the experience of the movement of wind through the folds of fabric. Architects can design buildings that let us *feel* space, and our place in it.

As you learn more about art and artists, you will develop skills that can help you use the forms of visual art to express your personal impressions and feelings about people, places, and things. It is like learning another language. In many ways, the language of visual art can be more accurate than words in telling others how we experience the world.

Figure 1.17. Ivan Albright. *Poor Room — There is No Time . . .* 1941-62. Oil on canvas, 121.9 cm. x 94 cm. Gift of Ivan Albright. 1977.35 Photograph ©1990, The Art Institute of Chicago. All Rights Reserved.

Cultural Heritage

The population of the United States is made up of people from many different cultural backgrounds. You may have heard people say that America's strength lies in the *diversity* of its people. Your parents, grandparents, or great-grandparents might have come to America from another country, or are of another culture. Your family ancestry could have its origins in Europe, South America, Africa, or Asia. All these cultures are rich in traditions and artistic heritage. In many cases, it is works of art

Figure 1.18. Grant Wood. *American Gothic.* 1930. Oil on beaver board, 76 cm. x 63.3 cm. Friends of American Art Collection. 1930.934 Photograph ©1990, The Art Institute of Chicago. All Rights Reserved.

that have preserved the details of a culture, its history, and its identity for generations to come.

Many artists of today use their own cultural heritage as inspiration and subject matter for the artworks they create. This not only preserves their heritage, but shows the pride these artists have in their cultural roots. You may want to explore your own family history for subjects for your artworks. The record of one's family history is called **genealogy** [jee • knee • AL • a • jee]. Examine the following works of art (Figures 1.18 through 1.21). How do you think each artist has shown pride in his or her cultural heritage? In his or her family history?

Politics

In our country, when we hear the word *politics* we tend to think about the President, Congress, the Supreme Court, or some other part of the structure of government. Art does not usually come to mind. But, think for a moment. What do you consider the most famous symbol or object representing the United States? Is it the flag (Figure 1.22)? The Statue of Liberty (Figure 1.23)? The

Figure 1.19. Harrison Begay. *Herding of the Sheep.* Undated. Casein painting, 20″ x 25″. Courtesy of Museum of the American Indian, Heye Foundation, N.Y.

Figure 1.20. Alma Gunter. *Twilight Games.* 1978. Acrylic, 14″ x 18″. Collection of Sally Griffiths.

Figure 1.21. Fernando Botero. *La Guitarista.* 1985. Oil on Canvas 53½″ x 40″. Private Collection. Courtesy Marlborough Gallery.

Capitol in Washington (Figure 1.24)? All have great power and meaning for the citizens of the United States, as well as people around the world. All are examples of art used to symbolize a political unit.

Most governments use some type of visual symbol or art to identify the country and citizens they represent. These symbols can take the form of a national flag, a government building, or a monumental sculpture of a heroic event. These images give identity to a nation and its people. They serve as rallying points in times of national celebration or crisis.

above. **Figure 1.22.** Childe Hassam. *Allies Day.* May 1917. 1917. Oil on canvas, 36¾" x 30¼". National Gallery of Art, Washington, D.C. Gift of Ethelyn McKinney in memory of G.F. McKinney.

left. **Figure 1.23.** *Statue of Liberty.* Statue given to U.S. by France, New York City. Courtesy National Park Service. below. **Figure 1.24.** *Capitol Building.* United States Capitol, Washington, D.C. Photo credit: Rosenthal Art Slides.

Figure 1.25. *Chartres Cathedral.* 1194-1220. Gothic Cathedral. Chartres, France. Photo credit: Giraudon/Art Resource.

Religious Beliefs

Many great works of art have been created to inspire religious feelings and devotion. The great cathedrals of Europe, constructed during a time period known as the **Middle Ages** (approximately from the 5th to the 15th century A.D.), are excellent examples of art used for religious purposes. These magnificent structures, with their soaring stone arches and brilliant stained-glass windows, took generations to build. The purpose behind these massive building projects was to inspire religious devotion in the citizens who daily lived and worked in their shadows. It would have been hard to forget one's religious duties with the towers of Chartres [CHAR•tre] cathedral (Figure 1.25), looming overhead. Or forget to pray with the peaceful faces of saints and angels carved into the stone front or **facade** [fa•SAHD] of the cathedral gazing down upon you.

Of course, cathedrals, are certainly not the only examples of art used for religious purposes. Many other cultures in all time periods have used artworks to inspire devotion to their gods or rulers.

At about the same time the great European cathedrals were being constructed, the Indian civilizations of Mexico were also creating amazing works of art and architecture. These works also had a religious purpose. The Christian religion that inspired the cathedrals was devoted to one God. The artists of the Mayan and Aztec civilizations created artworks to honor many different gods, such as the snake or jaguar (Figure 1.26).

You can probably think of many other uses for visual art. As you look around your school and neighborhood, find examples of visual art that are used to teach, to tell stories, to entertain, or to add beauty to the world. Art is everywhere.

Figure 1.26. Mexico. *Jaguar.* Toltec Culture. Limestone relief carving on ruins at Tula.

The Jaguar was one of many gods worshipped by the Indians of Pre-Columbian Mexico.

LEARNING TO LOOK

The Place:	The main gallery space of a large new art museum.
The Players:	A museum guide and four visitors
Guide:	"Welcome to our new gallery. We have many wonderful works for you to see today. Please, follow me."

Everyone stops in front of a large painting (Figure 1.27).

Guide:	"This work is called *The Tragedy*."
First Visitor:	"Who in the world painted that?"
Second Visitor:	"There isn't much movement, is there?"
Third Visitor:	"What are those people doing? Why is everything blue?"
Fourth Visitor:	"Well, I like it, even though it makes me feel sad."

This little scene is used to introduce you to the four main levels of **art criticism** or evaluation. You probably think that the word *criticism* means that you have to dislike everything you see. This isn't correct. Criticism, in this case, means that you are forming a judgment. You may decide that a work is very good, and you like it. You are making a judgment. This is still art criticism.

Each of the questions or comments made by the visitors in the scene represents one level in the process of looking at and evaluating works of art.

Level One—Description

The first question asked was, "Who painted that?" The answer would be a fact or a piece of information about the painting. This is **description**. Description is the first level of looking at a work of art for the first time. Description includes any facts about the painting. Who painted it? What is it painted on? What do I see? Look again at the painting shown in Figure 1.27. What do you see? Read the credit line (beneath the painting). All information in the credit line is part of the description as well.

Level Two—Analysis

When you **analyze** something you try to decide how it is put together or organized. The second question asked

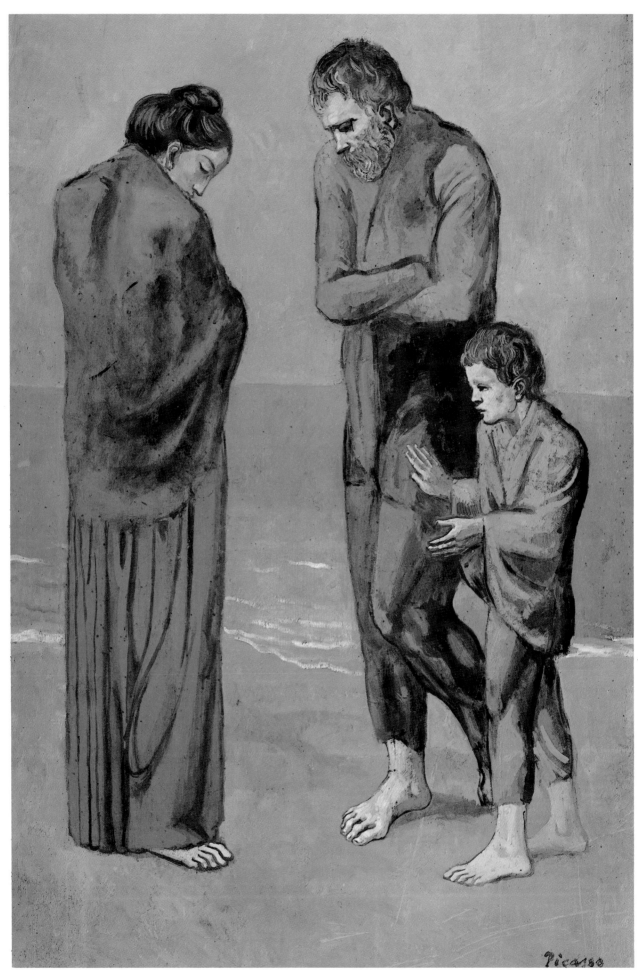

Figure 1.27. Pablo Picasso. *The Tragedy.* 1903. Oil on wood, 41½″ x 27⅛″. National Gallery of Art, Washington, D.C.,

22 Chester Dale Collection.

was, "There isn't much movement, is there?" Movement, as you will discover in the following chapters, is one of the principles of design used by artists to organize works of art. Analysis is the second level of art criticism. It is deciding how the artist has organized the work. In other words, how the art elements and design principles have been used.

Level Three—Interpretation

"What are those people doing? Why is everything so blue?" These are questions of **interpretation**, the third level in looking at art. When you give an interpretation of something, you try to decide what the artist is saying. Why do you think everything is so blue? What *are* those people doing?

Level Four—Evaluation.

Finally, you get to give your opinion! And the fourth visitor did just that. When you evaluate something, you judge it. You decide whether it seems good or bad to you. This step just needs your opinion to be complete. Do you like the painting shown in Figure 1.27? The catch is that you must always have a good reason for your opinion. This means that you have taken the time to look at a work carefully. It also means you have completed the other three levels before making your judgment. In this way, you should be able to discuss and defend your judgment with others who may not share your opinion.

As you continue reading about and looking at the art-works in this book, you will gain more experience in using the four levels of art criticism. Congratulations! You have just taken your first steps toward becoming an authentic art critic!

Leonardo da Vinci. *Self Portrait.* c. 1512-15. Red Chalk. Windsor Castle Royal Library ©1990 Her Majesty Queen Elizabeth II.

BORN: 1452
DIED: 1519
BIRTHPLACE: Vinci, Italy

Figure 1.28. Leonardo da Vinci. *Mona Lisa.* c. 1503-05. Panel, 30¼″ x 21″. Louvre, Paris, France.

A Renaissance Man

Leonardo da Vinci was considered one of the greatest artists of the Italian Renaissance, and one of the most gifted artists in all history. His genius was not limited to visual art, but included science, as well. From early youth, Leonardo was very curious about the way the world looked and worked. He spent much of his time studying nature and the way things worked.

When Leonardo was very young, he was apprenticed to the great artist and goldsmith, Verrocchio [ver • ROW • key • o] An apprentice works for a master artist to learn and develop special skills. Leonardo, as might be expected, soon caught the attention of Verrocchio. Leonardo was an outstanding student in many art forms, including drawing, painting, sculpture, and architecture. He was also an excellent math student!

Leonardo's great talent was soon noticed by the rich and powerful men of Florence where he worked. He began to be hired to design everything from costumes to war machines.

When not busy with his many designing tasks, Leonardo devoted himself to his nature studies and his inventions. Designs for airplanes, helicopters, cameras, tanks, and submarines can be found in his sketchbooks. These sketchbooks, many of which now belong to the Queen of England, record the detailed observations and drawings of a great genius. Unfortunately, Leonardo was a genius who had trouble finishing anything, because he was interested in everything.

Of course, it is Leonardo's great works of art that are most treasured today. You have probably seen some of these works in books and magazines. Two of the most famous are reproduced in Figures 1.28 and 1.29. The *Mona Lisa* (Figure 1.28) was Leonardo's favorite. It was the only artwork he took with him when he moved to France at the invitation of the French king Francis I. Leonardo never returned to Italy, although he lived to be sixty-seven years old. When Leonardo died, this famous painting became the property of the French king. It is now in the Louvre [LOOVE] Museum in Paris.

Figure 1.29. Leonardo da Vinci. *The Last Supper.* 1495-97. Mural, 460 cm. x 880 cm. Cloister St. Maria delle Grazie. Photo credit: Archiv fur Kunst und Geschichte, Berlin.

Did you learn

- The definitions of these words and phrases: aesthetics; art criticism; description; analysis; interpretation; evaluation; symbol; Renaissance; Middle Ages; facade?
- Four things art does for us?
- Four ways we use art?
- Four levels of art criticism?
- Why Leonardo da Vinci should be called a Renaissance man?
- Where the *Mona Lisa* painting is now?

Student work.

Understanding and Evaluating

- Select a work of art from the text and apply the four levels of art criticism to it. What did you learn about the work you didn't know before?
- Select an object, such as a tool or kitchen appliance, you do not usually consider a work of art. Apply the four levels of art criticism to it. What have you discovered about the object you never noticed before?
- Find a photograph of a well-known national monument, such as the Lincoln Memorial or the Washington Monument. Make a list of reasons why you think it represents the spirit of America.

Seeing and Creating

- Select a short story or part of a story you think paints a vivid word picture, or creates a powerful mood. Make a drawing or painting of the story. Compare the written version to the visual art version.
- Using construction paper, design a flag for a newly discovered country. On the back of your flag design, write a short description of the new country, where it is, what animals or plants are native to it. Describe how the flag's colors and images symbolize the spirit of the country or its character.
- Select a human-made object. Draw how it would look as it aged or decayed. Draw each stage of aging in a 3″x5″ box drawn on your paper. Draw at least five stages.

Georges Braque. *Still Life: Le Jour.* 1929. Oil on canvas, 45¼″ x 57¾″. National Gallery of Art, Washington, D.C., Chester Dale Collection.

Like other subjects you learn about, works of art are made up of parts that can be named and described. These parts are called the **elements of art**. The elements of art are line, color, value, shape, form, space, and texture. To help you remember the elements let's use something called a **mnemonic** [ne • MON • ik] (the first M is silent). Mnemonics are ways to assist memory. Using the first letter of the words you need to remember, you make up a silly sentence that is easy to recall. How about this for the art elements: Laziness Causes Very Sharp Folk Serious Trouble? You can make up mnemonics for word lists you need to remember in other classes.

Artists also need to know ways of arranging the art elements to create works of art that express a wide range of emotions, moods, and ideas. These ways of arrangement are called the **principles of design**. The principles of design are unity, balance, variety, repetition, emphasis, movement, and proportion. Here is a mnemonic that might help you remember them: Unless Bats Vacate Rooms, Every Man Pauses.

In the following chapters you will learn to recognize the art elements and principles of design in the world around you, as well as in the work of many artists. Seeing how different artists use the art elements and principles of design will help you learn to use them to express your own ideas and feelings in some form of visual art.

Unit II

THE ELEMENTS OF ART

Chapter 2
LINE

WORDWATCH
implied lines
natural environment
constellation
horizontal lines
parallel lines
vertical lines
diagonal lines

Look at the photographs on this page. Can you find lines in any of them? Take a piece of paper and write your name three or four times. Look carefully at your signature. What kind of lines did you use? Can you describe them? Is there a way to write your name without using lines?

Lines are everywhere. We see and use them all the time without thinking very much about them. But what is a line? In math a **line** is sometimes described as a moving point. As artists we are more concerned with the trail a line leaves behind when it moves! That trail can be rough, smooth, jagged, or curvy. It can be made with crayon, pencil, paint, or clay. It can be seen in marble statues and in the rows of windows in buildings. However, the trail left by the moving point can never be wider than the trail is long, or we have a shape. You will learn more about shapes later. What else do we know about lines in art?

- Lines can express feelings and moods.
- Lines can enclose space.
- Lines can show direction.
- Lines can show movement.
- Lines can make shapes.
- Lines can create texture.
- Lines can make value.

IMPLIED LINES: NOW YOU SEE THEM; NOW YOU DON'T

Look again at the photographs on this page. They are all taken from the **natural environment** [en • VI • ran • ment]. The natural environment includes all scenes or objects not human-made. Trees, rocks, mountains, and flowers are all part of the natural environment. The lines you found in the photograph are different from the lines you used to write your name. Many of the marks in the photographs that you may have identified as lines are really cracks, creases, or rows of dots that look like lines. These are **implied lines**. Implied lines are suggested by a particular arrangement of objects, shadows, or textures. Implied lines are created by human beings who always want to make sense of their surroundings by creating designs, patterns, and pictures. For example, the **constellations** [con • stel • A • shuns] create implied lines.

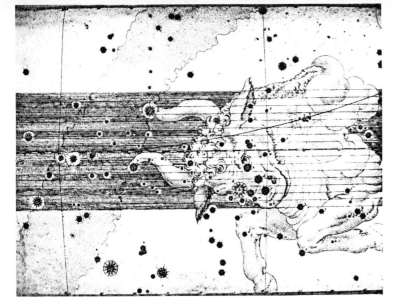

Figure 2.1. *Star Constellation.* Smithsonian Libraries, Rare Book Collection. The ancient Greeks saw the stars as points, that when connected or completed with implied lines, created the outline of Greek heroes. This illustration of the constellations came from an 18th-century book of etchings.

On a clear night you can look up and see patterns created by the stars. The ancient Greeks did the same thing, but gave them names we all now use. You may know some of these names: Orion [o • RI • on]; Cassiopeia [cas • e • o • PAY • ah]; and Pegasus [PAY • gah • sus]. The human eye connects the dots of the stars, creating the outlines of figures. These are the constellations. The outlines of the figures are made with implied lines (Figure 2.1).

? Look at the photographs once again. Can you pick out implied lines? Are there any "real" lines at all? Look around your classroom. Are there any implied lines? Is the classroom a natural environment? If you find implied lines, see if you can describe how they are created. Are the edges of objects implied lines?

VARIETIES OF LINE

Not only are lines everywhere, but they come in a wide assortment: fat, thin, wide, rough, bumpy, curved, jagged, zigzag, or wiggly. Lines also have direction: vertical, horizontal, or diagonal.

Vertical lines (Figure 2.2) stand upright like you do. **Horizontal lines** (Figure 2.3) lie down. They are said to be **parallel** to the horizon. **Parallel lines** (Figure 2.4) are an equal distance from each other along their entire length. **Diagonal lines** (Figure 2.5) can slant in any direction that is not vertical or horizontal.

SEEING AND UNDERSTANDING LINES

With all the different kinds and uses of line, it is easy to see why line is an important element to artists. In the following section, we will explore some of the many ways artists create with line. Pay close attention to each example. They will help you learn to use line in your own artworks.

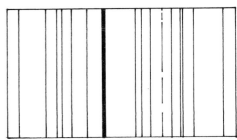

Figure 2.2. Vertical lines.

Figure 2.3. Horizontal lines.

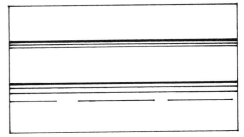

Figure 2.4. Parallel lines.

Figure 2.5. Diagonal lines.

Lines Can Express Feelings and Moods

Look at the work by Edvard Munch [ED • vard MOOCK] titled *The Shriek* (Figure 2.6). This work was created by a printing process called **lithography** [lith • OG • rah • fi] The prints are called **lithographs** [lith • o • GRAFS]. To create a lithograph, an artist draws an image on a large smooth stone with a special crayon. You can see how much Munch's print looks like a drawing. But look at the way Munch has used line.

The artist has created a special, powerful mood that each of us can experience. This has been accomplished not with words, but with line. Munch has used repeating, wavy lines everywhere. The imagined sound seems to make the very air vibrate. Since Munch, the visual artist, could not let us actually *hear* the sound of the scream, he did something better. He showed us, with line, how it *feels* to suddenly hear a scream. Have you ever been suddenly startled by the sound of a scream? How did you feel? Doesn't a loud noise or a scream seem to change everything around you for a few seconds?

Lines Can Enclose Space

Figure 2.7, *Landscape with a Solitary Traveler*, is a good example of how an artist can enclose and create the illusion of space with line. Yosa Buson, the Japanese artist who created this beautiful drawing, used many types of lines to show us different natural objects and textures in the landscape. Bold, heavy lines are used for close objects, like the tree trunks and the cracks in the rocks. In the distance, the top edge of the mountains is like a lid on a container, enclosing the space between. Notice the kinds of lines used in the middle of the drawing. They are very delicate and light. They give us a feeling of the space between the rocks and trees at the bottom of the drawing and the mountains at the top. They also create a feeling of atmosphere. Can you see the fog lying at the base of the mountains?

Lines Can Show Direction and Movement

Thomas Hart Benton, an American artist of the 1930s, was famous for his large wall paintings or **murals**. Like Edvard Munch, Benton also made lithographs. Figure 2.8, titled *Going West*, is a lithograph made by Benton. In this print he uses both real and implied lines to show us direction and movement.

The edge of the train, and most of the lines within it, bend forward. They seem to strain toward the left side of

Figure 2.6. Edvard Munch. *The Shriek.* 1895. Lithograph, 13 15/16″ x 10″. Collection, The Museum of Modern Art, New York. Matthew T. Mellon Fund. (By filling the landscape with repeated lines, the artist has created the visual sound of a scream).

Figure 2.7. Yosa Buson. *Landscape with a Solitary Traveler.* Painted about 1780. Hanging Scroll, ink and light color silk, 40″ x 14⅜″. Kimbell Art Museum, Ft. Worth, Texas.

the print. Imagine for a moment that you have a map of the United States lying on the desk in front of you. Which direction would be west on the map? Is Benton's rushing train going the right way? Look for other lines that show direction. What about the telegraph poles? Are they vertical, horizontal, or diagonal?

The telegraph poles seem to lean back, as the train speeds forward. This is a very clever use of line direction. It makes the forward motion of the train even more obvious. Can't you almost feel the rush of the wind against your face as the engine flies by?

When you think about line you probably think about drawing. This is natural, since you usually draw by making lines with a pencil, pen, crayon, or some other drawing tool. As you continue to learn about art, you will realize that drawings depend on other art elements as well. You will also learn that line as an art element is also used by painters, sculptors, and the makers of clay pots.

Figure 2.9 is a photograph of a famous ancient Greek sculpture known as *The Nike of Samothrace* [NI • key of SAM • o • thrace]. This figure, the Greek goddess of victory, was made by an unknown sculptor. It was created at a time in Greek history when artists were interested in showing their skill in creating realistic movement and action in figures. The sculptor of the *Nike* used implied lines (the edges and folds of the fabric) to make us feel the forward movement of the figure. It is as if the figure were walking into a breeze that whips the cloth around her feet. Look at the outstretched wings. It is easy to imagine that the figure is about to flap her wings and sail over our heads. The edges of the feathers (implied lines) direct our eyes forward. They seem to push the goddess against the wind.

Figure 2.9. Nike of Samothrace
Photo credit: Rosenthal Art Slides. The edges of flowing draperies and outspread feathers give movement to this masterpiece.

Figure 2.8. Thomas Hart Benton. *Going West.* 1934. Lithograph, 12 5/16″ x 23 3/8″. Courtesy Amon Carter Museum, Fort Worth, Texas.

Figure 2.10. Joan Miro. *People as Night Guided by the Phosphorescent Traces of Snails.* 1940. Gouache on paper, 14¾" x 17¾" Philadelphia Museum of Art: Louis E. Stern Collection.

Figure 2.11. *Japanese Storage Vessel.* c. 2,000 B.C. Middle Jomon Period, Japan. 61 cm. h. earthenware. Cleveland Museum of Art. John L. Severance Fund 84.68.

Lines Can Make Shapes

Spanish artist Joan Miró [wan me • ROW] is well known for his child-like, humorous paintings. *People At Night Guided By Snails* (Figure 2.10) is a good example of Miró's sense of fun and his skillful use of line to create interesting shapes.

Have you ever taken a pencil or crayon and scribbled lines over a sheet of paper, then filled in the enclosed areas with color? You get a wide variety of shape sizes and **profiles**. A profile is the edge of an object. Miró has done something similar in the painting shown in Figure 2.10. He has created shapes by enclosing spaces or areas of the background with line. He then filled some of the shapes with color.

But Miró has done something else. He has marked off areas of the background with lines also. Some areas are closed; some open. Even with color to fill them in, these areas circled by lines have importance. They add interest to the flat background. They also add space. They seem to carve up the background into chunks that place themselves in, around, and behind the solid-colored shapes.

Lines Can Create Texture

Makers of clay pottery also make use of line. Implied lines (edges and profiles) play an important part in shaping clay containers. Implied line is also used to create texture and surface decoration. Texture, you may recall, is one of the art elements. It means the surface quality or characteristic of an area. Sandpaper is rough to the touch; glass is smooth. Both have texture. You will learn more about how artists use texture later.

From earliest times, clay containers have been made for use as eating utensils and storage vessels. These ancient containers can be as simple and plain as a flattened clay circle, or as elaborate and textured as the one shown in Figure 2.11. This storage pot was made in Japan over 4,000 years ago. The unknown artist has made full use of line to create texture on the surface of the container.

Notice how the surface of the container appears to move with the swirling lines that cover it. Not content with texturing the surface, the artist has set the top of the pot in motion by shaping the line of the edge into dips, waves, and points. Because the artist knew how to use line to create texture, this container is much more interesting.

? What do you think was stored in such a fancy pot? The line texture on the surface looks familiar. Does it provide a clue to the contents?

Lines Can Create Value

Later you will read about the art element, value. Value in art doesn't always refer to the price of an artwork. Value can also refer to the amount or degree of lightness or darkness on a surface or in a color. Value plays an important part in visual art. Without value, artists would have few ways to show us how things look in sunlight or shadow. In fact, in drawing and painting, it is difficult to show how objects are shaped without value.

There are many ways to create value in painting and drawing. Some you probably already know. For example, when you smear charcoal or soft-pencil lead over paper you create "shading," or value. But you can also create value with line.

Artist John Biggers's drawing, *The Cradle* (Figure 2.12), is an excellent example of value created with line. The four figures in the drawing seem rounded and three-dimensional. Biggers has achieved this effect by creating shadowed areas and areas of light. Instead of smearing his lithographic crayon to create the shadows, he has built the shadows with hundreds of lines. The more lines he piles on top, the darker the shadow. Notice how, in some places, the lines change directions. Look at the arms of the mother. How have the value lines been drawn? Are they straight or curved? Why did Biggers use so many curved lines?

Creating value by drawing lines close together in one direction, then drawing them over other lines in a different direction is called crosshatching. As you continue to look at the artworks reproduced in this text, and those shown by your teacher, you will recognize many other examples of crosshatching. Later you will have an opportunity to try crosshatching for yourself.

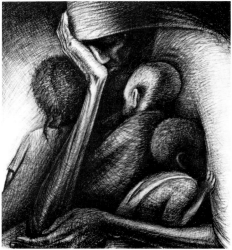

Figure 2.12. John T. Biggers. *The Cradle.* 1950. Charcoal on paper, 22⅜″ x 21½″. The Museum of Fine Arts, Houston. 25th Annual Houston Artists Exhibition, Museum Purchase Prize, 1950.

Self portrait. 1973. Lithograph, 30 cm. x 24 cm. National Portrait Gallery, Smithsonian Institution.

BORN: 1889
DIED: 1975
BIRTHPLACE: Neosho, Missouri

Artist of the American Scene

One of the first jobs Thomas Hart Benton ever had was as a cartoonist for a Missouri newspaper. This job lasted until he began his art studies in Chicago and Paris, France.

Thomas Hart Benton was a tough, stubborn individualist, who frequently got into arguments. His practical nature and no-nonsense approach to life were also carried into his study of art. When he arrived in Paris in 1908, the art movement known as Cubism was getting underway. Cubist painters simplified or reduced objects to their basic, geometric shapes. There was little interest in realism. For a while Benton tried his hand at this new style of art, but soon realized it wasn't for him. He returned home to America.

For several years he traveled the country roads of America. He drew and painted the rural landscape and the strong energetic people who worked the land, built the railroads, and cut the timber. After 1929, he and other artists of the American scene, like Grant Wood and John Curry, became very popular. They were hired to paint not only individual paintings, but also large wall paintings or murals. They began to call themselves Regionalist painters. They painted the common people working at common jobs. They wanted to show the dignity and importance of the ordinary individual and the work that made America great.

In many of his murals, Benton made fun of the flashy city life he hated. Instead, he idealized the small-town, rural life he found in the American South and Midwest. Even when he painted subjects taken from Greek mythology or the Bible, he used ordinary American figures. He often exaggerated the shape and proportion of his figures to give them dramatic power. This style of painting has been compared to cartooning. Not too difficult to imagine when one remembers Benton's first art job!

Figure 2.13. Thomas Hart Benton. *Boom Town.* 1927-28. Oil on canvas, 46⅛″ x 54¼″. Memorial Art Gallery of the University of Rochester, Marion S. Gould Fund.

Did you learn

- The definitions of these words and phrases: implied lines; natural environment; constellation; horizontal lines; parallel lines; vertical lines; diagonal lines?
- Seven ways line can be used for art?
- Where to find implied lines on the *Nike of Samothrace*?
- How to make value with lines? What is the word for this technique?
- The name of the art movement Thomas Hart Benton founded?
- Two ways movement is created in *Boom Town* (Figure 2.13)?

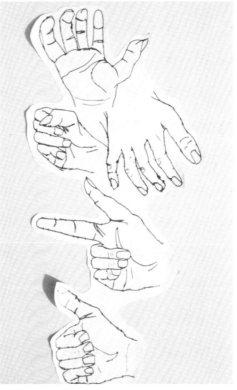

Student work.

Understanding and Evaluating

- Find five examples of implied lines in your classroom. How are these lines created?
- Compare the kinds of lines used in Figure 2.7 with those in Figure 2.8. Which shows the most movement?
- If you were going to redesign the clay pot pictured in Figure 2.11 to hold live fish, how would you change it? Does the new design "symbolize" or represent what it contains?

Seeing and Creating

- Fill a page with as many different kinds of lines as you can make with a pencil. Each line must be different from all the others. Tape a pencil on either side of a small box or eraser. Make sure the points are even. What kind of lines can you make now?
- Select a natural object such as a shell, pine cone, or tree limb. Make a contour-line drawing of the object. Once you begin, do not lift your pencil.
- Select a small section of your classroom or landscape. Draw it in contour line only.
- Try your hand at crosshatching to create value. Use a crayon or soft pencil. Select a simple human-made object for your drawing.
- Draw your hand in blind contour (don't look at your paper) from four different positions. Use four different colors of crayon, one for each view. Let each new drawing overlap the others.

Have you ever felt blue? Green with envy? Purple with rage? Funny, how we often use colors to describe feelings. Like line, color is taken for granted by most of us. But, can you imagine the world without color? Look at the photograph on the opposite page. What a boring place the world would be without color.

The study of color is interesting. Recent scientific studies have shown that color has more influence on the way we feel than previously thought. Did you know:

- Blue has a calming effect on people?
- Blue is the favorite color of most people in the United States?
- Red can actually make your heart beat faster, whether you like or not?
- Red is the first color babies are attracted to?
- Yellow is the color that the eye recognizes the quickest?
- Children cry more in yellow rooms?

Chapter 3
COLOR AND VALUE

WHAT IS COLOR?

Perhaps in one of your science classes you were allowed to experiment with a **prism**. This is a wedge of glass that separates light into individual colors. These colors are part of the **spectrum**: red, orange, yellow, green, blue, indigo and violet.

The rainbow is the largest and most famous prism in the world. The colors of the rainbow are created by light shining through the glass-like water drops floating in the air after a rain.

Light helps us see colors. Try an experiment. In the late evening, just before dark, turn off all the lights in your room. The colors of all the objects seem washed out, dull. The brilliance of the colors has disappeared. Human beings need light to see color. Each color you see is reflected back to your eyes. All the other colors in the light are absorbed. Color is an optical effect.

CHARACTERISTICS OF COLOR

All colors share certain properties or characteristics. By using these characteristics, we can describe and discuss color. We can begin to make judgments about the use of color in everything from a new sweater to a famous painting.

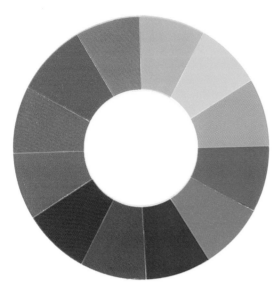

Figure 3.1. Color Wheel. A color wheel is one way of showing the relationship between hues or colors.

The first property of color is **hue**. Hue is simply the name of a color: red, blue, or yellow. These three colors are called **primary** colors. These are colors that cannot be made by mixing other colors or hues. When you *do* mix any of the primary colors together you get **secondary** colors: orange, green, or violet. The way all these colors work together can be shown on a **color wheel** like the one shown in Figure 3.1.

As you look at the color wheel, notice that there are colors between the primary and secondary colors. These are known as **intermediate** [in • ter • MEED • i • ate] colors. They are made by mixing a primary color with a secondary color. If you mix blue with violet, you create blue-violet.

Another characteristic of color is **value**. Remember that we mentioned value when we discussed line. Value is the amount of lightness or darkness in an area or in a color.

How often have you heard someone say, "I love pink. It is such a beautiful shade of red."? This statement isn't really correct. But, most people use the word **shade** to indicate any variation in a hue. Pink is made by mixing red with white. When you mix white with a hue, the color is called a **tint**. When black is mixed with a hue, the color is a **shade**. (Figure 3.2).

Look again at the color wheel. Which color would you select as having the highest value or the lightest value? Which has the darkest? If you picked yellow for the lightest and violet for the darkest, you understand **color value**.

But what about black and white? Are these colors? Black, white, and gray are called **neutral colors**. They are very useful in changing other colors. The value of all hues can be altered by adding black or white. Adding white raises or lightens the value of a hue; black lowers or darkens the value.

The final characteristic of color is **intensity**. Intensity is sometimes confused with value. If you keep in mind two words—brightness and dullness—you can understand intensity.

Look around the classroom. There are probably several students wearing clothing of the same hue: red, blue, or yellow. Compare all the reds; all the blues; all the yellows. Some of the blues seem brighter, or more intense, than some of the other blues. These blues are of high intensity. These hues have very little of other colors mixed with them. They are called pure hues. High intensity or pure hues can be altered or made duller by adding black or another hue. Mixing **color complements** (colors opposite each other on the color wheel) dulls the intensity of a color.

Figure 3.2. Color range showing tints and shades of one color. Tints are made by mixing white with a color. Shades are made by mixing black with a color.

ORGANIZING COLOR

In addition to describing the properties or characteristics of color, we can organize and categorize color. Let's look at some ways to organize color.

We can begin with a division you may know: **warm** and **cool**. Colors such as red, yellow, and orange are known as warm colors. Blue, green, and violet are cool. The reason for this division is easy to understand. Warm colors remind us of things that are warm—the sun or fire. Cool colors, on the other hand, suggest coolness: water, sky, grass. Skillful artists know how to use these color divisions to make us see and feel in particular ways.

It is fairly easy to understand color divisions when we look at individual hues. But, colors have a tricky way of not always behaving in a way we expect. For example, a color can change from cool to warm depending on where we put it. If we put a dark red on a bright yellow background, the red seems cool in comparison with the yellow (Figure 3.3).

Figure 3.3. Color example of a red square on yellow. Warm colors can appear cool when used next to other warm colors.

COLOR SCHEMES

Through experimentation over many years, artists have discovered that some colors go well together. Artists have also discovered that by arranging certain colors together they can create moods and feelings. Because of the power of color on our emotions, these moods and feelings can be created even without subject matter. These color arrangement systems are called **color schemes**. We will look at three: **monochromatic**, **analogous**, and **complementary**.

Monochromatic

The word **monochromatic** [mono • cro • MAT • ic] means "one color." This is a very good description of how a monochromatic color scheme is made. Using one hue or color, the artist creates different values and intensities by mixing the color with varying amounts of black or white. While a monochromatic color scheme may not be very exciting, it does create a feeling of unity. All parts of the artwork seem to belong together. The challenge of using a monochromatic color scheme is seeing how many variations in value and intensity you can create with one color. You might be surprised at the range of tints and shades possible. (Figure 3.4)

Figure 3.4. Color example showing a monochromatic color scheme. A monochromatic color is created by mixing a hue or color with black and white to create tints and shades.

Figure 3.5. Color example showing analogous color scheme. An analogous color scheme is created from a related group of colors on the color wheel.

Figure 3.6. Color example showing a complementary color scheme. A complementary color scheme can be used to express feelings or mood.

Analogous

An **analogous** [a•NAL•a•gus] color scheme makes use of a family of colors. Look back at the color wheel. Analogous colors are next to each other on the color wheel. You might say they live in the same neighborhood on the color wheel. The neighborhood is located between any two primary colors. (Figure 3.5). The reason for this rule is that analogous colors must have one hue in common. For example, look at yellow, yellow-green, green, blue-green, and blue. All the colors bounded by the two primaries—yellow and blue—have yellow in common.

An analogous color scheme can create a feeling of unity similar to the monochromatic color scheme. However, an analogous color scheme allows for more variety and more interest.

When you go home, open the door of your closet and look at your clothes. They will likely be within an analogous color arrangement. We, as individual personalities, tend to like a limited range of colors for our dress and environment. When you choose clothes to wear, see if you don't select items that "go together" or "match." These matches are usually analogous.

Complementary

Have you ever heard the phrase "opposites attract"? Well, that is certainly true of **complementary colors**.

The word *complement*, like *monochromatic*, tells you a good deal about the kind of color arrangement it describes. Complements are items that go together or help each other. Complementary colors look good together. They "assist" each other when placed side by side (Figure 3.6).

Look once again at the color wheel. Complementary colors are those opposite each other: red-green; blue-orange; violet-yellow. Complementary colors also share some strange characteristics.

When placed side by side, complementary colors intensify the brilliance of each other. It is hardly an accident that red and green were chosen for a holiday celebration. It would be hard to select two other colors that look so well together, unless it would be two other complements.

You would think that since complements go together so well, mixing them would create a spectacular hue. Not true! Complementary colors, when mixed together, cancel each other. In other words, the intensity of each is dulled to a muddy gray-brown. What a mess! But you have just learned how to make gray-brown. And the gray-brown color made by mixing complements is usually much more interesting than the plain brown that comes from the jar, bottle, or tube you buy.

Artworks which use complementary color schemes can be very exciting. Feelings of tension and competition can be created with these color schemes.

Keep in mind that color schemes are *guidelines* for using color, not unbreakable rules. As you will see in the works to follow, it is rare for an artist to use a color scheme in its pure form. Artists have freedom to make changes, and to create new color arrangements. As you continue to learn about art, you will be able to identify easily the dominant or main color scheme in an artwork. Even when an artist has altered it to achieve a new mood, or to magnify a feeling.

SEEING AND UNDERSTANDING COLOR

The following artists have one thing in common. Color is as important to the meaning of their artworks as any scene, object, or design they have chosen. In fact, you could say that color, and the way it makes the viewer feel, *is* the subject of their work.

Andre Derain [AHN • drey day • RAN] was a French painter who worked in the early part of the 20th century. He was a member of a group of artists who took the name **Fauve** [FOV] to identify their style of painting. In French the word "fauve" means "wild beast." An odd name for a group of painters! But look at the work pictured in Figure 3.7, titled *The Turning Road*.

When the critics saw this work with its blast of glowing colors and cartoon-like landscape, they decided that such a strange way of painting could only have been created by a "wild beast."

The Turning Road may not seem as unusual to us today as it did in 1906 when it was painted. At that time, many artists were still painting in a very realistic way. They used soft, realistic colors in the landscapes they painted. Derain and the other Fauves must have seemed wild and crazy.

Let's look at *The Turning Road* and see how color was used. It is fairly easy to see that the subject of the painting is a landscape. There are trees, a road, houses, and people going about their business. But look at those colors! Derain has used warm colors that seem on fire—hot reds, yellows, and oranges. These colors are all of very high values and intensities. Even the dark, cooler

Figure 3.7. Andre Derain. *The Turning Road, L'Estaque.* 1906. Oil on canvas, 51″ x 76¾″. The Museum of Fine Arts, Houston, The John A. and Audrey Jones Beck Collection.

colors are not dull. They make the warm colors appear warmer by contrast.

It is easy to see that Derain has used a complementary color scheme. But it is not a simple one. More than one pair of complementary colors has been used. Can you pick them out?

With complementary color schemes, it is possible to create feelings of tension. These opposite colors also create a mood of excitement and energy.

What an interesting, lively place Derain shows us. Look how quickly the people seem to move. Painted in such explosive colors, even the trees seem to bend and sway.

Though Derain painted his landscape in some very wild colors, you can still recognize trees, hills, and other landscape objects. The following three painters really do use color as the subject of their work. These paintings are **abstract** [AB • stract] or **non-objective**. Remember, this means that they have not used any objects we can recognize and name, such as a chair, a tree, or a dog.

As you continue studying this book and working in your art class, you are going to learn more about how and why artists create abstract or non-objective artworks. You may be puzzled by it now. Many people are. They sometimes say things like, "A two-year-old child could paint like that." or "It doesn't mean anything." You may agree, but by looking at examples of abstract works and learning about artists who created them, you will develop an understanding of non-objective artworks. You must, however, keep an open mind! Be willing to give the new and different a chance. Now, let's look at some non-objective artworks in which color is the subject.

Figure 3.8, *Vega-Nor*, was painted by Victor Vasarely [vas • a • REL • ee]. This kind of painting is known as **Op art**. "Op" is short for **optical**. Optical means having to do with the eyes or vision. Op art is art that tries to fool the eye. It tries to make the viewer see something that may or may not be true. Victor Vasarely was a master of optical art.

In Figure 3.8 Vasarely is fooling our eyes into seeing an area in the flat-painted surface area swell up into a rounded shape. The flat, two-dimensional surface of the painting has turned into a three-dimensional object. How has he done this?

First, he has made use of line. See how he has changed not only the width of the lines, but their direction as well. The lines around the ball-like shape seem to be flat.

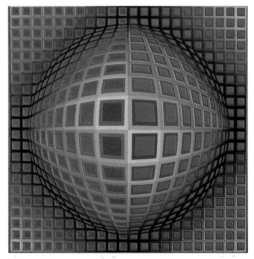

Figure 3.8. Victor Vasarely. *Vega-Nor.* 1969. Oil on canvas, 78¾" x 78¾". Albright-Knox Art Gallery, Buffalo, New York. Gift of Seymour H. Knox, 1969. Vasarely creates an eye-fooling example of Op art.

They form a grid like a chessboard. But, as the lines approach the ball they change! Can you see what happens? They change direction and curve. Our eyes are tricked into seeing something round, when it is really flat.

Color also helps the optical trick or illusion [e•LU•shun]. Notice first what colors have been selected. They are various shades and tints of both warm and cool colors. The cool colors have been used mainly around the base of the ball-like shape. They act as a kind of shadow. This makes us believe the ball is three-dimensional or rounded. But cool colors have another quality. When used with warm colors, like the reds and yellows here, they *recede*. When something recedes, it pushes into the background. How does this help the optical illusion here?

[?] In contrast, warm colors come forward. Notice the colors used in the lines across the center of the ball. What kind of color scheme has Vasarely used? Do you remember what feelings or moods this color scheme can create? Does the color scheme help the optical illusion? Does the ball-like shape seem solid or empty? Why?

Hans Hofmann works with color in a different way than Vasarely. He does, however, make use of the strange way that certain colors seem to recede, while others advance.

Figure 3.9 is a work called *Towards Crepuscule* [kri•PUS•cool]. *Crepuscule* means dim or twilight. A strange title for so bright a painting! The hues are very high in value and intensity. The background colors are spread on with heavy, bold brush strokes. In some places the artist has even mixed the colors together with his brush right on the canvas. These colors create shapes. The edges of these shapes are rough and uneven. These are called organic or free-form shapes. There are other kinds of shapes in this painting. Can you find them?

The three rectangular shapes are green, red, and a small orange shape stuck to the edge of the painting. Different from the background shapes, the rectangular shapes have sharp, even edges. The differences in the shapes make these three shapes stand out from the others. They seem to float just above the other colors on the painting. The artist has created this effect in several ways.

First, he has used geometric shapes. Second, he has used very pure colors within the rectangles. Third, and most importantly, he has used a very quiet brush! You can probably see some brushstrokes if you look very closely, but they are pretty smooth compared to those in the background. But, there is something else unusual about these three shapes. Can you tell which one is closest to you? Remember, warm colors advance; cool colors recede.

Figure 3.9. Hans Hofmann. *Towards Crepuscule.* 1963. Oil on canvas, 60″ x 72″. Cincinnati Art Museum. Edwin and Virginia Irwin Memorial.

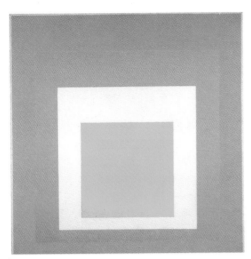

Figure 3.10. Josef Albers. *Homage to the Square: "Ascending".* 1953. Oil on composition board, 43½" x 43½". Collection of Whitney Museum of American Art, Purchase 54.34.

Figure 3.11. New Mexico. *Navajo Wool Blanket.* National Museum of the American Indian, New York. William M. Fitzhugh Collection.

Although the green shape appears to overlap the red shape and to be larger in size, it is having a hard time staying in front! The red shape is fighting for first place. That warm red pushes itself forward like a rude person cutting into a movie line. And look at that little orange intruder! Why does it seem even closer than the other ⟦?⟧ two? Could it have an advantage by hanging on to the edge like that? This painting seems to be a battle of the colors!

Do you remember when we talked about how the behavior of colors can be altered by their surroundings? Warm colors appear cool; cool colors warm, depending on the colors used behind them. Something like that is happening in this painting. Look carefully around each rectangle. What colors has the artist used in the neighborhood of each shape?

Figure 3.10, titled *Homage To A Square: "Ascending"*, was painted by another abstract artist who was very interested in the way colors can make us see and feel in certain ways. Josef Albers [JO • sef AL • burs] uses only geometric shapes to contain his colors. He was especially fond of squares. This painting is one of many that he created to pay homage or "honor" to the square.

By reducing all subject matter to the very simplest squares, Albers makes us really look at and feel the colors within the squares. Like Hoffman, he was interested in how some colors change, advance, or recede, depending on where they are placed in a painting.

In *Homage To A Square: "Ascending"*, the central square ⟦?⟧ is a strong yellow. Is this a warm or cool color? In this painting does it appear to recede or come forward? Compare its position with the other squares. Does it seem closer than the blue? The grey? The white? Why? Which color is the highest in value? The lowest?

Why do you think the artist placed the painted squares near the bottom of the canvas?

We know color is an important art element for many modern painters. But, look how a Native American weaver used color almost one hundred years ago.

Figure 3.11 shows a wool blanket. The Navajo artist who created this blanket used color to add interest and beauty to what was a very common, everyday object for the tribe. Maximum color contrast was created by selecting a complementary color scheme. The color opposites intensify each other. The zig-zag lines appear to dance across the surface. Although the design is a simple one, the artist has made the most of it. Straight lines fence in the dancing zig-zags. Diamond shapes highlight the center.

The colors that the artist has used were probably created from natural dyes. The desert of the American Southwest, where the Navajos lived, provided many plants and minerals for making fabric dyes and paints. The colors selected remind us of the desert landscape itself. The red-orange, yellow, and black can be seen in the hills and rocks. The vivid blue is like the cloudless sky of a desert morning.

? For more practice in recognizing color schemes, study the paintings reproduced in Figures 3.12 through 3.15. What color scheme is used in each? Is it predominantly monochromatic, complementary, or analogous? Think about why the artists chose the colors used. What moods or feelings do the paintings convey?

Figure 3.12. Henri Rousseau. *Landscape with Milkmaids.* 1900. Oil on canvas, 16¼″ x 20¾″. Bequest of Marion Koogler McNay, Marion Koogler McNay Art Museum, San Antonio, Texas.

Figure 3.14. Frederic Remington. *The Grass Fire.* 1908. Oil on canvas, 27⅛″ x 40⅛″. Amon Carter Museum, Fort Worth, Texas.

Figure 3.13. Ellsworth Kelly. *High Yellow.* 1960. Oil on canvas, 80½″ x 57¾″. Archer M. Huntington Art Gallery, The University of Texas at Austin, lent by James and Mari Michener.

Figure 3.15. Georgia O'Keeffe. *From the Plains I.* 1953. Oil on canvas, 47 11/16″ x 83 5/8″. Marion Koogler McNay Art Museum, San Antonio, Texas. Gift of the Estate of Tom Slick.

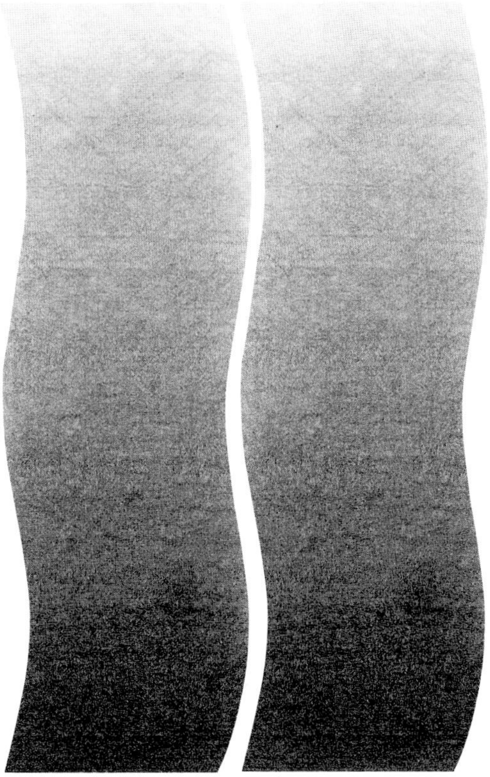

Figure 3.16. Example of shading.

VALUE

The art element **value** has to do with the varying degrees of lights and darks that are found in a work of art. Value is often created with **shading**. This is a way of adding dark areas to indicate shadows and light or bright areas to indicate reflected light. Artists who want to make a convincing illusion of form on a two-dimensional surface, such as paper or canvas, must learn to use value skillfully. They have to learn to **modulate** [MOD•u•late] values. Value modulation means that the change from one value, or degree of darkness, to another is softened and smoothed (Figure 3.16).

In the next section, you will read more about how forms (three-dimensional shapes) are created on a two-dimensional surface using value. In Unit Five, you will learn how to improve your own drawings by modulating values.

SEEING AND UNDERSTANDING VALUE

Do you remember how line could be used to create value? Look again at John Biggers's work in Figure 2.12. As lines are piled on top of each other, the value darkens. Artists also have other ways of creating value.

Artist Chuck Close is famous for creating large portraits of himself and his friends. In Figure 3.17, titled *Self Portrait,* he uses pencil shading to change the value from very dark to very light. With much skill and patience, he is able to make a drawing that is almost as detailed as a photograph. Pay particular attention to the smooth blending of one value into another (modulation). There are no visible lines where one value stops and another begins.

This style of drawing or painting is called **Photo-realism**. As the parts of this word tell you, these artworks seem as realistic as a photograph. You will see other examples of Photo-realism throughout this book. As you look at each, try to determine if there is anything about them that is not like a photograph. Can you always be fooled?

Figure 3.17. Chuck Close. *Self Portrait/58424.* 1973. Ink and pencil on paper, 70½″ x 58″. Photo credit: Bevan Davies. Photo courtesy of The Pace Gallery, New York.

Another work by Chuck Close creates value in a very different way (Figure 3.18). This work is a portrait of a friend named *Jud*. Rather than pencil, charcoal, or any other type of drawing material, Chuck Close uses small circles or dots of paper shaded in hundreds of different values from brightest white to darkest black. Each dot is glued in place until all the shadows and lights tell our eyes that this is the face of a particular man.

Both newspaper photographs and computer art are created in a very similar way. In newspaper print the image is made up of dots and spaces. The more or larger the dots, the darker the value. Open or white spaces become the light values. When dots are used to create value it is called *stipple* or **pointillism**. [POIN • te • lizm]. (Figure 3.19)

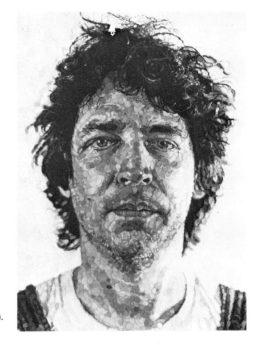

Figure 3.18. Chuck Close. *Jud.* 1982. Pulp paper collage on canvas, 96″ x 72″ (#10784). Photo credit: Zindman/Fremont. Photo courtesy of The Pace Gallery, New York.

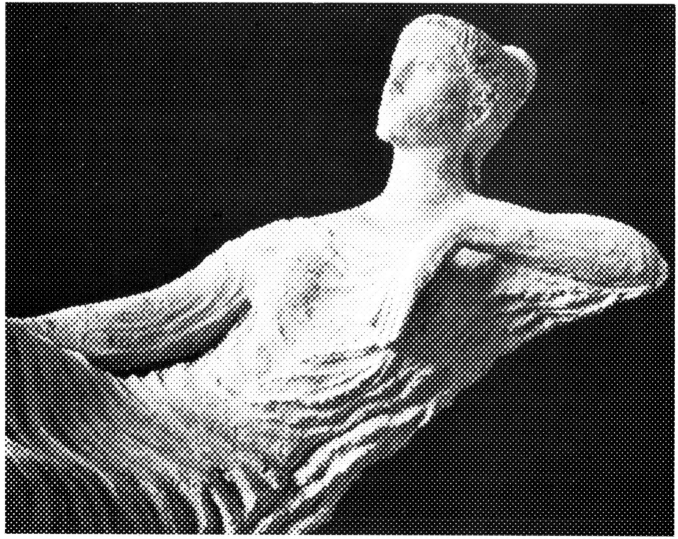

Figure 3.19. Newspaper and magazine print and graphics are created by dots. More dots for dark values and fewer dots for light values.

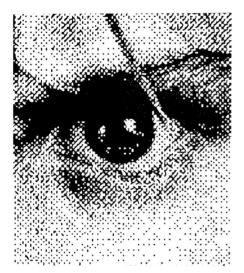

Figure 3.20. In place of dots, computers use pixels or small squares to create value changes.

Computers, on the other hand, use small squares in place of dots (3.20). These squares are called *pixels* [PIC•suls].

Figure 3.21, *Feline Felicity* by Charles Sheeler, is a wonderful example of how simple materials (black crayon on white paper) can be used to create a masterpiece of value modulation.

The artist has used values to tell us not only about the textures and patterns seen on the sleeping cat and the surrounding objects, but about the forms and cast shadows as well.

Notice first the shadows of the chair. Can you tell from which direction the light is coming? How do you know? Look at the area under the seat of the chair. There seem to be other shadows there. What could be making them? ?

The soft markings on the fur of the cat are drawn as convincingly as the hard, rounded forms of the legs and woven seat of the chair.

Sheeler has used a wide range of values in this drawing. He has created very dark values (black); very light values (white); and many degrees of value (gray) between the black and white. This is one reason the drawing is so interesting. Most drawings can be made more exciting when a full range of values are used. This drawing uses a wide range of values to show **contrast**. Contrast is a way of showing strong differences between colors, values, shapes, forms, lines, and textures. You will find that you often need contrast to show shape.

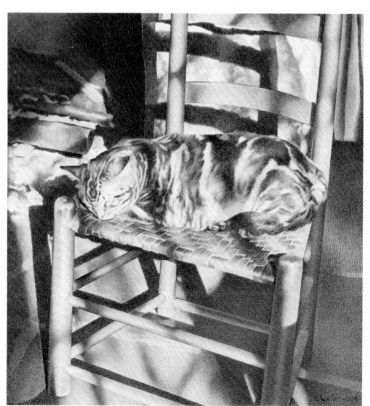

Figure 3.21. Charles Sheeler. *Feline Felicity*. 1934. Conte crayon on white paper, 559mm. x 457mm. Courtesy of The Fogg Art Museum, Harvard University, Cambridge, Massachusetts. Purchase of Louise E. Bettens Fund.

48

Artist of Industry

Charles Sheeler began his artistic career in a school of industrial design. This early art training in the world of machines, factories, and industry greatly influenced Sheeler's art throughout his life.

Like Thomas Hart Benton, Sheeler went to Europe to study art. He too encountered the new art movement of the age—Cubism. Unlike Benton, who rejected Cubism for a more realistic style of painting, Sheeler accepted the basic ideas of Cubism. However, always an individualist, he invented an American style of Cubism which he called Precisionism.

Like the Cubist painters he admired, Sheeler was not interested in realistic details. He reduced subjects to their basic geometric forms. Machines, factories, oil refineries, and skyscrapers were excellent subjects for this type of painting.

About 1917 Sheeler renewed his interest in photography. He often used his photographs for art ideas and compositions. His photographs received praise and won him jobs with several magazines. He even helped make a film called *Manahatta*.

During the 1930s Sheeler's art subjects changed. In place of the cityscapes and architectural subjects he had painted and photographed, he turned to country and rural life. While he appreciated and painted many of the same subjects as Regionalist painters like Thomas Hart Benton, Sheeler retained his own precise drawing and painting style.

The 1950s saw Sheeler returning once again to his original love—the architecture of the cities and the industrial world. Unfortunately, in 1959 he suffered a severe stroke. He was never able to draw, paint, or photograph again.

Self-portrait, c. 1924. Pastel and Charcoal on paper, 24″ x 20 1/8″. Purchased with funds from the Mr. and Mrs. M. Anthony Fisher Purchase Fund and the Martin and Agnete Gruss Foundation. Whitney Museum of Art.

BORN: 1883
DIED: 1965
BIRTHPLACE:
Philadelphia, Pennsylvania

Figure 3.22. Charles Sheeler. *Continuity.* 1957. Oil on canvas, 29″ x 23″. Collection of the Modern Art Museum of Fort Worth. Gift of William E. Scott.

Student work.

Student work.

Did you learn

The definitions of these words and phrases: hue; primary and secondary colors; intermediate colors; value; shade; tint; intensity; warm and cool colors; color schemes; monochromatic; analogous; complementary; Fauve; abstract; Op art; modulate; contrast?

- How to make the secondary colors? The intermediates?
- How to make shades? Tints?
- How to dull the intensity of a color?
- Why the Fauves were called "wild beasts"?
- Why Figure 3.8 is called Op art?

Understanding and Evaluating

- Collect as many samples of paper or material scraps of one hue or color as possible. Put them together and compare the differences in value and intensity.
- Open your closet. Squint your eyes and look at the main color or color group you clothes fall into. Can you tell? Do you wear mostly blue, green, or red? Are they mostly warm or cool colors?
- The next time you are in a supermarket, check the shelves where the laundry detergents are kept. What colors are used on the boxes? What colors are not used at all?

Seeing and Creating

- Practice mixing tints and shades. On a sheet of white paper, mark off three rows of seven one-inch squares. Fill the first square of each row with one primary color. In the squares underneath each primary, mix and fill in the tints. Each square should contain a lighter tint than the one above it. Repeat the exercise by mixing shades for each primary color. Use liquid tempera paint. (**CAUTION:** ©Some tempera can stain. Wear an old shirt or smock.)
- Paint a still life using a particular color scheme. Have a specific mood in mind when you select your color.
- Paint a landscape in the style of the Fauves.

Our world is filled with objects. As young children, we learn to identify objects by their characteristic **silhouette** [SIL•oo•ette] or **shape.** A shape or silhouette is a *two-dimensional* image of an object. Something that is two-dimensional has only height and width.

SHAPE

We become so skilled at identifying by shape alone, that we do not need to see details of an object to name it. For example, can't you name all the objects on the following page just by the contours of their shadows? (Figure 4.1). Like lines, shapes come in a wide variety. There are, however, two basic classifications: **geometric** and **organic** or **free-form.**

Geometric shapes, just as their name implies, are shapes that are created by geometry. They have clean, smooth edges that can be measured and drawn with rulers, compasses, or protractors. Some familiar geometric shapes are circles, rectangles, squares, and triangles (Figure 4.2).

We usually find geometric shapes in human-made objects. Because most of us live in a human-made environment, we find geometric shapes all around us. Road signs, billboards, movie screens, doors, windows, cassette tapes, and compact discs are all designed from geometric shapes.

Organic shapes, on the other hand, are shapes that appear to be created by nature. The contour or edge of an organic shape is very uneven. It can curve, angle, or bump along without any need to follow a geometric formula. Organic is a good name for these shapes, since they look as if they were grown or created in a natural environment. You may also hear these irregular shapes called **free-form shapes.**

SEEING AND UNDERSTANDING SHAPE

Artists can create shapes in several ways. Shapes can be made with line, color, or texture. Take a pencil or crayon and draw a line. Continue to draw the line until the beginning meets the end. You have created a shape with line. A blob of red paint and a bright green cut-paper silhouette create shapes with color. Different textures can also be used to make shapes. Areas of dots or crosshatched lines on a page, or ridges and bumps on a clay pot, make an area whose contours create shapes. The

Chapter 4
SHAPE AND FORM

WORDWATCH
silhouette
geometric
organic
free-form
positive shapes
negative shapes
caricature
three-dimensional
utilitarian
stylized
calligraphy

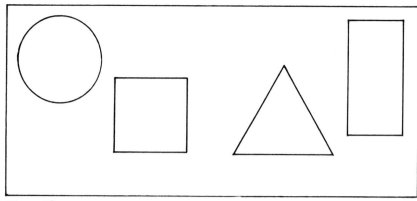

Figure 4.2.

following artists use both geometric and organic shapes in their work.

Both categories of shapes have specific meaning for us when we see them. In other words we feel one way about shapes with very precise, straight edges, and quite another way about shapes that are rough and irregular. Some shapes are so familiar that we associate them with a particular event, activity, or idea. The letters of the English alphabet are a good example of this. By the time you are in the seventh grade, the letters of the alphabet are as well-known to you as your own name. In fact, it is difficult to see them as *shapes*.

Look at the work by Stuart Davis (Figure 4.3). The artist has used letters, even whole words. He also wants us to see the shapes created by the familiar letters and words. To do this he makes use of different styles of lettering or **calligraphy**.

He uses many other shapes, as well. They seem more shape-like simply because we can't read them! How would you categorize most of the shapes—geometric or organic? Can you point out places where the background makes a shape?

Davis has created his shapes with colors. Every time a new color or color value is used, a new shape is created. Is there any place where texture makes a shape?

Look at the work shown in Figure 4.4. This painting is by the American artist Georgia O'Keeffe. For the latter part of her very long life (she lived to be 99!), Georgia O'Keeffe lived and painted near Taos, New Mexico. The landscape of the Southwest, its shapes and colors, inspired most of her paintings. Can you identify the source of the subject for Figure 4.4?

The artist has left out all details that would make the painting "realistic." Instead, she has carefully selected just those shapes that identify these characteristic Southwestern objects—a window and the wall of an adobe [a • DOE • bee] house.

Adobe is a building material made of sun-dried mud bricks. Frequently, the core of mud bricks is smoothed over with a coating of plaster. It is a popular way of constructing houses in the desert.

Figure 4.1. Photos by John Smithers.

As rainfall is limited in such areas, there is little danger of the bricks falling apart. It is an inexpensive and attractive building material, perfectly suited to the hot, dry climate of the desert. You will see adobe buildings featured in many Southwestern artworks. Artists find its smooth, but slightly irregular surface, interesting, without being fussy. In many ways the adobe wall surface is like that of a hand-made clay pot or sculpture. Small changes in surface texture and form are possible by compressing an area with the palm of a hand.

Georgia O'Keeffe also loved to paint the simple shapes and forms of adobe buildings. She even had one built for her own house and lived in it until her death in 1986.

At first glance, the shapes in Figure 4.4. appear geometric. They do share many of the characteristics of geometric shapes: smooth, clean edges. But O'Keeffe has introduced some very small curves which alter the shapes ever so slightly. Can you see them? The edge of the roof against the sky; the top of the window opening. These small changes add interest and hold our attention in a painting that *appears* simple and plain.

As we continue to look at this work, we notice other changes. Notice how the artist has altered the color value of the wall from the right corner to the left. The left side is noticeably darker. How does this change the shape of the wall? Can you tell which part of the wall is closest to you? The more you study this painting, the more you find! And it is all created by very simple shapes—shapes created with color.

This painting not only provides visual interest with simple shapes and colors, but it also creates a very special mood. The desert of the American Southwest was and still is a landscape of great beauty. But it is not a land easily tamed by humans. The climate is either blazing hot during the day or freezing cold at night. The animal and plant life that live there has to make special provisions to survive. It is a stark and barren place, where even today, humans find it difficult to be comfortable. However, the wide-open landscape continues to inspire artists like Georgia O'Keeffe. Human beings, especially artists, seem attracted to the vast, untamed regions of the world. Few have been as successful in sharing that wild beauty as Georgia O'Keeffe.

Now, let's focus on another artist who uses shape in many inventive ways. Henri Matisse [on • REE maa • TEESE) was a French artist who originally started as a painter. It was not until he was seventy-three and unable

Figure 4.3. Stuart Davis. *Blips and Ifs.* 1963-64. Oil on canvas, 71⅛" x 53⅛". Courtesy Amon Carter Museum, Fort Worth, Texas.

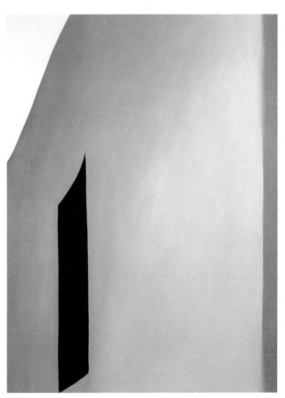

Figure 4.4. Georgia O'Keeffe. *Black Patio Door.* 1955. Oil on canvas, 40⅛" x 30". Courtesy Amon Carter Museum, Fort Worth, Texas.

to leave his bed, that he developed a wonderful new way of making art—cut-paper collage [co•LOGE].

Rather than create shapes with line by drawing or painting them, he cut fantastic shapes out of large sheets of colored paper. He then arranged them onto a background and glued them down. Working only with paper and scissors didn't stop Matisse from inventing some unusual shapes.

The Horse, Bareback Rider, and The Clown (Figure 4.5) shows Matisse's love of strong shapes and colors. This work, with all its bright colors and decorative shapes, does seem to call up images of the circus. The dazzle, movement, and excitement of the center ring are all there. Those small, yellow shapes seem to whiz around like confetti. The large, red shape we recognize as the profile of a horse seems about to prance out of the picture frame.

Matisse has selected as his subject what could be a very complicated scene. Without losing any of the mood and feeling of the circus, he has simplified it with shape and color. Like O'Keeffe, he has used color, rather than lines and texture, to create his shapes.

Look at the variety of sizes and shapes Matisse has used. Notice how the silhouettes of the shapes constantly change from one to the other. How would you classify these shapes—organic or geometric? Are they all one kind? Look at the yellow shape in the upper left-hand corner. Is it a piece of yellow paper with a black shape on top, or a yellow shape cutout? If you look around at the other shapes, you can find the answer!

Figure 4.5. Henri Matisse. *Le Cheval, L'Ecuyere, et le Clown from Jazz.* Pochoir, 16⅝" x 25½". Marion Koogler McNay Art Museum, San Antonio, Texas. Gift of M.B. Pace and others.

Matisse frequently used both **positive** and **negative** shapes. The horse is a **positive shape**. The space in the paper left by the shape also creates a shape. If you glue that piece of paper down so the space shows against another color, it is a **negative shape**. In a later chapter on the art element, space, you will read about negative and positive spaces and shapes again.

Figure 4.6, titled *The Mocker Mocked* by Paul Klee [CLAY] is a good example of shapes created with line. Klee has made an exaggerated portrait or **caricature**.

By swinging a single, unbroken line from one direction to another, Klee has managed to make a wide variety of shapes. As his line dips and jumps under and over other lines, he is able to create the illusion that some shapes are closer, some farther away. Like Georgia O'Keeffe, Klee has managed to show much through simple, limited means. How would you categorize the shapes used in the *The Mocker Mocked?* Are they geometric or organic? Or both?

Figure 4.6. Paul Klee. *The Mocker Mocked.* 1930. Oil on canvas, 17″ x 20⅝″. Collection, The Museum of Modern Art, New York. Gift of J.B. Neumann.

FORM

Shapes are *two-dimensional;* **forms** are three-dimensional shapes. If an object is three-dimensional, it has height, width, and depth—three dimensions. Forms differ from shapes in that we can walk around them. Furniture, houses, sculpture, cars, and you are all forms (Figure 4.7). Like shapes, forms can be either geometric or organic. You can probably name some of the more familiar geometric forms (Figure 4.8). As with shapes, artists have different ways of creating forms and different uses for them in works of art.

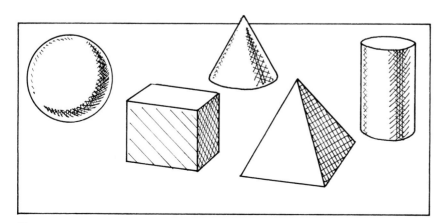

Figure 4.8.

Figure 4.7.

Figure 4.9. *Portrait of Egyptian Boy.* Undated. Encaustic on wood, 38cm. x 19cm. Roman Period II Century A.D. The Metropolitan Museum of Art, All Rights Reserved. Gift of Edward S. Harkness, 1918. (18.9.2)

SEEING AND UNDERSTANDING FORM

What if you woke up one morning and discovered you had forgotten how to tie your shoe. "Impossible," you say. "I have known how to tie my shoe since I was just a little kid. I can't forget that!" You probably feel the same way about the progress of history. Once something is discovered or invented, it can't be lost or forgotten. Strangely enough, it can. One of the basic skills of art *was* forgotten for many centuries. That skill was how to create the illusion or appearance of three-dimensional forms on a flat surface, such as a wall, a wooden board, paper, or canvas.

To convince a viewer that a painted object has form, when they can't pick it up and touch it, takes skill in the use of value or shading. An artist must know how to change smoothly from one shade to another to create the illusion. It is a skill that you, yourself, will develop as you continue to create your own artworks.

We take this illusion so much for granted, it is difficult to imagine works of art without it. Look at the three works shown in Figures 4.9 through 4.11.

The first, Figure 4.9, is a portrait of an Egyptian boy. It was painted in the 2nd century A.D. At this time Rome had conquered Egypt. In fact, the artist was very likely a Roman.

Notice how realistic it seems for such an ancient work of art. The artist has created an illusion of the roundness of the boy's face by using shadows under the chin and around the nose.

Look how the light seems to fall on the top of his nose, on his forehead, and on his cheek. If he were sitting behind you in math, wearing a shirt, jeans, and sneakers, you would never guess that he lived over 1,800 years ago!

Now look at Figure 4.10. *Enthroned Madonna and Child* was painted in the 13th century A.D. That is over 1,000 years *later* than the Egyptian boy. Things have certainly changed! The figures seem to be getting *less* realistic, more two-dimensional. The figures of the Madonna and child appear to be cut out of paper and pasted onto the background. The folds of the Madonna's robe are not very convincing. They fail to create the illusion of real fabric. The illusion of form has been lost.

Enthroned Madonna and Child was painted during a period called "The Dark Ages." One reason for the name was that much knowledge and skill from the ancient world, the world of Greece and Rome, was lost. Most of the scientific knowledge of the Greeks and Romans was forgotten or surpressed. Scientific knowledge was often considered "pagan" or "unholy" by the church. Drawing skill, the ability to create the illusion of form on a flat surface, was also either forgotten or dismissed as unimportant. Flat, beautifully decorated images of religious subjects were wanted, not realistic portraits that reminded people of earthly life.

Now look at Figure 4.11. This is another *Madonna and Child* painted by an artist in the century following the century when *Enthroned Madonna and Child* was painted. Notice the soft shading that is used to give roundness to the figures. The folds of the clothing seem very realistic and natural when compared to the robes of the *Enthroned Madonna and Child*. This work, although a religious subject, is much closer in spirit and artistic tradition to the Roman portrait, than to *Enthroned Madonna and Child*.

Madonna and Child was painted by Giotto [JOT•toe]. Giotto was the first artist to "rediscover" and appreciate the secret skill of the ancient artists for creating the appearance of three-dimensional form on a flat surface. He was interested in giving his religious subjects more realism. He wanted the everyday people who saw his work to feel closer to the religious subjects of his paintings. One way he did this was to give them form. He studied the human figure and the way light and shadow defined the form. Giotto was a master of making us feel the weight and substance of forms. At times his figures seem more like sculptures than paintings.

All artists who paint and draw realistically owe a great debt to Giotto. He rediscovered the lost art skill of the ancients. The following two painters made excellent use of Giotto's legacy or gift.

Figure 4.10. *Enthroned Madonna and Child.* Undated. Wood, 51⅝" x 30¼". National Gallery of Art, Washington, D.C. Gift of Mrs. Otto H. Kahn.

Figure 4.11. Giotto. *Madonna and Child.* c. 1320/1330. Wood, 33⅝" x 24⅝". National Gallery of Art, Washington, D.C. Samuel H. Kress Collection.

Wood Boatmen On A River (Figure 4.12) was painted by the American artist George Caleb Bingham in 1854. The subject of much of Bingham's art was the settling of the American West. He provided us, as did many other artists, with a pictorial history of our country. He became a camera of history, long before cameras were popular. Figure 4.12 shows his skill in creating the illusion of form on the flat surface of a stretched canvas.

The figures gathered around the campfire seem to project from out of the darkness of the background. Their forms are highlighted by the firelight. This, together with the encircling shadows, gives the figures a rounded, realistic appearance.

Can you see the small, dark figure in the background? He is silhouetted against the bright light of a full moon. Because we can only see his profile, or the edge of his form, he seems flat in comparison to the other figures in the painting. The interplay of *both* light and shadow is necessary for a realistic illusion of form.

Bingham has placed his figures in such a way that the viewer seems part of the scene. One man has his back to us, as all listen to the music of the harmonica player. If we move a little closer, we can hear the music and feel the warmth of the fire.

The sphere is one of the more difficult geometric forms to present convincingly on a flat surface. On a cube, corners stop each highlight and shade. But when light strikes a sphere, it is smoothly washed over the whole surface with no breaks between values.

Figure 4.13 by William McCloskey is an excellent example of how realistic an illusion of form an artist can create with paint and canvas. In this painting the oranges seem to sit, not on a flat canvas, but in an open box. Surely, if we just reach out our hand, we can pick up an orange and feel its weight and curved form.

Look at the oranges wrapped in paper. The creases and wrinkles of the paper *curve* around the surface of the oranges. This helps create the illusion of three-dimensional form. And what about the reflections in the shiny table? Don't they help convince us these oranges are real?

Sculptors and ceramists [sir • RAM • ists] are the artists that most often come to mind when we discuss **form** as an art element. Unlike painters, sculptors and ceramists work with materials that actually have three-dimensional form. A block of marble or a chunk of clay has real

Figure 4.12. George Caleb Bingham. *Wood Boatmen on a River.* 1854. Oil on canvas, 29″ x 36¼″. Courtesy Amon Carter Museum, Fort Worth, Texas.

Figure 4.13. William J. McCloskey. *Wrapped Oranges.* 1889. Oil on canvas, 12″ x 16″. Courtesy Amon Carter Museum, Fort Worth, Texas. Acquisition in memory of Katrine Deakins, Trustee, Amon Carter Museum.

dimension. You can lift it in your hands and feel its weight and mass. From these raw materials and many others, sculptors and ceramists fashion new, expressive forms. We can admire their art by walking all the way around it. We can see how each work creates its own shadows on the surroundings. We admire how real light plays over its surface.

The three artists discussed below have all borrowed the forms for their work from nature. As you will discover, the natural environment is a great source of ideas for both two- and three-dimensional art.

Figure 4.14 shows the work of sculptor Evaline Sellors. It is titled *Winter (Sleeping Fawn)*. The artist has chosen to show the fawn, or baby deer, tightly curled upon itself against the winter cold. The work is made of limestone. This stone is favored by many sculptors. It is a strong stone, but allows small details to be carved into its surface. However, Evaline Sellors hasn't used very many details.

She has shown us the basic **form** of the deer, but none of its details, such as the texture of the fur. She is more concerned with showing us the simple, yet beautiful, form of the deer. In fact, if you trace your finger around the outline of the deer's body, you can know the shape of the limestone block the artist started with. What geometric shape do you think it was?

Evaline Sellors wants us to remember, as we look at her work, that it is a sculpture, carved from a block of stone. She makes no attempt to convince us that the deer is real. In other words, the subject of the sculpture is not just a deer. She gives special value to the stone itself, and to the act of carving it. It is easy to test this. Ask yourself what other animals could have been substituted for the deer. If the artist had sculpted a dog, a colt, or a calf, would the work have been very different?

[?] Does the "thing" in Figure 4.15 look familiar? You may have seen a slightly smaller version before! The title of this sculpture is *El Cucaracho* [el Koo•ka•RAH•cho]. This word is Spanish for "cockroach."

What a strange subject for a sculpture! Why would an artist want to use as a subject something that is so hated and feared as the cockroach? The "creepy crawlies" of the animal kingdom do seem unusual as subject matter for artworks. But, one of the main tasks of art is to reveal something new about the world around us, to make us look with fresh eyes at the ordinary.

Sculptor José Rivera [hoe•SAY ree•VAY•rah] has certainly succeeded in creating an artwork that will definitely make you look twice. Carved of mesquite [mess•keet] wood, *El Cucaracho* both attracts and repels

Figure 4.14. Evaline Sellors. *Winter (Sleeping Fawn)*. 1947. Limestone, 6½" x 9½". Collection of the Modern Art Museum of Fort Worth, Museum Purchase.

Figure 4.15. José Luis Rivera. *El Cucaracho*. 1982. Mesquite wood carving, 24" x 11" x 7". Collection of Cesar Martinez.

us. The artist has carefully studied the complicated structure of the cockroach. Each part has been simplified, smoothed, and polished like the parts of a machine.

While we recognize the image, we see it in a new way. We notice, for example, how well the parts fit together; how the form of one part repeats the form of another. But, look how many different forms make up the whole. In fact, we see what an interesting and beautiful object this really is.

? Why do you think the artist chose wood for his sculpture material? How would the work be changed if it had been made out of another material, such as marble or clay?

Fortunately, we never have to encounter a roach this large in real life, or one that approaches us on its hind legs! Why do you think the artist selected the size (twenty-four inches tall) and the position for his work? Can you picture in your mind how the sculpture would appear lying flat as we usually see cockroaches? If you walked around the sculpture, what would you see? Although unusual, insects do make interesting subjects for artworks. What other kinds of insects would be good ? for a sculpture?

Ceramic artists or potters, work with "real" forms as well. They fashion the forms for their artworks either by hand or on a potter's wheel. Figure 4.16 shows a pot made over 600 years ago.

The unknown artist who created this beautiful pot used animal life as the inspiration for his work. Can you recognize the animal? At first, it looks something like a turtle. But, in reality, it is a parrot. The artist has used the form of the parrot's head, with its curved beak, as a spout. The parrot's tail serves as a handle. The body of the pot looks just like a pot, not the body of a parrot. Can you picture in your mind how parrots and other birds are shaped? Why did the artist choose not to use the form of the parrot's body for his pot?

This pot is known as a **utilitarian** [u•teel•i•TEAR•e•un] object. This means that it was made to be used for everyday tasks, such as holding water or cooking food. We don't always think of everyday objects as works of art. But a well-designed pot, telephone, or table shares many of the same qualities we appreciate in artworks. If an object is made with good craftsmanship; that is they are easy to use in the tasks they were created for, and are pleasing to our eyes, as well, we might consider them works of art.

Figure 4.16. Unknown American Indian, Casas Grandes. *Effigy Bowl in the Form of a Macaw.* ca. 1300 A.D. Ceramic, polychrome buffware, h. 5⅛″. The Museum of Fine Arts, Houston. Gift of Miss Ima Hogg.

The artist who created the parrot pot, like Evaline Sellors (Figure 4.14), didn't feel the need to show us many small details. We aren't given any information about the texture of the feathers or the actual colors of the parrot. The colors and designs used on the pot are not realistic. Instead, the artist has used geometric shapes created by lines and colors. These repeated designs and colors seem to fit the form of the pot, although they are created with sharp angles. What part of the pot uses forms that are sharp and angular?

Let's look at another sculpture. Figure 4.17 uses the human head as the basis for its form. This wooden sculpture was created by an artist in the West African republic of Gabon. The features of the head—eyes, nose, mouth—have been simplified or **stylized** into geometric-like shapes. The sculptor has left out all details except those that we need to identify the form as a human head.

Notice the hair. Or is it a cap? The two long shapes extending on either side of the head seem to represent hair or some type of headdress. It is interesting how little information we need to decide that this is a representation of a human head.

Do you notice anything else unusual about this head? Do you know anyone with a neck that long or a mouth that small? The sculptor has exaggerated the proportions of the human head. He stretches some out and squeezes others together.

As you look at artworks throughout this book, you will find other artists who do the same thing. They change the proportion of familiar objects, until we suddenly see them in a new way. The objects are familiar, but different. In this way, artists reveal new meanings to us. In Figure 4.17 the exaggerated form of the human head has become more than a face. It is also an interesting combination of geometric shapes. This work seems to give new dignity and importance to the human head as a work of art.

There is something else that makes this work interesting. It was designed as a **reliquary** [REL • eh • kwer • ee]. This is an object that is used to hold a **relic** or the remains of something or someone. As a container for some precious or religious item, this sculpture is also an object of worship. What do you think would be preserved in such an impressive container?

Figure 4.17. *African Reliquary Head.* Gabon. Wood, 17.5cm.

Gelatin silver print, 28.5 cm. x 25.7 cm. National Portrait Gallery, Smithsonian Institution. Gift of George R. Rinhart. Photo by Philippe Halsman, 1967.

BORN: 1887
DIED: 1986
BIRTHPLACE:
Sun Prairie, Wisconsin

An Artist of the Desert's Soul

Georgia O'Keeffe began her art career as a teacher and supervisor of other art teachers in Amarillo, Texas. However, after attracting a great deal of attention with her first art exhibit in 1916, she decided to devote all her time to painting.

In 1924 she married one of the greatest photographers of the century, Alfred Stieglitz [STIG•list]. The two, living in New York City, became part of a very important group of artists and gallery owners. This group encouraged the work of new, abstract artists working in the city. O'Keeffe soon established herself as one of the leaders of modern art in America.

Like so many other artists, Georgia O'Keeffe fell under the spell of the towering skyscrapers of New York. She admired their geometric forms and the compositions they made against the sky. She painted numerous works using the city as her subject.

O'Keeffe was also interested in the beauty and structure of natural objects. To call this perfection to the attention of everyone, she painted flowers so that they fill huge canvasses.

Flowers soon gave way to other natural objects, such as bones. Again, these were enlarged until they filled the canvas. Their forms became more like sculptures than simple animal bones.

Georgia O'Keeffe lived out her final years in a plain, adobe house in New Mexico. Even in her nineties she continued to paint. The vivid blue sky and the endless miles of sand and rock of the desert became the subjects of her paintings. Few details remained in the objects she painted. They had become as pure and simple in form as O'Keeffe's life in art.

Figure 4.18. Georgia O'Keeffe. *Yellow Cactus Flowers.* 1929. Oil on canvas, 41½″ x 29¾″. Private Collection.

Student work.

Did you learn

- The definitions of these words and phrases: silhouette; shape; geometric; organic; free-form; negative and positive shapes; caricature; form; three-dimensional; utilitarian?
- The difference between a shape and a form?
- Why Figure 4.6 is called a caricature?
- Why Figure 4.10, *Enthroned Madonna and Child,* looks flatter than Figure 4.11, *Madonna and Child?*
- Two things needed to create an illusion of three-dimensional form in a painting?
- One way sculptures differ from paintings in their use of form?

Understanding and Evaluating

- What kinds of shapes, organic or geometric, are most often used to advertise food? Why?
- Collect some magazine photographs of other art-works from the Middle Ages. Do they share any similarities with those reproduced in this chapter? Name three things that would help someone recognize artworks from this time.
- Write a short story about the Egyptian boy pictured in Figure 4.9. Study his face carefully. What can you decide from looking at him?

Student work.

Seeing and Creating

- On a sheet of white paper, practice going from the darkest value your pencil will make to the lightest value (the white of the paper). Practice modulating (smoothing the changes) from one value to the next.
- Try your hand at shading the following geometric shapes: cube; cone; sphere. Use either pencil or char-coal. If possible, shine a light onto the forms to see the values better.
- Make a cut-paper collage. Use both positive and negative shapes. Cut some shapes out with scissors and tear out other shapes. Add details with black
- Ⓒ crayon or water-based felt markers. [**CAUTION:** Water-based felt-markers can stain clothes. Wear an old shirt or smock.]

Chapter 5
SPACE

These days the word *space* probably calls to mind images of starships, ringed planets, and remote galaxies. However, **space** is an art element, with other meanings as well. When we talk about the space in a painting or piece of sculpture we may be talking about **negative space**. Negative space surrounds everything else. It is the distance or area between shapes, forms, colors, lines, or textures. It is sometimes called **background**.

Shapes and spaces are not always what they seem. In some artworks they can change places. For an example, look at Figure 5.1.

[?] This painting is by American artist Nicholas Krushenick [CREW•she•nick]. As you look at this work, can you be sure what is negative space or background and what is positive shape? Look at the painting again. Can you make the spaces and shapes switch places?

HOW TO CREATE SPACE

Just as with form, artists can create illusions of space in paintings, drawings, and prints. Or they can work with actual or "real" space in sculpture and architecture. In two-dimensional artworks, there are several ways to fool the eye of the viewer into believing there is space between one object and another.

Figure 5.1. Nicholas Kruchenick. *Jungle Jim Lieberman.* 1969. Acrylic on canvas, 82″ x 72″. Virginia Museum of Fine Arts, Richmond. Gift of Sydney and Frances Lewis.

Overlapping

This is probably the method you used to create space in your first painting or drawing. One object, color, line, or texture covers or overlaps another. This creates the illusion that the one on top is closer than the one behind (Figure 5.2).

Position

Look out over the classroom from your desk. If you were going to draw the view you see on a piece of paper, you would want to draw those objects closest to you, near the bottom of the paper, or in the **foreground**. Objects farthest away from you would be part of the **background**. They would be placed higher on your paper. All objects falling in between, or in the **middle ground**, would be positioned between foreground and background (Figure 5.3) on the **picture plane** or surface of your paper.

Size Change

An illusion of space or depth can be created by adjusting the size of objects (Figure 5.4). When we look at objects in the distance, they appear to be smaller in size than objects close up. And while we know that the tall, pine tree in the distance is much larger than our hand, we can cover the tree with our hand because of the distances between them. When this illusion is created on a flat, two-dimensional surface, like canvas or paper, it is called **linear perspective**.

In the 15th century, artists, painters in particular, decided that when there were hundreds of objects to place in a painting, guessing at their relative sizes was just too difficult. What was needed was a system or formula for calculating how big each item should be in relation to other objects in the same scene. So they invented **linear perspective**.

Figure 5.2. An illusion of shallow space can be created by overlapping.

Figure 5.4. Drawing objects larger creates the illusion they are closer. Smaller objects appear farther away.

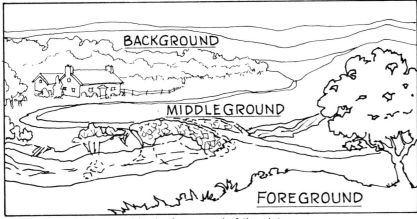

Figure 5.3. Objects placed in the foreground of the picture appear closer to us. Objects placed in the background appear farther away.

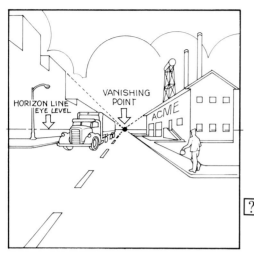

Figure 5.5. Horizontal edges of structures drawn in one-point perspective converge on the vanishing point located on the horizon.

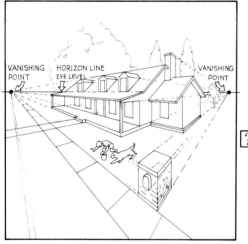

Figure 5.6. Two-point perspective drawing.

Figure 5.5 shows a simple scene drawn with **one-point** linear perspective. It is really quite simple to use this system to add depth and interest to your drawings.

First, notice two things in Figure 5.5—the **vanishing point** and the **horizon line** or **eye-level line**. The tops and bottoms of the buildings, windows, and doors all **converge** (come together) at the vanishing point. All other lines—sides or corners of buildings, windows, doors—are **parallel** to the sides of the page or the top and bottom of the page.

Figure 5.6 shows a drawing in **two-point** linear perspective. As you can see, two vanishing points are used rather than one. Can you tell what else is different about the scene pictured in Figure 5.5 and the one pictured in Figure 5.6? Does the difference have something to do with your **point of view?**

Much of the way we experience objects and the space around them has to do with **point of view**—that is, the position from which we see an object. Take off your shoe. Hold it up in front of your face with one side facing you. This represents one viewpoint. You see certain shapes and details from this view. Now, turn your shoe so that you are looking directly at the front. Position it so that the toe is close to your face. You now see a very different form, with new details revealed. How does your shoe change when you hold the sole or bottom in front of your eyes? What details are now invisible? Is it ever possible to see more than one point of view at a time?

Our point of view can be changed by moving the object we see or by moving ourselves. Artists sometimes use an unusual point of view to add interest and mystery to an artwork. Later you will see some examples of painting with unusual points of view.

SEEING AND UNDERSTANDING SPACE IN DRAWING AND PAINTING

Often the space that surrounds the objects in a painting, drawing, or print is as important as the objects themselves. Artists working on two-dimensional surfaces, such as canvas or paper, have several methods by which they can create the illusion of depth or space. They can use **overlapping, position,** or **size changes** (linear perspective) to create these illusions. Many times, as we will see in the following examples, artists use more than one of these methods to fool our eyes.

Remember, from our discussion of **form,** that during the Dark Ages, artists had very little interest in showing depth or space in their work (Figure 4.10). Any space shown was very shallow and created primarily by overlapping shapes. And then the great Giotto rediscovered the ancient Roman way of making two-dimensional shapes appear three-dimensional (Figure 4.11). Three-dimensional forms need a three-dimensional space to move about in. Artists began to be interested in creating an illusion of *deeper* space in their paintings. We will look at and compare three paintings that show this growing interest and ability to create an illusion of space.

First, look at the work in Figure 5.7. This painting was completed some two hundred years after the *Enthroned Madonna and Child* (Figure 4.10). Things are still pretty crowded. However, the artist Gentile da Fabriano [jen • TEE • lay dah fah • bree • AH • no] has made a serious effort to open up more space behind the people and animals. There is even an attempt to use linear perspective. Can you find it? Can you tell whether it is one-point or two-point?

Figure 5.7 titled *The Adoration of the Magi,* was painted as an altarpiece. That is, it was created to be placed above the altar of a church. For this reason it is very large, over nine feet high! It tells the Biblical story of the birth of Jesus. In the large panel you see the Three Wise Men, or Magi, bringing gifts to the infant Jesus. The three smaller panels below illustrate other parts of the story.

Even with nine feet of area to use, Fabriano still had trouble squeezing all his people and animals into the space he created. The frame of the altarpiece is barely able to contain the excitement of barking dogs, pushing people, and impatient horses. If you wanted to join the group, where would you stand?

The space or depth in the large panel is created by using all three methods: overlapping, position, and size change. The figures in the **foreground,** overlap the figures in the middle ground, leaving very little space between. Without a convincing space between them, the people and animals appear cut from paper and pasted on top of each other. There couldn't be enough room for all of that crowd on the right-hand side!

As you look toward the top of the painting, a landscape view opens out. Here, Fabriano makes use of position to convince us that the objects and landscape seen at the *top* of the painting are farther away. He also changes the size of the **background** objects, making them

Figure 5.7. Gentile da Fabriano. *The Adoration of the Magi.* 1423. 300 cm. x 282 cm. Uffizi Gallery, Florence. Photo credit: Scala/Art Resource.

Figure 5.8. Pieter De Hooch. *Interior with People.* c. 1658. Oil on canvas, 24½″ x 21″. Reproduced by courtesy of the Trustees, The National Gallery, London.

Figure 5.9. Kay Sage. *No Passing.* 1954. Oil on canvas, 51¼″ x 38″. Collection, Whitney Museum of American Art, Purchase 55.10.

smaller. This creates the illusion that they are at some distance from the figures painted at the bottom.

Now, before you give Fabriano a "D" for failing to create a convincing illusion of space, notice the small panels at the bottom of the altarpiece. The spaces created here are more convincing and better able to contain the figures. While bending the rules somewhat, Fabriano does use linear perspective quite successfully.

Remember, the creation of space in a painting can be of great concern to an artist. However, the *purpose* and *meaning* of the painting does not always call for deep, or realistic, space. Some artists choose to make the spaces between objects or colors shallow. This close, cramped space can be very effective in helping the viewer experience a certain mood or emotion.

[?] With this in mind, reconsider for a moment *The Adoration of the Magi*. Would the excitement of this great event be shown and felt as vividly if the figures were spaced farther apart over a wide landscape?

Let's jump ahead another two hundred years and look at how another painter creates space. This artist's name is Pieter De Hooch [peter du HOOCK].

Interior With People (Figure 5.8) was painted in the 17th century. It shows the interior of a large room, where four people seem to be enjoying a friendly conversation. But look at the space! De Hooch seems to create more space in a room than Fabriano did in a landscape! If you study the painting for a moment, it isn't too difficult to discover why De Hooch's space appears so large.

Look at the black-and-white tiled floor. It not only gives the illusion that it is firmly beneath the feet of the people, but it also spreads out and continues far into the distance. Obviously, De Hooch was a master in the use of linear perspective.

[?] Can you find other examples of linear perspective at work in Figure 5.8? Where would you, the viewer, be standing if you were invited into this painting? Does the artist use one- or two-point perspective?

Moving ahead another two hundred years brings us to modern times. Artists are still concerned with ways to create space in their work. Look at the painting (Figure 5.9) by Kay Sage. It is titled *No Passing*.

Sage has painted a place that may only exist in her imagination. We recognize a deserted street, some kind of buildings or box-like structures, banners, and flags. The artist has used linear perspective to make the buildings [?] recede into the distance. What a lonely place this is? Doesn't that deep, endless space make it seem even more lonely?

Here again, an artist uses space, deep space this time, to create a mood and a feeling in a painting. If we didn't have that long, empty street to gaze down, the mood of the painting would be very different. Compare Figure 5.8 with Figure 5.9. Is Kay Sage's perspective point of view the same as De Hooch's? Is her use of perspective as accurate?

SEEING AND UNDERSTANDING SPACE IN SCULPTURE AND ARCHITECTURE

Artists who work on two-dimensional surfaces, that is artists who paint, draw, or make prints, rely on illusion to create space. Some artists use actual or "real" space to add interest and meaning to their work. Sculptors, ceramists, and architects work with both form and space.

Make a big circle with your arms. Close the circle by clasping your hands together. You have just created two spaces—the area *outside* of your arms and the area *inside* your arms. Both areas or spaces are important to artists who work in three dimensions.

The soaring arch of *Gateway Arch* in St. Louis (Figure 5.10) is a work of art that is both sculpture and architecture. Designed by Eero Saarinen [A • row SAR • eh • nin], this structure is also known as the *Jefferson Westward Expansion Memorial.*

The gleaming stainless-steel band arches overhead to a height of 630 feet. Its interior space is large enough to allow visitors to take an elevator to the top of the arch for a spectacular view. The very simple design of the structure makes full use of **negative space.** Just as your circled arms carved out a space, the span of the arch does the same, but on a much grander scale.

To Saarinen, the area of space inside the arch is a part of the sculpture. It is every bit as important as the stainless-steel form that frames it. And what about the space *outside* the form? Can you also see that as part of the work?

This artwork was created to commemorate or honor one of the great movements in American history—the [?] Westward Expansion. Do you know what this was? The city of St. Louis is a very good choice as a site for this monument. Do you know why?

On a smaller scale, artist Julio Gonzales [WHO • lee • o gone • ZAL • es] has used "real" space to create an interesting sculpture in wrought iron titled *Head* (Figure 5.11).

Different parts of the sculpture cut through the surrounding space, creating space/shapes that remind one of a human head. In this work, the negative spaces are as important to the work as the iron structure itself. If you could walk around the sculpture, you would discover that the "head" changes. The artist makes use of the viewer's changing point of view to add even more interest to his work.

Figure 5.10. Eero Saarinen. *Jefferson Westward Expansion Memorial.* Courtesy National Park Service.

Figure 5.11. Julio Gonzales. *Head.* 1935. Wrought iron, 17¾" x 15¼". Collection, The Museum of Modern Art, New York. Purchase.

Figure 5.12. Alexander Calder. *Lobster Trap and Fish Tail.* 1939. Hanging Mobile: painted steel wire and sheet aluminum, about 8'6" high x 9'6" diameter. Collection, The Museum of Modern Art, New York. Commissioned by the Advisory Committee for the stairwell of the Museum.

The sculpture shown in Figure 5.12 doesn't have to rely on the viewer to change point of view. The work itself moves. Art that moves is called **kinetic** [ken • NET • ik] **art.**

Figure 5.12 is a type of kinetic art called a **mobile** [MO • beel]. This work was created by Alexander Calder, an artist who became famous for his mobiles.

Calder mobiles are usually very large, and must be hung in large, open spaces. Balanced with precision, the sculptures gently move with the air currents. Their movement constantly cuts the surrounding space into ever-changing shapes for viewers. Calder mobiles are delightful works of art.

They also can have amusing titles. The mobile in Figure 5.12 is titled *Lobster Trap and Fish Tail.* Can you spot the trap? What about the fish? Why would undersea life be a good subject for parts of a mobile?

ARCHITECTURE

Architecture, or the design of buildings, is an art form that is more closely related to human beings than any other. First of all, people live, work, and play *in* buildings. We walk through their spaces, touch their floors and walls, and look out of their windows. In other words, we use buildings in ways that we don't use paintings, drawings, or sculpture. For this reason, we are more likely to take the design of our houses, schools, shopping malls, movie theatres, and government buildings for granted. We rarely look at them as works of art, or even as structures that may be designed for their beauty, as well as for their function.

We only worry about a building's space when we need more room in our closet or a place to put our new wide-screen television! Nevertheless, architects, throughout history, have been concerned with the best way to use space—space that will be functional and pleasing to the eye—in the design of buildings. Let's look at some examples of architecture where space is used to create a certain feeling or mood.

If you are the ruler of a country and want to impress your friends *and* enemies, you need large buildings in which to live and conduct business. These buildings must be large in the exterior space they cover and the interior space they enclose.

Figure 5.13. Karnack. *Temple of Khonsu.* South View. 20th dynasty.
Art Resource/Giraudon.

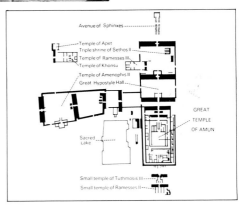

Few architects in history were more skilled at creating enormous buildings with awe-inspiring space than the architects of ancient Egypt.

One of the greatest of all ancient Egyptian structures was the temple complex at Karnak [CAR • nak] (Figure 5.13). Constructed many centuries ago, this enormous group, or complex, of buildings is large enough to hold six European cathedrals! One of the most famous structures is known as the Hypostyle [HIP • po • style] Hall. (Figure 5.14).

All that remains today of the Hypostyle Hall is a forest of gigantic columns. These columns are so large that it takes six people to encircle one with their outstretched arms!

The huge space of the hall was once roofed over, enclosing a temple room that must have rivaled the largest Hollywood movie set. One can imagine the fear and respect such a building must have inspired among visitors. With megaton columns crowding the space of the hall, the visitor, dwarfed by this forest of stone, could have little doubt of the power and majesty of the pharoah, supreme ruler of Egypt.

Figure 5.14. Karnak. Temple of Ammon. Hypostyle Hall. 1530 B.C. Egypt.

Figure 5.15. Reims Cathedral.

Figure 5.15 shows an interior view of the famous 13th-century French cathedral, Reims [REEMS]. The architect of this great building used high-soaring arches to create an interior space that must have made quite an impression on the people who came to worship there. Can you imagine how the poor people of Medieval France must have felt as they left their dark, low-ceilinged houses and entered that huge space! Looking up at the roof so far above their heads, they must have thought they were entering heaven itself.

Even today, walking into a cathedral like Reims is an awesome experience. The arches seem so light and fragile, one wonders that they can actually support the roof. These structures are examples of how successfully space can be used to inspire awe and a feeling of religious devotion.

That vast space is still filled at times with the echoes of singing voices and the dazzling colors of the great stained-glass windows. Larger structures have been built since the 13th century, but few have been designed with more sensitivity to the use of space.

The next example of space in architecture is taken from more recent times. Figure 5.16 shows an exterior view of a contemporary house designed by architect John C. Watson. Notice how the outside space around the pool seems to push into the spaces of the house. The house, at the same time, curves and pushes out toward the pool and surrounding courtyard.

The architect has skillfully created spaces that overlap and interact with each other. Could he be trying to make the outdoor space appear part of the inside space? Many people like large windows and open areas around their houses. This helps them enjoy the out-of-doors all year long. This architect, designing this house, seems to believe the same thing.

[?] As you look around your school and at other buildings in your neighborhood, notice how architects have used space. Have they used it to inspire awe or religious devotion? Have they tried to bring the outside spaces into the building? How does the space make you feel when you stand in it? Do you feel small and lost? Do you feel the space of the building?

Figure 5.16. John C. Watson. Contemporary House.

Gelatin silver print, 32.5 cm. x 22.1 cm. National Portrait Gallery, Smithsonian Institution. Gift of photographer B.J. Fernandez, 1968.

BORN: 1898
DIED: 1976
BIRTHPLACE:
Philadelphia, Pennsylvania

Motion Magician

Alexander Calder was lucky enough to be born into a very artistic family. His grandfather and father were sculptors; his mother was a painter. Everyone expected that Calder would study art. But, as everyone soon discovered, Calder never did what was expected. Instead, he decided that mechanical engineering was what he wanted to study. But, something about art kept attracting him.

In 1923 he finally enrolled in art school. Calder soon distinguished himself in a popular game among the art students. They would compete to see who could make the quickest and best sketch of the people who were moving rapidly through the streets and subways. Alexander became famous for his ability to show movement with a continuous contour line. This ability for sketching quickly and an interest in sports led to the publication of some of his drawings in the *National Police Gazette!*

Calder's interest and ability to use line soon became the source for his famous wire sculptures and mobiles. Another job provided more experience in the science of movement. In 1927 he went to work for the Gould Manufacturing Co. This company specialized in the manufacture of mechanical toys!

During the 1930s, Calder became well known as a sculptor and mobile artist. His first mobiles, like mechanical toys, were powered by hand or small motors. These mobiles were described by Calder as "four-dimensional drawings." Later, he began to make the unpowered mobiles for which he is most famous. Many of these works, constructed during the 1960s, are enormous. A famous example hangs at the Dallas-Fort Worth International Airport. It is called *Red, Black, and Blue.*

Calder had always been interested in animals and the circus as subjects for artworks. During the 1970s, he created several large pieces with animals as their inspiration. Like all of Calder's work, these sculptures delight us with the shapes, lines, colors, and movement of natural things. They also represent the humor and wit that always seems to be a part of Alexander Calder's life and art.

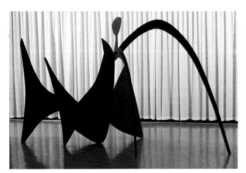

Figure 5.17. Alexander Calder. *Black Widow.* 1959. Standing stabile: painted sheet steel, 7'8" x 14'3" x 7'5". Collection, The Museum of Modern Art, New York. Mrs. Simon Guggenheim Fund.

Did you learn

* The definitions of these words and phrases: negative space; foreground; middle ground; background; picture plane; linear perspective; one-point perspective; two-point perspective; horizon/eye-level line; vanishing point; converge; point of view; kinetic art; mobile; architecture; architect?
* Three ways to create an illusion of space on a flat surface?
* Why architecture is such a personal and human art form?

Student work.

Understanding and Evaluating

* Look through magazines and newspapers for examples of architectural drawings or photographs. The Sunday newspaper usually has a number of sketches or photographs of houses for sale. Using a marker and straight edge, find and mark the eye-level line and the vanishing point of the houses. Determine whether the point of view is one- or two-point perspective.
* Locate other examples of architect Eero Saarinen's work. Compare them with the "arch." Write a two- to three-page essay on Saarinen. Can you find similarities between his designs?
* Think about the building design in your town you dislike most. Make a list of reasons for your dislike. Try to concentrate on the architectural design. Make a list of ways it could be improved.

Seeing and Creating

* Practice linear perspective by making a simple one-point drawing of a street or hallway. Make a similar study in two-point. Rulers aren't necessary, just a straight edge, such as a folded sheet of paper.
* Use perspective to create a future city. Be sure there are objects in the foreground, middle ground, and background. Add details to give the buildings and objects a realistic look. Use value in your designs.
* Make a light, pencil drawing of the front of a very old house. Pay attention to the shapes and spaces of windows and doorways. Notice details or decoration. Finish your drawing in pen and ink, water-based felt
* marker or crayon. [CAUTION: India ink stains. Wear an old shirt or smock. You may even wish to add color with a watercolor wash or colored pencils.]

Figure 6.1.

Chapter 6
TEXTURE

The final art element to learn is **texture**. Texture is the surface quality or character of an object. Texture is found in both natural and human-made environments. [?] Can you identify all the textures in Figure 6.1? Which are natural and which human-made? How can you tell?

Rub your hand over the top of your desk. How does it feel? Is it rough or smooth? Sometimes we don't think of objects with smooth textures as having texture at all. But they do. Everything that we touch has texture.

Most textures can be identified and described with words—slick, bumpy, scratchy, lumpy, slippery, gooey, or soft. Human beings are very sensitive to various textures, because our hands, especially our fingers, are designed to handle objects and identify them. Even with your eyes closed, you are able to identify a wide range of textures and the objects they belong to. With eyes only, we can still recognize and name textures, just as you did with those shown in Figure 6.1.

In art there are two basic kinds of textures that we recognize: real or **tactile** textures and visual or **simulated** textures.

Tactile textures are identified by both sight and touch. For example, the roughness of the soles of your gym shoes can be *felt* with your hand and *seen* with your eyes. As you will discover, it is frequently possible to fool the eyes, but rarely possible to fool your hands. With special-effects, movie artists do this all the time. What to the eyes is an avalanche of huge heavy boulders, becomes light-as-air chunks of styrofoam when lifted with the hands.

Artists who work in three-dimensions, such as sculptors, ceramists, and architects, are more likely to use tactile textures to add variety and meaning to their work. However, artists who create **collages** [co • LAHGE • ez] also use the tactile quality of objects to enhance their work. You have probably made collages before. They are simply a collection of textures—cloth, paper, cardboard— that are attached to a flat surface. You will see many examples of collages throughout this book.

WORDWATCH
texture
tactile
simulated
collage
Photo-realism
association
decalcomania
impression
addition

Figure 6.2. Closeup of surface of the moon. Photo credit: NASA

Visual or **simulated** texture is identified by your eyes only. Figure 6.2 shows a photograph of the surface of the moon. Although you may visit its surface sometime in the future (2010?), it is unlikely that you have yet had an opportunity to touch its texture with your hands. In fact, this may never be possible. Do you know why?

Not being able to touch the moon's surface with our hands, does not keep us from *seeing* and *imagining* what the texture would feel like. We can also, as artists, create an illusion or simulation of the texture of the moon. This presents us with many new creative possibilities for making interesting textures in our own work. As you will see in the examples that follow, natural textures are a great source of inspiration for artists in both two- and three-dimensions.

Simulated texture is also created for reasons other than art. Look again at the top of your desk. Does it look like wood? Does it feel like wood? It might be a wood simulation. Modern technology makes the reproduction and simulation of natural textures a fairly simple matter. As you look around your school building, how many texture simulations can you identify? Ask yourself how you are able to identify each. Is there something about them that isn't quite natural? What is it?

You will see in the following artworks that texture, both tactile and simulated, is an important art element used for adding interest and meaning. Artists throughout the centuries have developed many ways to use both actual textures and simulated textures. As with space, some artists have perfected the illusion of textures. In other words, they are able to convince our eyes that the bark on a tree is rough or that the fur of a rabbit is soft.

Other artists use the variety of textural surfaces to enhance the quality of a colored area, a line, or a curved shape. Some artists use our natural human responses to certain textures to give their artworks strong emotional impact. These artists understand that texture is one of the most powerful art elements, because it involves the two most powerful human senses—touch and sight.

SEEING AND UNDERSTANDING TEXTURE IN TWO-DIMENSIONS

Is It Real?

Do you remember that artist Chuck Close's working style was called **Photo-realism**? Although the term *Photo-realism* is fairly new, artists have been able to paint and draw with amazing realism for many centuries.

Creating a convincing illusion of a texture on the flat surface of a board, canvas, or paper takes not only a steady, skillful hand, but a sharp eye as well. Artists who want to paint and draw realistically must learn to look carefully at objects and their textures. They must learn how the texture of objects feels to the touch, as well as how it looks to the eye.

The following artists have learned to observe the world around them with great attention and precision. They rarely miss a detail of the objects they draw or paint.

Long before the invention of the camera, artists wanted to portray the beauty, variety, and detail of the world. Few artists were more accomplished at this than Jan Van Eyck [YAN van IK].

Van Eyck lived in Belgium during the 15th century. He was the first artist to use oil paints. Working on wooden panels, rather than on canvas, Van Eyck could mix and blend his colors until they matched exactly the hues, tints, and shades he found in the objects and textures of his world.

Figure 6.3 shows one of his most famous paintings. Known as *Arnolfini Marriage,* it is both a remarkable work of art and a kind of marriage contract, as well. Let's study this amazing painting more carefully.

Figure 6.3. Jan Van Eyck. *Arnolfini Marriage.* 1434. Oil on wood, 33″ x 22½″. Reproduced by courtesy of the Trustees, The National Gallery, London.

The first thing you may notice is the photographic realism of the painting. Every detail is recorded, from the fur edging on the velvet clothes to the shine of the brass chandelier. Did you notice that there is only one candle? There is a reason for this, as you will soon discover. But first, let's test your eyes!

Look at the mirror on the back wall. Can you see figures in the mirror? You should be able to see the backs of the happy couple and the artist! He is the official witness to the wedding. He has signed his name just above the mirror. This painting is a record, like a wedding photograph, of the great event.

The simulated textures found in this work are painted with such realism that we wouldn't be surprised if the little dog stepped from the frame so we could scratch his ears. But look around the room a little more. What other objects and textures can you identify? Are those the groom's shoes to the left? One would think the groom would wear his shoes at his wedding!

This painting serves many purposes. We know it is a wonderful work of art and we now know that it was used to record a special event. But, there is something else that this remarkable painting does. It teaches!

When you think about it, a pet dog is a rather strange member for a wedding party. Why is he there? Is he the bride's special favorite? Maybe. But, he also serves as a symbol. Symbols, you may recall, stand for other things. Everyday items can symbolize or represent ideas and feelings. For example, the American flag has come to symbolize freedom and democracy throughout the world.

When Van Eyck painted this work, people were very religious. Many artists of the time liked to put Christian symbolism into their artworks. It then could be used to teach, or remind the viewer, that God was everywhere and expected certain things from human beings.

Marriage, as portrayed in this painting, was thought to be a very sacred event. Most of the objects in the room were chosen to symbolize certain religious ideas about marriage. For example, the one burning candle represents the presence of God at the ceremony. The little dog symbolizes fidelity or faithfulness. The abandoned shoes, (can you find the bride's) means that the couple are standing on sacred or holy ground.

Symbolism in art is a fascinating subject. Unraveling the symbolic meanings of artworks can be similar to playing detective. Discovering the meanings of symbols can be fun and also informative, but you shouldn't worry too much if you don't have all the answers. A work like

The *Arnolfini Marriage* can be enjoyed just for its beauty and the technical mastery of the artist. Even though many hundreds of years separate us from Van Eyck and his time, we can still understand the delight he must have taken in the variety of objects and textures in his world. One wonder's what he would have thought of plastic, stainless steel, and vinyl!

Another artist, Albrecht Dürer [AL•breck DUR•rur], also enjoyed drawing and painting the textures of nature. Figure 6.4 titled *Young Field Hare,* was drawn in 1502. The date is clearly seen, as are the distinctive initials of the artist.

Even if Dürer had possessed a camera, he could not have recorded more accurately the texture and form of a rabbit.

He has drawn the texture and varied color of the fur with great skill. Looking at this drawing, it is almost possible to feel the softness of the fur. Notice the position of the rabbit. The artist has not allowed the fur's texture to hide the form of the body. One can see how the long, back legs are folded beneath the body.

If you have ever observed rabbits, you know that even when they are still, they seem to move. Whiskers tremble, ears flick, and the nose twitches. Dürer's rabbit seems about to jump from the paper. This kind of realism is only possible through careful observation *from life.*

Dürer had no photographs to copy. He only had the objects, themselves, which he studied and drew many times. In the chapter on drawing, you will learn more about the importance of drawing from life. Drawing from life, rather than copying from a photograph, is more difficult, but it is worth the effort.

The tradition of realism begun by artists like Van Eyck and Dürer has continued to the present. As you saw in the works of Chuck Close, realism is still popular. But one important change has been made—the invention of the camera.

Realism in art today does not serve the same purpose it did before the invention of the camera. Artists, as you will see throughout this book, are no longer obligated to paint and draw realistically. They can devote their time to creating works that are more about feelings, emotions, and moods than about how an apple looks sitting on a table.

As you continue to read about and to look at art, you will come to appreciate how varied visual art can be, and how much it can say to us as human beings. Far beyond simply showing us the objects and environments of our world, art can tell us about dreams, imagination, and the deepest fears of our hearts.

Figure 6.4. Albrecht Dürer. *Young Field Hare.* 1502. Watercolor, 25.1cm. x 22.6cm. Collection Albertina Museum, Vienna. Photo credit: Archiv fur Kunst und Geschichte, Berlin.

Perhaps of all the art elements we have discussed, color and texture have the greatest emotional power. As you read earlier, science has discovered how our reactions to certain colors can be physical. In a similar way, various textures can make us react with pleasure or horror. Artists frequently use this natural human response to advantage as you will see in the artworks in this chapter.

The two most powerful senses we have are sight and touch. Our eyes describe the world to us; our hands confirm its reality. Therefore, an art element like texture, which uses both sight and touch, can add much to creative expression.

Look at the work pictured in Figure 6.5. It is titled *Object*. This sculpture was created by artist Meret Oppenheim [may • ret OP • pen • hihm]. What reaction do you experience when you look at this work? Does your mouth feel funny? Would you look forward to drinking a cup of hot chocolate out of that cup!

Oppenheim has very cleverly combined two opposite ideas to give us a work of art that can actually create a physical reaction. First, when we see objects, such as cups and saucers, plates, or forks and knives, we make an **association** or mental connection. Put very simply, we think about food or eating. The second object we associate with is the fur. Fur is something we enjoy feeling with our hands, but not with our tongues. The very thought of hair or fur in our mouths makes us gag!

Oppenheim combined these two very different associations into a new image. The new image—a fur-covered cup and saucer—is so powerful that we have a physical reaction to it.

Putting together two very different images to create a new one, or placing an ordinary object in an unusual setting, are both favorite tricks of the art movement called **Surrealism**. Oppenheim was definitely a member!

Surrealism means "more than real" or "super real." Surrealist artists, and you will meet more later, were very interested in creating artworks that touch on the bizarre. They liked to shock and mystify the public with their dream-like, or nightmarish, visions of the world. Creating new and strange textures was the means they used to give an other-world quality to their work. The science fiction and fantasy artists of today are their creative heirs.

Figure 6.5. Meret Oppenheim. *Object.* 1936. Fur-covered cup, saucer, and spoon; cup 4⅜″ diameter, spoon 8″ long: overall 2⅞″ high. Collection, The Museum of Modern Art, New York, Purchase.

Figure 6.6 by Max Ernst [URNST] is titled *The Eye of Silence*. Talk about your alien landscapes! Such a place could only exist in the imagination.

To create this place of dreams, Ernst developed a new method for making texture in paint. He called it **decalcomania.** The method is really quite simple. Paint is applied to a surface. While the paint is still wet, wrinkled paper, plastic, or cloth is then pressed into it. The wrinkle marks are left in the paint.

Obviously, Ernst did more to his painting. He used the process of decalcomania to provide the background for his imagination. Looking into the textured paint, he found shapes that reminded him of rock formations and strange creatures. These he highlighted with color and value.

While the world around us provides many interesting textures to use in our art, we can also create our own textures with techniques such as decalcomania.

Figure 6.6. Max Ernst. *The Eye of Silence.* 1943-44. Oil on canvas, 108cm. x 141cm. Washington University of Gallery of Art, St. Louis.

SEEING AND UNDERSTANDING TEXTURE IN THREE DIMENSIONS

Sculptors and potters (ceramists) also use texture to add interest and meaning to their works. These artists

Figure 6.7. *Sumerian seal and impression.*
Seal is lapis lazuli, with a gold cap and
bronze stem, 2.8 cm. high. Oriental Institute
Museum, University of Chicago.

In place of a written signature,
ancient Sumerians pressed carved stones into
wet clay to identify themselves on
documents.

use "real" or tactile texture. Texture on a sculpture or a
clay container can be felt, as well as seen.

There are two ways, **addition** and **subtraction,** to add
texture to sculpture and ceramics made from clay.

Since clay is a soft, pliable material, many different
textures can be created by pushing objects into the surface. These objects then leave behind an **impression** or
mark in the clay. An example of impressed texture is
shown in Figure 6.7.

The small, tube-shaped object is a cylinder seal.
Created in Sumeria more than 5,000 years ago, it was
used to identify its owner. Just the way you sign your
name to your school papers, ancient Sumerians "signed"
with cylinder seals.

The seals were made of some hard stone. The images,
usually animals or human figures, were carved into the
surface of the stone. The cylinder of stone was then
rolled across a small slab of damp clay. The carvings on
the surface left their impressions in the clay. When the
clay dried, the slab could be sent to someone or attached
to an object.

⬚? Can you recognize what is impressed in the clay
sample? Wouldn't this design look good around the
middle of a clay container! If you were going to design
a cylinder seal for your own use, what images would
you use?

The Japanese artist who created the clay container in
Figure 6.8 many thousands of years ago used both
impression and addition to add interest and beauty.

Notice the raised, curved lines that decorate the top
section. It is easy to imagine how these were created.
You, yourself, have probably made clay "snakes" or coils
by rolling a piece of soft clay between your hands. Surely
the maker of this pot did something similar. By adding
them to the surface of the container, a tactile texture was
created, as well as a flowing design that leads our eyes
⬚? around the pot. Can you see how the end of one coil
points to the next?

There seem to be two small handles on either side of
the vessel. Could these have been made with clay coils
also?

⬚? Other texture designs on the surface of the container
appear to be made by impression. Can you find them?
What kind of tool could have made these textures? Look
carefully at the top of each raised line. Can you see the
impressions left by a tool? Have you seen a similar container pictured in this book? See if you can remember

Figure 6.8. *Japanese Urn.* c. 1000 B.C. Middle Jomon Period. Terra Cotta, 15½″h. x 13″d. Cleveland Musuem of Art. John L. Severance Fund.

where. When you find it, compare the two. What do you think was kept in this pot?

The sculpture of the laughing boy (Figure 6.9) is also very old. It was made by a sculptor who lived in Pre-Columbian (the time before the arrival of Columbus in the New World) Mexico. Made of a reddish clay, it shows how the sculptor used addition to create a tactile texture that looks like fish scales. Small, flat pieces of clay are overlapped to form the fish-scale texture.

Notice how the scales stick out from the surface of the figure. Each one throws a little shadow on the one beneath. This adds *visual* interest, as well as *tactile* interest. The artist has also used impressed texture. Can you find it?

☐? We called this a sculpture of a laughing boy, but maybe he isn't laughing. Could he be crying? How has the sculptor shown emotion in the boy's face? Do you think he is happy or sad?

Figure 6.9. Pre-Columbian. Xipe Toltec. A.D. 600-750. Clay sculpture, 15¾″ x 6⅝″ x 3⅞″. Kimbell Art Museum, Fort Worth, Texas.

Figure 6.10. Albrecht Dürer. *Self Portrait.* 1500. Oil on wood, 67cm. x 49cm. Collection Alte Pinakothek, Munich. Photo credit: Archiv fur Kunst und Geschichte, Berlin.

BORN: 1471
DIED: 1528
BIRTHPLACE:
Nuremburg, Germany

The Mirror of Nature

Albrecht Dürer was one of the greatest artists of the Renaissance in Germany, just as Leonardo was in Italy. Like Leonardo, Dürer excelled in many different art forms, including drawing, painting, and printmaking. After visiting Venice, Italy, as a young man, Dürer returned to Germany with many new ideas about art and the role of the artist in the world of the 15th century.

Dürer decided that artists needed to be objective, careful observers. They also needed to understand the technical side of their art. They needed the ability to create convincing illusions of space through linear perspective. Dürer even wrote a kind of textbook on geometry and perspective, illustrating it with his own prints. His woodcuts and engravings are considered some of the finest ever created.

As you might imagine, Dürer had great confidence and pride in his artistic abilities. It became characteristic of him to identify his artworks with his unique monogram. You can usually find it prominently displayed somewhere in his drawings, paintings, or prints. The "A" of his first name is written large with the "D" of his last name written between the legs of the "A."

Dürer was also fond of self-portraits. He painted and drew himself many times throughout his life. He liked to show himself in an elegant pose, dressed in rich and elaborate clothes. The love of detail that is seen in the wonderful drawing of the rabbit is also obvious in his self-portrait. Every curled lock of hair, every rich detail of clothing is lovingly presented with amazing skill. Few artists in history have had the ability to reproduce textures like Albrecht Dürer.

Figure 6.11. Albrecht Dürer. *St. Eustace.* 1500-02. Copper engraving, 357cm. x 260cm. Photo credit: Archiv fur Kunst und Geschichte, Berlin.

Did you learn

- The meaning of these words and phrases: texture; tactile; simulated; Photo-realism; association; decalcomania; impression; addition?
- Why Figure 6.3, *Arnolfini Marriage,* is considered a marriage contract?
- The symbolism of the little dog; of the one candle?
- How Oppenheim's fur-covered cup uses two associations?
- How to create decalcomania? Who used it? Why it is good for making strange textures?
- Two methods for creating texture in clay?

Student work.

Understanding and Evaluating

- In one column, make a list of objects or surfaces with textures you dislike touching. Make another list of objects or surfaces with textures you enjoy touching. Make a list of at least five each. Now, randomly draw lines between a pair of items in the rows. Imagine the texture of one on the other.
- Design a game in which texture recognition is the purpose.
- Look around your classroom or your room at home. How many different textures (not objects) can you find? Do you live in a relatively smooth or rough environment? Which do you prefer?

Seeing and Creating

- Collect four samples of very different textures. On a piece of drawing paper, mark off four boxes 3"x 3". Fill each box with a drawing of each of the textures.
- Select two objects, one human-made, one natural. Study them carefully. Reverse the textures. Either draw the natural texture on the human-made object, or the reverse. Use pencil.
- With your teacher's help, try decalcomania. Tempera paint works well for this project. Once your paper surface is covered, complete the painting by adding other people, animals, or objects. Before deciding, turn your paper in several directions.

Unit III
THE PRINCIPLES OF DESIGN

Now that you have learned about the art elements and how artists use them to create different works of art, you are ready to find out how artworks are put together.

You may recall that the **principles of design** are guides or general directions for putting a work of art together. Just as a piece of music is composed, a work of art is composed also.

A work of art is a **visual** composition, arranged according to certain guidelines. These guidelines are the principles of design: **unity, balance, variety, repetition, emphasis, movement,** and **proportion.** Can you remember the mnemonic we used to remember them? (*U*nless *B*ats *V*acate *R*ooms, *E*very *M*an *P*auses)

Though the principles of design can be helpful to artists in organizing and composing their artworks, they should never be thought of as hard and fast rules. Using the principles of design cannot guarantee a great work of art, or even a good one.

Why then, you may ask, should I learn about something that is not going to guarantee a successful artwork? As with language, the more words we are able to recognize and use in different ways, the better we can write and express our thoughts and feelings.

As you learn about the many ways artists throughout the centuries have used art elements and design principles to express themselves visually, you will find that your own artworks will improve. You will be able to "say" things with images in ways that you had not thought of before. You will also be able to "read" a work of art for meaning, just the way you read a book. Although some works of art may remain mysterious, you will still be far ahead of most people in understanding art.

While the art elements are fairly easy to identify as separate parts in an artwork, the principles of design are more difficult to isolate. They overlap each other and are never used alone.

Max Weber. *Chinese Restaurant.* 1915. Oil on canvas, 40″ x 48″. Collection, Whitney Museum of American Art. Gift of Gertrude Vanderbilt Whitney, 31.382.

Look at the object pictured in Figure 7.1. As a method of transportation, it probably wouldn't take you very far! And although it is fun to look at, the parts just don't fit together. They don't make a workable whole, nor do they have **unity**.

Chapter 7
UNITY AND BALANCE

UNITY

Have you ever listened to the school band when everyone is tuning their instrument? What a noise! Although bits of music can be heard from some instruments, there is no **unity** to the sounds. Everyone is playing their instruments without thinking how they all sound together.

Unity in a visual art composition works much the same way as it does in music. Works of art that show unity appear to have an order and oneness that says to the viewer, "These parts have meaning and go well together."

You might be surprised to find that an artwork can have unity, even though many art elements are present in a complicated arrangement. You will also discover in the examples that follow, that artists have many ways of creating visual unity.

WORDWATCH
unity
symmetrical balance
asymmetrical balance
axis

Figure 7.1. An image that has unity appears whole. Parts seem to belong or go well together.

Figure 7.2. Example of symmetrical balance.

Figure 7.3. Example of asymmetrical balance.

When you stand on one foot, you sometimes need to extend your arms to keep your balance. Artists must also make adjustments to their artworks so that they appear balanced to viewers. A work of art that is **balanced** appears to have an equal arrangement of art elements.

However, visual balance does not mean that the art elements must be used *equally*. As you will discover through the following works of art, artists have many different ways of creating balance.

There are two kinds of visual balance—**formal** or **symmetrical** [sim • MET • tree • cul] and **informal** or **asymmetrical** [a • sim • MET • tree • cul].

Symmetrical Balance

Symmetrical balance is like a mirror image. Everything on one side of a center line or **axis** [AX • is] is the same as everything on the other side (Figure 7.2).

An art composition that is formally or symmetrically balanced can be very pleasing to the eye. Human beings like symmetrical balance. Can you guess why?

Although a symmetrically balanced design can be very appealing, it can also be boring. To prevent this, artists use a wide variety of colors, lines, shapes, and textures to add interest to a symmetrically balanced composition. Sometimes artists change one or two small details, so that the symmetry isn't exact.

The use of symmetrical balance can express feelings of order, strength, and calmness.

Asymmetrical Balance

Informal or asymmetrical balance is created by changing the arrangement of colors, shapes, other art elements, or subjects so that they are not equally positioned (Figure 7.3).

Although asymmetrical balance is fairly easy to recognize, it is sometimes difficult to discover exactly how and why it works in an art composition. This is because there are usually a number of art elements involved in creating asymmetrical balance.

When you look at a work of art that is asymmetrically balanced, you may "feel" the balance more than see what creates it. This is why it is important to look at a wide variety of works by artists who have used asymmetrical balance. As you examine or analyze the following artworks, you will discover that there are many different ways of creating asymmetrical balance.

Asymmetrical balance can be very interesting. It is an

effective way to express feelings of tension, anxiety, or instability.

SEEING AND UNDERSTANDING UNITY AND BALANCE

Artist Richard Lindner, in his work titled *42nd Street* (Figure 7.4), uses symmetrical balance to give order to a painting that has many different shapes and colors.

[?] At first glance, we are convinced that this is a mirror-image design. The central axis runs down the center from top to bottom. But look again! Is this really a mirror image?

The artist may have tricked us into believing the design is symmetrically balanced. Like the mirrors in a carnival funhouse, you look, but don't necessarily see what you expect. If you look closely at *42nd Street*, you will see small differences from one side of the design to [?] the other. Can you tell what has been changed?

Are you ever bothered by a picture that hangs crooked on a wall? Some people are very uncomfortable unless everything hanging on their walls is straight. Part of our discomfort with objects that are not perfectly horizontal or vertical to us, is our own physical symmetry. As human beings we are very sensitive about keeping our balance. When we become dizzy, or unbalanced, we are very uncomfortable and frequently ill. And although we may love to challenge our body to keep its balance on a wild ride at the amusement park, we could not stand the feeling for very long.

The human need to feel stable and balanced has been used by artists to make us experience new sensations and emotions.

Figure 7.5 shows a work by Dutch artist Piet Mondrian [PEET MON • dree • on]. Mondrian takes advantage of our need to straighten pictures and stand on a flat, stable surface. By turning a square canvas until it rests on one point or corner, he creates a very unstable image. But notice the arrangement of lines and geometric shapes. They are painted as if the canvas hangs parallel to the ground!

This composition of straight lines, squares, and rectangles seems to lock the canvas in place, even though it is balanced on one point. The composition of the painting is informal or asymmetrically balanced. Let's analyze why.

[?] What color has been used at the very bottom of the canvas? Can you guess why?

Dark colors, like black, blue, and purple usually appear *heavier* to us than higher-value colors, such as yellow,

Figure 7.4. Richard Lindner. *42nd Street.* 1964. Oil on canvas 70″ x 60″. Private collection.

Figure 7.5. Piet Mondrian. *Diamond Painting in Red, Yellow, and Blue.* 1921/25. Canvas on hardboard, diagonal 56¼″ x 56″. National Gallery of Art, Washington, D.C. Gift of Herbert and Nanette Rothschild.

91

red, and orange. Mondrian has taken advantage of the visual weight of color in his painting.

The black at the bottom point acts as a kind of anchor that seems to keep the composition from falling to the right or to the left.

Mondrian also uses shapes and lines to balance his painting. For example, the violet triangle on the right is balanced by red and yellow triangles and thicker, heavier lines. Can you find them?

Even though nothing in the painting is matched or equal, it still appears to be balanced. The balance is *felt* by the viewer, because of the way the artist has arranged the art elements.

This painting is also a good example of how visual unity can be created through the use of repeated shapes and lines. The elements or parts of the composition seem to belong together.

Figure 7.6, titled *J.F.K. 1963*, is by artist James Brooks. It is another example of asymmetrical balance. Unlike the painting by Mondrian, this work does not use geometric shapes. The colors are also more varied and complex. However, line does play an important role in balancing the composition.

Look at the thin, red lines that cross the bottom of the canvas. They draw our eyes toward the bottom of the painting. They help balance the red shape on the left. Can you find other areas of the painting where repetition of colors, shapes, or lines provide visual balance?

Notice the dark rectangular shape at the bottom right. This shape and color, just as in Mondrian's painting, serves to anchor the composition in place. It is not necessary to balance a shape or color by an exact copy. Sometimes a variation is more effective and interesting.

BALANCE IN THREE DIMENSIONS

Artists working with three-dimensional materials also use both symmetrical and asymmetrical balance. Even sculptors who use the symmetrical form of the human body as a subject, often pose their subjects in asymmetrical positions. Remember, asymmetrical balance can be used by artists to create a feeling of tension and energy. Symmetrical balance, on the other hand, expresses permanence and stability.

Let's compare two sculptures that were created in different times and by different cultures, as well as having different purposes. As you will discover, each sculptor used a different kind of visual balance to express something quite unique in both works.

Figure 7.6. James Brooks. *J.F.K. 1963.* Oil on canvas, 72″ x 72″. The Museum of Fine Arts, Houston. Gift of Skidmore, Owings, and Merrill, New York.

Figure 7.7 shows a huge sculpture of the great Egyptian pharoah, Ramesses [RAM • ah • ses]. The figure of the king faces forward. The features of the face being equally placed on either side of a center line represents a example of a symmetrically balanced sculpture.

Remember our discussion of the great Egyptian temple of Karnak? The ancient Egyptians were very concerned with telling the world about the importance of their culture and the greatness and power of their Pharoah or king. They were also very concerned that the art they created would last forever. They built big, and they built permanently. What better way to show timeless power and importance than through symmetrically balanced artworks. It is very difficult to find an example of art from ancient Egypt that is not symmetrically balanced.

The civilization of ancient Egypt lasted many thousands of years. During this long period it changed very little. This stability and permanence is reflected in both the architecture and sculpture of this remarkable culture.

In contrast, the sculpture shown in Figure 7.8 is from a very different time. It also has a very different expressive purpose.

Sculptor Gianlorenzo Bernini [gee • ahn • low • RENS • o bear • NEE • nee] lived and worked in Italy during the 17th century. He was one of the great artists of the Italian Renaissance.

The sculpture shown in Figure 7.8 is one of his most famous works. It is called *David*, and represents an important moment in the Bible story of David and Goliath. Do you know the story? David, the brave, shepherd boy, has been challenged to a battle by the giant Goliath. Armed with only a stone and slingshot, David kills Goliath with one fatal blow.

Bernini has captured the young David just before he throws the stone. In order to show us the energy and power about to be released with the stone, the sculptor has twisted the figure of David into an asymmetrically balanced position. Like a coiled spring, the twisted figure seems just on the point of unwinding and hurling his deadly rock.

In the sculpture of Ramesses, you could easily locate the center line or axis of the composition. The sculptor has positioned equal parts on either side of this line. The figure is rigid in its symmetry. In contrast, if you drew the central axis down the figure of *David*, you would not have a mirror-image on both sides.

Each sculptor had a very different expressive purpose in mind when he created his work. As you can see, the choice of symmetrical or asymmetrical balance in a work of art often has much to do with what the artist wants to say.

Figure 7.7. Egyptian Pharoah Ramesses.

Figure 7.8. Gianlorenzo Bernini. *David*. 1619. Marble. Collection Borghese Gallery, Rome. Photo credit: Archiv fur Kunst und Geschichte, Berlin.

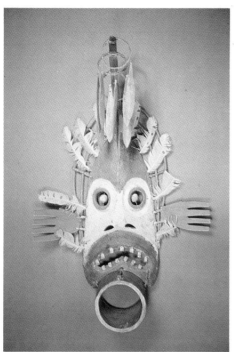

Figure 7.9

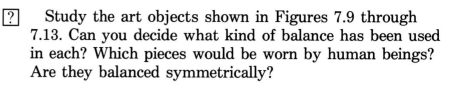

Study the art objects shown in Figures 7.9 through 7.13. Can you decide what kind of balance has been used in each? Which pieces would be worn by human beings? Are they balanced symmetrically?

Figure 7.10

Figure 7.11

Figure 7.12

Figure 7.13

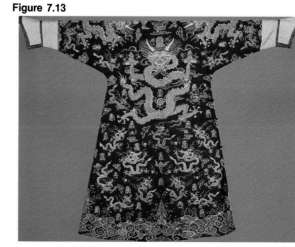

The Framework of Nature

Piet Mondrian began his art career by painting landscapes. These first works were very different from the pure line, shape, and color paintings that later became his trademark.

Like other artists of his time, Mondrian was attracted to Paris as the center of everything exciting about art. He, too, became fascinated with Cubism. But reducing objects to simpler shapes didn't go far enough for Mondrian. He wanted all hints of the original subject matter eliminated. He would say everything he needed to say in art through the use of pure art elements.

In 1914 Mondrian returned home to continue his work in pure abstraction. In 1917 he helped form a group of artists with ideas similiar to his own. They called themselves De Stijl. [day STYLE] or "The Style."

After returning to Paris in 1919, Mondrian continued to paint, but he separated himself from De Stijl, because he felt they were not following his strict formula for painting pure form!

In 1938 he moved to London. Unfortunately, his studio was destroyed in a bombing raid during World War II. Not to be stopped, even by war, Mondrian moved to New York in 1940 and began the last phase of his painting career.

The energy and rhythm of the big city inspired one of Mondrian's most famous series of paintings known as *Boogie-Woogie.* The characteristic squares, rectangles, and lines are still there, but they have been energized with color. They seem to have a restless beat all their own.

Portrait of Piet Mondrian. 1940-41. Photographer Harry Holtzman. ©Estate of Harry Holtzman, New York, New York.

BORN: 1872
DIED: 1944
BIRTHPLACE:
Aarsfoort, Holland

Opposite page. **Figure 7.9.** *Painted Wooden Mask.* Eskimo Mask representing Negakfok, the cold weather spirit. Eskimo, Near Bethel, Kuskokwim Rimever, Alaska. National Museum of the American Indian, New York.

Figure 7.10. Joseph Stella. *The Brooklyn Bridge; Variation on an Old Theme.* 1939. Oil on canvas. 70" x 42". Collection, Whitney Museum of American Art. Purchase 42.15.

Figure 7.11. *Pre-Columbian Pendant: Two Deer Heads.* 800-1200 A.D. Cast gold, 7.2cm. h. Kimbell Art Museum, Fort Worth, Texas.

Figure 7.12. Paul Gauguin. *Portrait of the Artist with the Idol.* c. 1893. Oil on canvas, 17¼" x 12⅞". Marion Koogler McNay Art Museum, San Antonio, Texas. Bequest of Marion Koogler McNay.

Figure 7.13. Chinese Dragon Robe. 17-18 century. Silk, 144cm. Photo credit: Rosenthal.

Figure 7.14. Piet Mondrian. *Composition in White, Black, and Red.* 1936. Oil on canvas, 40¼" x 41". Collection, The Museum of Modern Art, New York. Gift of the Advisory Committee.

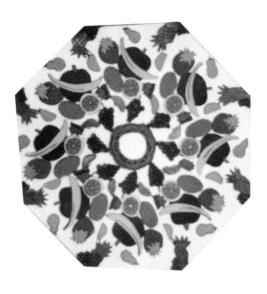

Student work.

Did you learn

- The definition of these words and phrases: unity; symmetrical balance; asymmetrical balance; axis?
- The difference between symmetrical and asymmetrical balance?
- The name of the group founded by Mondrian?
- One of the greatest rulers of Egypt?

Understanding and Evaluation

- Apply the four levels of art criticism to Figure 7.5. Write down your observations for each level.
- Find a number of examples of symmetrical and asymmetrical designs. Compare them. Which do you prefer?
- Are the designs on clothes always symmetrical? If so, why.
- Select another artwork from a previous chapter. Try to decide how balance was achieved. Review the discussion of artworks in this chapter if necessary.

Seeing and Creating

- Using an analogous color scheme, create a symmetrical design from cut construction paper.
- Make a kaleidoscope design. Draw a large circle or rectangle on white construction or drawing paper. Divide into equal parts. Make a pattern that fits one of the sections. Draw a design on that section. Transfer the design to each of the other sections. Color the design with crayon or tempera paint.

Chapter 8
VARIETY, REPETITION, AND EMPHASIS

Can you imagine a world in which everything and every person looked the same? What if you went into a department store and found only one kind of shoe to wear? What if there were nothing in the supermarket but apples—red apples? How boring!

Most people soon tire of wearing the same clothing, eating the same food, or doing the same activity. Human beings love variety and need change to keep them interested (Figure 8.1).

Artists use the principle of **variety** to make their art interesting. Variety in artworks can be recognized by the use of different art elements or subjects or the **contrast** between them.

Repetition can be thought of as the opposite of **variety**. Repetition in an artwork concerns the use of exact or similar elements or subjects. Artists may repeat colors, lines, shapes, forms, textures, or values. They can also repeat subject matter, either completely or in parts (Figure 8.2).

Variety and repetition are frequently used in the same work of art. These two principles complement each other.

While the use of repetition is one way to create unity in a visual composition, used alone it can be very monotonous. The use of variety then becomes very important. Like the salt and pepper we use to enliven the flavor of our food, it adds interest and pleasure.

EMPHASIS

Visual **emphasis** in a work of art is a way of calling attention to a particular area.

When you circle a word in a sentence or whistle and clap your hands at a thrilling point in a football game, you are adding **emphasis.** You are saying, "Notice this part," or "What a great play!"

The part or area emphasized in a work of art is said to be the **focal point.** In other words, it is the point where the artist wants us to focus our attention. The following works show how artists are able to create emphasis and focal points in many different ways.

WORDWATCH
variety
repetition
emphasis
focal point

Figure 8.2. Andy Warhol. *100 Cans.* 1962. Oil on canvas, 72″ x 52″. Albright-Knox Art Gallery, Buffalo, New York. Gift of Seymour H. Knox, 1963.

The design principles of variety, repetition, and emphasis all work together to create visual compositions that can be both unified and expressive. Let's examine how artists organize their works using these principles. And, don't forget balance. As you examine the following works, see if you can determine the kind of visual balance in each.

SEEING AND UNDERSTANDING VARIETY, REPETITION, AND EMPHASIS

When people talk about repetition in art, they sometimes refer to **pattern**. They are not really the same. A visual **pattern** can be the result of the use of **repetition**. (Figure 8.2).

For example, if you press your finger into some ink or paint and then onto a sheet of paper ten times, you have used **repetition** to create a **pattern**. This kind of pattern is familiar to us from many everyday items, especially the designs on our clothes.

But pattern does not always have to be created by repetition. The shadows of leaves and tree limbs on a sidewalk or the reflected colors of a stained-glass window on a wall create pattern also.

The use of repetition is sometimes not so obvious. For example, look at the work by Diego Rivera [dee•A•go ree•VER•ra] in Figure 8.3. In this work, the artist has created unity by repeating similar shapes. With few expectations, all the shapes have rounded corners. They are simple, with few details. Notice how the bent shape of the man is repeated in the shape of the basket of cotton and in the woman's shoulders.

The shapes almost remind us of the block-like forms found in natural rock formations. The artist has emphasized this feeling by leaving out small details. Do these large, bulky shapes add to the expressive quality of his work? What do you think the artist is trying to say about these two people and the work they are doing?

Rivera has also added variety to his work through the use of color, value, and texture. How would you describe the color scheme he has used? Can you identify the textures?

Artist Henri Rousseau [ON•ree ru•SEW] loved to paint imaginary scenes of the jungle with its plant and animal life. Figure 8.4, *Jungle: Tiger Attacking Buffalo*, shows his interest in this subject.

Opposite page. **Figure 8.1.**

Figure 8.3. Diego Rivera. *The Flower Carrier.* 1935. Oil and tempera on Masonite, 48″ x 47¾″. San Francisco Museum of Modern Art. Albert M. Bender Collection, Gift of Albert M. Bender in memory of Caroline Walter.

Figure 8.4. Henri Rousseau. *Jungle: Tiger Attacking Buffalo.* Oil on canvas, 67¾″ x 75⅜″. The Cleveland Museum of Art. Gift of Hanna Fund.

Since Rousseau never visited a jungle, he depended on his vivid imagination and books to fill in the details. His paintings have been described as "childlike." Though skillfully painted, they do have a storybook quality to them. The animals don't really seem very threatening, or the jungle very wild.

One of the first things that catches your attention in this painting is the pattern created by the overlapping leaves and tree branches. Strongly outlined, the leaves and branches break up the negative or background space into even more patterns. Can you see how the artist has used repetition of both shape and space to create unity? Even the bunches of bananas repeat the shapes of the jungle plants. The tiger, camouflaged by his striped coat, can barely be seen among the twisted foliage.

Rousseau has altered the size or proportion of leaves and branches to add variety. Variety in color values adds even more interest to the work.

Though not very realistic, the imaginary jungles of Rousseau are pleasing to look at. They remind us of elaborate puzzles in which each part is related, but slightly different. They are simple in detail, but complex in composition.

EMPHASIS

Artists use emphasis to call attention to some part of an artwork. They may want the viewer to look there first, or to pay particular attention to the area because it has special meaning. There are many ways to create emphasis in a visual art composition. An area may be highlighted or cast in deep shadow. There may be an object that is different or in contrast to other objects in the work. For example, something round may be placed among straight-edged objects. The emphasized area may be isolated by color or value. This always draws attention.

The object or area of the artwork may be different in size from the surroundings. This changes the **proportions** of the elements within the work. You will learn more of how artists use proportion as a design principle in the next section.

The following artists have used a combination of these methods to focus attention on a specific area of their works. As you study their works, see if you can decide why the artists wanted to emphasize these specific parts.

Figure 8.5. Rembrandt van Rijn. *The Philosopher in Meditation.* Oil on canvas, 21⅛″ x 16¼″. Collection: The Louvre, Paris. Photo © R.M.N.

How does the placement of emphasis or focal point change the meaning of the work?

Rembrandt van Rijn [RIM•brant von RINE] was one of the most famous Dutch artists who ever lived. Recognized for his life-like portraits, he painted the ordinary people of Holland during the 17th century. He often had members of his own family sit for their portraits. He was also very interested in his own face as a subject for painting. This wasn't because he was vain or thought himself handsome! He was interested in how the passing years changed the features of his face.

Rembrandt painted with oil paint on canvas. At times, he used quite a bit of paint! Some of his artworks have such thick paint on them that it sticks out one-fourth-inch beyond the canvas.

A fine example of his painting technique and use of emphasis is shown in Figure 8.5, titled *Philosopher in Meditation.* When you look at the painting, where are your eyes first attracted? Where do you look next? Can there be more than one focal point or area of emphasis in a painting? Of course, there can be. Anything is possible in art!

The primary focal point is the head of the old philosopher. Light floods into the scene spotlighting his head. Much of the background and body of the old man is lost in heavy shadow. Rembrandt is using high contrast in values here. This creates a very dramatic impression. In fact, the word *dramatic* describes this work very well. Doesn't it look like a scene from a stage play? The old philosopher could easily be an actor performing his "big" scene under a dazzling theater spotlight. Did you decide where the second area of emphasis is?

Rembrandt had a purpose for choosing these two areas of the human figure for emphasis. Can you guess why?

Look at the face of the other figure in the painting. What is this person doing? If you guessed that this is the second area of emphasis, you are right. Rembrandt has made you look from one side of the painting to the other. He has also called attention to the quiet concentration of the old man and the busy activity of the servant.

The paintings of the American artist Edward Hopper are frequently about very ordinary subjects—stores, houses, simple things, and simple people. Figure 8.6, *Seven a.m.*, is a good example of his favorite subjects and how clearly he used emphasis to add meaning and expression to his work.

? Can you find the focal point of this painting? Look carefully. It is not as obvious as in the work by Rembrandt. Remember that isolation of an object or an art element can create emphasis.

If you picked the clock in the window of the store, you are correct. Our eyes are attracted to that shape for a number of reasons. First, it is somewhat isolated from other objects. There is space between it and everything else. The shape of the clock is also different from other shapes in the painting. For example, notice the shapes of the other objects in the window of the store. There isn't another rounded shape like the clock anywhere else in the painting. Hopper has used contrast of shape to focus our attention on the clock.

The clock is a dark value against a wall of light value. More contrast there. Can you identify what parts of the painting balance the dark stand of trees to the left? Remember what you have learned about the weight of certain colors.

Figure 8.6. Edward Hopper. *Seven a.m.* 1948. Oil on canvas, 30″ x 40″. Purchase and exchange 50.8. Collection of Whitney Museum of American Art, New York.

Figure 8.7. Andrew Wyeth. *The Chambered Nautilus.* 1956. Tempera on panel, 24¾" x 48¼". ©1990 Wadsworth Atheneum Museum, Hartford. From the collection of Mr. and Mrs. Robert Montgomery.

But, why call our attention to the clock? Why do you think the artist has used it as the focal point of the painting?

Figure 8.7, titled *Chambered Nautilus,* by American artist Andrew Wyeth [WYTH], is another good example of how an artist can use emphasis to express something special through art.

But first, where and what is the chambered nautilus? Can you find it? Look on the chest at the foot of the bed. The shell is called a chambered nautilus. But is it the focal point of this painting? What about the large, lighted window? Is that what draws your attention first?

This painting is another example of a work with more than one focal point. Because of its size and brightness the window captures our attention. It floods the room and all objects in it with light. But at the same time it highlights other areas of emphasis—the shell and the girl sitting in bed.

There are several interesting things about this painting. The title of the painting seems to refer to the shell at the lower right. But is that the only chambered nautilus here?

The shell of the sea creature, known as a nautilus, is divided into compartments or separate chambers. You might have seen one of the shells cut in half. As the creature inside grows, it builds a bigger and bigger shell, closing each outgrown chamber. Why name a painting of a girl sitting in a canopied bed (a bed with a top and curtains) *Chambered Nautilus?* Is the artist trying to help us make a connection between the areas of the painting that have been emphasized? What do you think is the connection? Are there other details that have special meaning? Are the curtains of the bed moving?

Diego Rivera. *Self Portrait.* 1941. Oil on canvas, 61 cm. x 43 cm. Smith College Museum of Art, Northampton, Massachusetts. Gift of Irene Rich Clifford, 1977.

BORN: 1886
DIED: 1957
BIRTHPLACE:
Guanajuato, Mexico

The Spirit of Mexico

Diego Rivera's art talent was recognized when he was very young. At age ten, he was enrolled in the San Carlos Academy. Here he studied traditional styles of painting, especially landscape.

In 1907 his work came to the attention of the governor of Vera Cruz. The governor was so impressed with young Rivera's work that he gave him a scholarship to study in Europe. While in Europe, Rivera too fell under the influence of Cubism. Unlike Mondrian and others, he did not reject all realism. He did, however, simplify the details of figures and objects. The shapes of objects in his paintings are very rounded. They seem to have both weight and substance.

It was his visit to Italy that probably had the greatest effect on Rivera's art. In Rome and Florence he began to study the murals and frescos (wall paintings) of the great Renaissance artists. In 1919 he met another Mexican artist, David Alfaro Siqueiros [SEE • KAY • eros]. They were both excited by the art they had seen, but wanted to return home to use what they had learned to transform Mexican art. They wanted to give the art of Mexico an identity as strong as that they had seen in Europe. Rivera was very excited about this idea and returned to Mexico in 1921.

The very next year he began his first mural. Many other murals followed, including ones for the National Palace, the Ministry of Education, and the Palace of Fine Arts in Mexico City.

Working with bold, simple shapes and vivid colors, Rivera illustrated the historical and political struggles of Mexico. His work influenced many mural painters, such as Thomas Hart Benton in the United States.

Figure 8.8. Diego Rivera. *Flower Day.* 1925. Oil on canvas, 58″ x 47½″. Los Angeles County Museum of Art. Los Angeles County Fund.

Did you learn

- The definitions of these words and phrases: variety; repetition; emphasis; focal point?
- At least three ways to create emphasis?
- Why Rembrandt emphasized the hands and face?

Student work.

Understanding and Evaluating

- Look again at *Chambered Nautilus* (Figure 8.7) by Wyeth. Apply the four levels of art criticism to this work. Can you find symbolism here? What do you think the symbols are?
- Look at *Philosopher* (Figure 8.5) by Rembrandt. Is there symbolism in this work? If so, what do you think it is?
- Search out patterns in your school. Are they natural or human-made? What purpose do they serve—decorative or functional?

Seeing and Creating

- Make a pattern by using stamp printing. Make your stamps by folding or rolling scraps of posterboard. Tape and use the edge for the stamp. Use tempera paint, lightly brushed on the edge of the posterboard stamp. Cover a sheet of white or colored construction paper with a repeating pattern. Vary your pattern by combining more than one stamp into a design.
- Divide a sheet of white drawing or construction paper into an equal number of one-half-inch squares. Using a water-based felt marker or India ink and pen, fill each square with a different repeating line. The lines can vary in width and direction. Use this line-patterned background for an ink drawing of a natural object.
- Create a design in which a shape is repeated, but with variations. Your design can be painted or made from cut paper.

Student work.

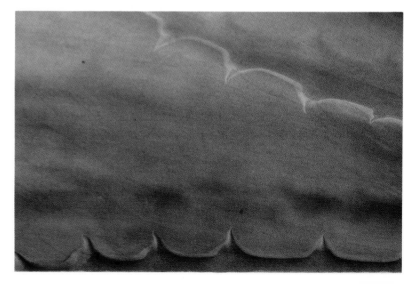

Figure 9.1.

Like music, visual art can have rhythm. Instead of your ears hearing sounds or your hands and feet starting to move in tempo with a beat, your eyes move from image to image. Sometimes the visual beat is slow and regular; sometimes fast and jazzy. Once you become aware of visual rhythm, you notice it everywhere. How would you describe each of the visual rhythms shown in Figure 9.1? Can you translate the visual rhythms you see into sound by clapping your hands?

As principles of design, **rhythm** and **movement** are usually discussed together. This is because they are very closely related. As in music, the sound cannot move without the rhythm or beat to drive it forward. Anytime visual movement is shown in a work of art, there will also be a **visual rhythm.**

Chapter 9
RHYTHM AND MOVEMENT

SEEING AND UNDERSTANDING RHYTHM AND MOVEMENT

Do you remember the name given to artworks that move? The word was **kinetic.** Artists who create kinetic art usually have to rely on motors hidden inside the artwork, or as the case with the Calder mobile, air currents, to provide the motion. But some artists want to *show* movement and rhythm without making the work of art actually move.

Our eyes and brains interpret certain arrangements of art elements as having more movement than others. Knowing this, artists use a variety of arrangements of lines, shapes, and colors to create feelings and illusions of motion. In other words, they use the design principles of **visual rhythm** and **movement.**

Artist Ben Shahn [SHAWN] has made a very clever connection between movement and rhythm in music, and movement and rhythm in visual art (Figure 9.2). Even the title, *Still Music,* is a play on words.

Figure 9.2. Ben Shahn. *Still Music.* 1948. Casein on fabric mounted on plywood panel, 48″ x 83½″. ©The Phillips Collection, Washington, D.C.

Figure 9.3. Jackson Pollock. *Water Birds.* 1943. Oil on Canvas, 26" x 21". Baltimore Museum of Art. Bequest of Saidie A. May

The subjects of the work are the folding chairs and music stands used by the members of an orchestra or band. Shahn has drawn them from every angle, overlapping each other. It is as if the musicians had just finished a long rehearsal, and eager to get home, left their chairs and music stands in a jumble.

But the artist has a purpose behind this arrangement. Notice, for example, how the lines of the chairs and stands cut up the negative space into sections. Our eyes are forced to dance from line to space without resting. The entire space of the picture plane is filled with lines and divided spaces. This creates a visual rhythm for our eyes.

Can you see the solid black wedges that serve as hinges for the folding chairs? They run from side to side, and up and down, like the background beat of a drum.

Through this imaginative work, Ben Shahn reminds us that even without the music and musicians, the **visual** beat goes on!

In his work titled *Water Birds* (Figure 9.3), artist Jackson Pollock [POL•luck] uses a special arrangement of several art elements to create an illusion of swirling motion.

The first element that catches our attention is line. Wildly swerving lines cover the picture plane. How do you make lines like that with paint? Surely, not by moving your hand and brushing slowly and carefully! In fact, maybe they were not brushed on at all.

Have you ever squirted water out of a water pistol onto the sidewalk? As you quickly move your arm, the water makes lines very much like those in Pollock's painting.

Notice the use and placement of color in this painting. Your eyes leap from one color to the next, with no resting place on those twisting lines. By forcing our eyes to move rapidly around the composition, Pollock creates a sensation of movement. To appreciate how energetic this work really is, look back at the work of Piet Mondrian (Figure 7.5).

When you compare the two paintings, it is easy to see how much movement the Pollock work has. This does not mean that the work by Mondrian is inferior. It simply means that each artist wanted to express a different feeling, a different mood.

In musical terms, how would you describe the rhythm or beat of the Pollock work? Is this heavy metal rock or a military march?

Some artists use visual movement and rhythm not to mimic real motion, but to share with us something beautiful or amazing about our world or ourselves.

A famous painting (Figure 9.4) by Dutch artist Vincent Van Gogh [VIN • cent van GO] uses a very different movement and visual rhythm than the works by Ben Shahn and Jackson Pollock.

Starry Night, unlike the Pollock painting, is not totally abstract nor non-objective. We recognize a landscape with buildings, trees, and hills. But these objects are not painted in a completely realistic style. Van Gogh has not tried to smooth out the marks made by his brush. In fact, he has used the brush strokes to create a feeling of movement throughout the starlit landscape.

The trees to the left twist and curl as if blown by the wind. The normally quiet, peaceful night sky is set ablaze with the swirling colors of stars and moon. The movement created by Van Gogh's brush seems to roll like waves across the distant hills. The movement is so obvious, that you can trace its path with your finger. The motion is even repeated in the curve of the hills and the rounded clumps of distant trees.

Why do you think Van Gogh wanted to create so much movement in a nighttime landscape? Could he be trying to make us feel more intensely, more vividly, the beauty and magnificence of the night sky? Have you ever seen

Figure 9.4. Vincent Van Gogh. *Starry Night.* 1889. Oil on canvas, 29″ x 36¼″. Collection, The Museum of Modern Art, New York. Acquired through the Lillie P. Bliss Bequest.

Figure 9.5. Umberto Boccioni. *Unique Forms of Continuity in Space.* 1913. Bronze (cast 1931), 43⅞″ x 34⅞″ x 15¾″. Collection, The Museum of Modern Art, New York. Acquired through the Lillie P. Bliss Bequest.

the stars and moon when they seemed close enough to touch?

Van Gogh was a man who felt strongly about many things. That he was able to express these feelings through art, was one of the few joys of his otherwise unhappy life. Troubled by an overly sensitive nature and recurring mental illness, Van Gogh found in art, an outlet for his most intense feelings. In *Starry Night* and many other great works, Van Gogh was able to share these feelings.

Do you remember the sculpture known as the *Nike of Samothrace* (Figure 2.9). With its outspread wings and flowing drapery, it seemed to be moving forward against the wind. Look at Figure 9.5 by 20th-century Italian artist Umberto Boccioni [um • BEAR • toe BOCH • chee • o • nee]. Does it remind you of the *Nike?*

Even without the realistic detail of the *Nike*, it is easy to see that the sculpture by Boccioni is a figure in motion. The artist has abstracted the human figure, leaving only a hint of the body's shape. But like the *Nike*, the figure seems to move forward. Shapes similar to cloth flow around the figure, creating the feeling of motion.

Boccioni was a member of a group of artists who called themselves **Futurists**. Formed at the beginning of the 20th century, **Futurism** was concerned, as its name suggests, with the future. This future was one in which the machine was all-important. As artists, Futurists loved the sleek, streamlined look of objects in early 20th-century art. They also loved the idea of motion and high speed promised by the new age of cars, trains, and airplanes.

Boccioni's sculpture is a tribute to speed and movement, and to the future that would make both commonplace for everyone.

Striding forward, the figure seems eager to enter that future. Every edge of every shape is curved with movement. Our eyes flow along the edges, unable to rest, before pushing forward. Not satisfied to work only with positive space, Boccioni carves the negative space into moving shapes, as well. Parts of the figure appear to enfold the surrounding spaces. Boccioni was one of the first sculptors to use negative space in this way. He knew that the space surrounding a sculpture was as important as the sculpture itself. Truly, he was an artist for the future!

The Face of Madness

Almost from the moment of his birth, Vincent Van Gogh's life was filled with drama and tragedy. Born the son of a minister, he felt unwanted by his parents. They, in turn, had great difficulty dealing with their son's violent temper. Van Gogh's fits of anger were so extreme that his parents finally sent him away to school.

The rigid discipline of a private school did little for the dangerously disturbed little boy. His relief came when he went to work in an art gallery owned by a friend of his father. This was his first exposure to the art world, and he loved it. He was soon transferred to the gallery's branch in London. Here, Van Gogh became even more dedicated to art. He also fell in love for the first time. Unfortunately, the young lady was already engaged. Van Gogh flew into a rage and left.

Before finally turning to art as his life's work, Van Gogh worked at many other jobs. His love of humanity drew him to the ministry. As a preacher, working among the poor, Van Gogh did everything he could to ease their situation, but in the end, he was fired for his efforts.

At the age of twenty-seven, Vincent Van Gogh became an artist. As with everything he did in life, Vincent devoted himself completely to his art. He wanted to paint as intensely as he felt.

His works were filled with vivid colors. Paint was slashed onto the canvas with furious energy. The surface of these works seems alive with movement. But, time was short. Continuing to battle increasing spells of depression, he began checking himself into mental hospitals, trying to get help.

These episodes of madness had all but driven away what few friends he had. His only remaining friend was his brother Theo. Ten years after he began to paint, Vincent Van Gogh committed suicide. Although now his artworks are some of the most prized and valuable in the world, he sold only one painting during his short, tragic life.

Vincent van Gogh. *Self-Portrait.* 1887. Oil on canvas mounted on wood panel, 13¾" x 10½". ©The Detroit Institute of Arts, City of Detroit Purchase.

BORN: 1853
DIED: 1890
BIRTHPLACE:
Groot-Zundert, Holland

Figure 9.6. Vincent van Gogh. *The Bedroom of Van Gogh at Arles.* 1889. Oil on canvas, 575 cm. x 740 cm. Collection: Musee d'Orsay, Paris. Photo ©R.N.M.

Student work.

Student work.

Did you learn

- The definitions of these words and phrases: movement; visual rhythm; Futurists; Futurism?
- At least three ways artists can indicate movement in a painting.
- Why artists like Boccioni called themselves Futurists?

Understanding and Evaluating.

- Try to find out more about Futurism. Look it up in the library. What other historical events were going on at the same time that Futurism was popular? Are they related? How?
- Van Gogh's life was a tragic, but fascinating, one. Try to find out more about Van Gogh. Write a short paper (3 to 5 pages) about his life. Are there any other artists you have read about that were working in France during this time?
- Rhythm and movement are design principles that are used in advertising. Find examples of ads where movement can be plainly seen as part of the design. What products seem to use movement in their ads? Why? Find at least four different examples.

Seeing and Creating

- Create a Futurist-type drawing. Try to give as much motion to your work as possible. Under the direction of your teacher, make a small clay figure of your drawing. How are you able to show motion in clay?
- Ⓒ [CAUTION: If you are allergic to clay dust, be sure to tell your teacher. Wear a mask if necessary.]
- Make a drawing composed of texture rubbings in which a particular rhythm is visualized.
- Paint a landscape in tempera. Along with a brush, use cardboard, sticks, or other tools. Try to create motion in your work as Van Gogh did.

What if

- shoes came in only one size?
- the ceilings of buildings were limited to five feet in height?
- chair seats were six feet above the floor?
- pizzas came with only one topping—oysters?

Fortunately, we live in a world where these "what if's" don't exist. Most of the everyday objects we wear and use are created with human proportion and scale in mind. These two words, **proportion** and **scale**, are also very important to artists.

As a principle of design, **proportion** has to do with the size of one part in comparison to another, or of one art element to another. **Scale**, on the other hand, is a size comparison made against some common standard. For example, furniture must be designed with the average size of most human beings in mind.

The human form and size is the **scale** that is used to determine the general size of furniture. This scale can be varied for special purposes. The desks and chairs in a first-grade classroom are designed with the average size of first graders as their reference scale. Have you ever tried to sit in a chair or eat from a table that didn't take human scale into account?

Artists use the design principle of proportion, in combination with other elements and principles, to express a wide variety of feelings and moods. The scale, for instance, of the human figure, can be presented realistically (Figure 10.1) or exaggerated for effect (Figure 10.2). The following artworks will give you an idea about the expressive power of proportion and scale as design principles.

Chapter 10
PROPORTION

WORDWATCH
proportion
scale
allegory

Figure 10.1. Andrea Del Verocchio. *Equestrian Monument of Collioni.* 1479-88. Photo credit: Archiv fur Kunst und Geschichte, Berlin.

Figure 10.2. *Bronze Equestrian Statuette of Charlemagne.* Collection: The Louvre, Paris. Photo ©R.N.M.

Figure 10.3, by Surrealist René Magritte [rah • NAY
ma • GREET], is a famous example of how proportion
and scale can effect the meaning of a work of art.

Magritte is playing around with our sense of scale. The
room he has painted looks like an average room in an
average house. This provides the scale for comparison.

But that apple! It fills the room, squeezing the space,
until we feel we should step back to give it more room.

Both the room and the apple are common, everyday
objects. However, Magritte has changed the meaning and
expressive quality of both by putting them together. He
has also altered the proportions and scale of both the
room and the apple. Their size relationship is no longer
realistic.

Think how the mood of the painting would be changed
if you could repaint the apple to normal scale. Would the
focal point or emphasis be changed? How? Why do you
think Magritte chose to paint a green apple? What color
or tint are the surrounding walls?

Like Max Ernst (Figure 6.6), Magritte was a Surrealist
painter. He frequently used proportion and scale to
achieve that mysterious, dream-like quality favored by
the Surrealists. As you look at the works of other
Surrealists, pay particular attention to their use of
proportion and scale. You will find that they often
change the size of everyday objects and place them in
unusual places, with other objects of unusual scale.

Figure 10.3. René Magritte. *The Listening
Chamber.* 1953. Oil on canvas, 31½″ x
39¾″. Private Collection.

Figure 10.4. Andrew Wyeth. *Soaring.* 1950. Tempera on masonite, 12¾″ x 23 9/16″. Shelburne Museum, Shelburne Vermont.

You are already familiar with the work of Andrew Wyeth (Figure 8.7). Figure 10.4, titled *Soaring*, is a good example of how size or scale can be altered within a painting and still be realistic.

In order to help us understand the sensation of flight that a bird must feel, Wyeth has painted his work from the perspective or viewpoint of soaring hawks. Our point of view is just behind the last hawk, whose wingspan covers most of the picture plane. We seem to fly with them, rather than just observing them from a distance.

The other birds are painted to a scale that makes them appear smaller and farther away. Do you remember the name of the technique for creating space in this way?

Notice, also, how the wings of each hawk are angled in a different direction. Our eyes are forced to swing back and forth along these lines, just as the hawks must tilt their wings to catch updrafts of wind. This is a very successful way to show movement. Can you find other parts of the painting that repeat the shape of the hawks' wings?

Changing the proportion and scale of birds and animals has been used by many artists. Sometimes it serves to produce a mood of mystery or fantasy; at other times, it is done for humor. In the work by Edward Hicks, *Peaceable Kingdom*, (Figure 10.5) it is used as a visual **allegory.**

An allegory is a symbolic story or fable that teaches something of importance. Most fairy tales, for example, were written as allegories. Good, represented by the brave prince or princess, always defeats evil, represented by the wicked witch, the sorcerer, or the dragon.

In *Peaceable Kingdom*, Edward Hicks has created a visual allegory of the American dream. He represents the beauty and bounty of the New World by showing people and animals living in peace and harmony in a landscape that offers opportunity for both growth and expansion. This is a theme that Hicks painted more than twenty times!

Figure 10.5. Edward Hicks. *Peaceable Kingdom.* c. 1840-45. Oil on canvas, 18″ x 24⅛″. The Brooklyn Museum, Dick S. Ramsay Fund.

Figure 10.6. Luis Jimenez. *Progress II.* 1974. Fiberglass, 10½′ x 22′ x 10′1″. Private collection.

You probably notice that the proportions of both the people and the animals are out of scale. Hicks has used the principle of proportion as part of the allegory. He shows oversized animals sitting and lying quietly together, next to the very small children in the foreground. According to Hicks's view of the New World, everyone and everything could exist in harmony and peace, no matter how large and fierce they might be. Have you noticed the figures in the background? They represent the settlers and Indians quietly and peacefully exchanging greetings. All is contentment and serenity.

Hicks has painted all the figures in a landscape of child-like simplicity. In fact, the animals look more like stuffed toys than realistic beasts. What are lions and tigers doing in America anyway? Do you see other animals that are not native to America? Why do you think the artist included them? Are there any clues to tell you when this work might have been painted?

Sculptors also use proportion and scale in many creative ways. Sculptor Luis Jimenez [lu•ees he•MEN•nez] portrays the characters of the American West with both energy and humor.

Progress II (Figure 10.6) is made of fiberglass. Fiberglass, a material often used in boats, is very strong and waterproof. As a material for sculpture, it permits the artist to fashion shapes that can withstand both stress and weight. It also allows the sculptor to mix intense color directly into the liquid fiberglass. The color becomes part of the sculpture, rather than being just painted on.

Jimenez takes full advantage of the properties of fiberglass in *Progress II*. The subject, a fast-riding cowboy roping a very large steer, is right out of the colorful history of the West.

To emphasize the tension and dynamic energy of steer and rider, Jimenez has changed the proportions between the two. The scale has been altered, increasing the size of the steer. This not only gives a certain humor to the work, but makes us more aware of the strength and agility needed to rope a wild steer.

Did you notice that the tension on the rope ties the two parts of the sculpture together? The straining steer seems to drag both cowboy and horse as if they were on water skis!

Sculptor Claes Oldenburg [CLOSS OLD•den•burg] is known for the wit and humor of his art. He likes to poke fun at the objects and products of modern culture.

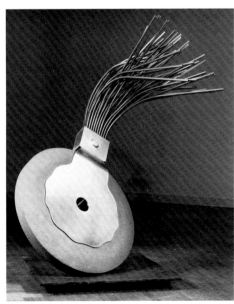

Figure 10.7. Claes Oldenburg. *Typewriter Eraser.* 1976. Aluminum, stainless steel, ferroconcrete, 84″h., base 48″l. x 48″w. Virginia Museum of Fine Arts. Gift of Sydney and Frances Lewis.

Figure 10.8. Claes Oldenburg and Coosje Van Bruggen. *Stake Hitch.* 1984. Aluminum, H. 642″ x w.182″ x d.534″. Dallas Museum of Art. Commission to honor John H. Murchison, Sr.

Although many of the objects he uses for subjects are small, Oldenburg alters the scale so that they tower over our heads.

Figure 10.7 is a good example of Oldenburg's humorous style. You may recognize this object as a typewriter eraser. You may even own one. This eraser, so realistically portrayed, is over eight feet tall! Such an ordinary object seems a strange subject for a large sculpture.

But this is exactly Oldenburg's intent. He wants us to pay more attention to the shape and detail of everyday objects we take for granted. It is as if he is saying, "Look how interesting and diverse the form of a simple object can be." If the eraser were not over eight feet high, would we notice how cunningly the rubber wheel rides inside the metal support? How the bristles of the brush divide negative space into varying triangles?

Figure 10.8 shows another Oldenburg sculpture. Titled *Stake Hitch*, it represents the much smaller version of a stake found at the corners of tents (Figure 10.9).

The photograph shows the surrounding museum space and the scale of this enormous (twelve-feet high!) sculpture. After seeing Oldenburg's *Stake Hitch*, it is difficult to overlook the interesting contrast of shapes found in the regular-sized version.

Figure 10.9. Photograph of stake hitch. Photo credit: Hans Beacham.

Photograph of Claes Oldenburg. 1985.
Courtesy Castelli Gallery.
Photo Credit: Chris Felver.

BORN: 1929
BIRTHPLACE:
Stockholm, Sweden

The Soft Side of Life

Although he was born in Sweden, Claes Oldenburg became a U.S. citizen in 1953. He did not begin his career in art until 1952. During the early 1960s, Oldenburg became well known for his colossal objects and soft sculptures.

As a member of the Pop art movement, Oldenburg used objects from American popular culture as subjects for his sculptures. He also used unusual materials, such as burlap soaked in plaster or canvas filled with foam rubber, for sculptures. The following titles give you an idea about the scale and humor of some of these works: *Giant Ice-Cream Cone; Giant Wedge of Pecan Pie; A Skyscraper in the Form of a Chicago Light Plug.*

Oldenburg also liked to stage "happenings." These were usually spontaneous events at which anything could happen! Some artist might decide to throw buckets of paint at a wall. This would be watched, sometimes filmed, like a performance. The idea was to reject traditional ideas about what art is. For the "happening" participants, art could occur anywhere and be anything, not just a painting or sculpture in a museum. A radical thought to be sure!

The pleasure of Oldenburg's work is in the surprise we experience when we see an everyday, small object transformed into a towering monument. To further tease us, he constructs it out of some soft material, so that it seems to sag and melt into the surrounding space. It is difficult not to smile when looking at an Oldenburg sculpture.

Figure 10.11. Claes Oldenburg. *Falling Shoestring Potatoes.* 1965. Painted canvas, kapok, 108″ x 46″ x 42″. Walker Art Center, Minneapolis. Gift of T.B. Walker Foundation.

Figure 10.10. Claes Oldenburg. *Two Cheeseburgers, with Everything (Dual Hamburger).* 1962. Burlap soaked in plaster, painted with enamel, 7″ x 14¾″ x 8⅝″. Collection, The Museum of Modern Art, New York, Philip Johnson Fund.

Did you learn

- The definitions of these words: proportion; scale; allegory?
- Why scale is important in furniture design?
- The differences between scale and proportion?
- Why Hicks's *Peaceable Kingdom* is an **allegory**?

Seeing and Understanding

- Where have you seen other examples of altered scale? You may even own some? Make a list of objects or scenes that use altered or changed scale.
- Look through this book to see if you can find another painting or sculpture that could be called an **allegory**. Make a list of reasons for your choice. Discuss your reasons with the class.

Seeing and Creating

- Choose a fruit or vegetable. Using crayon or felt marker, make a drawing of it in a landscape or put a scene inside the fruit or vegetable. Change the scale of the fruit or vegetable, so that it appears monumental.
- Under your teacher's direction, make a soft sculpture. Choose an ordinary object. You can sew, stuff, or glue fabric or large butcher paper together for your sculpture.
- Choose a famous folk legend or myth about someone or something. (Paul Bunyon, maybe). Make your hero or heroine change proportion or scale in your story. Make a drawing or painting to illustrate your legend or myth.

Student work.

Student work.

Student work.

119

Part Two
SEEING AND CREATING

Cristoforo Monari. *Still Life with Musical Instruments.* c. 1710-15. Oil on canvas, 53¾" x 39". The Museum of Fine Arts, Houston. Samuel H. Kress Collection.

Before creating visual art in any medium, artists need to be aware of the world around them. Information about the world comes to us through our five senses: sight, touch, smell, hearing, and taste. Although sight and touch are the two senses most often used by visual artists, other senses may also be used to give us creative ideas.

While we all see to know about the world, artists see to create. This means they have special ways of combining their five senses with their imagination. With this impressive set of physical and mental tools, anything is possible!

Now that you have learned about why and how people use art, and the many ways the art elements and design principles can be used to express ideas and emotions, you need to know where and how to get ideas for your own artworks.

You have the whole universe to choose from—both natural and human-made environments, plus all the objects and inhabitants of both. You also have a private universe that only you have access to. It is a very secret and special source for creative ideas—the universe of the imagination.

In the following chapters, you will read about how and where to look for ideas. You will also see how various artists use ideas from the natural and human-made environments in a variety of art media. You will find suggestions on using these subjects in your own artworks. But, first, you must learn how to see!

Unit IV
THE WORLD OF IDEAS

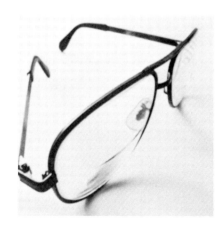

Chapter 11

SEEING TO KNOW— SEEING TO CREATE

WORDWATCH
visual analysis
naturalist
zoologist
botanist
sketch
working drawing

Being observant is important for everyone. We need to know where the chair is before we sit in it. We need to know how large an apple is before we take a bite. Did you notice that small, bright flash of light from the road-side? Is it a piece of glass, a bottle cap, or a diamond?

Although you have five senses with which to perceive the world, sight accounts for more than 90% of all that you perceive and know about the world. Your eyes are your personal, custom-designed cameras. They observe the environment, as your brain records and processes the images. It is little wonder that visual artists rely so heavily on the sense of sight for gathering information about the external world.

For artists, learning to be sensitive observers is just as important as learning to draw, paint, or sculpt.

"But I know how to see. I just open my eyes and look." Yes, but just "looking" may not be enough. To become a skilled observer, you need to learn to use your eyes in ways that will allow you not only to focus on details, but also to see the relationship between parts and wholes.

SEEING TO KNOW

When you examine something new, such as an object you have never seen before, you look closely at it. You hold it in your hand, turning it slowly and letting your eyes wander over its surface. You look at the whole shape or form, and you examine the details. You might even use a magnifying instrument, such as a magnifying glass or microscope to get an even closer look. You come to know the object by seeing both its structure and its details. You have made a **visual analysis** of the object.

Artists need good observational skills. To reproduce an object through drawing, painting, or sculpture, an artist needs to be able to see and understand how parts and details of an object relate or fit into the overall form.

If you think you are already a good and careful observer, you can become an even better one by following these simple suggestions:

- Relax. It is difficult to concentrate and study something closely, if you are uncomfortable.
- Give yourself plenty of time. Don't rush your observation. Reexamine the object at different times.
- Let your eyes pause to look closely, then move on. Staring is not a good idea. If you stare at some-

thing, your eyes will not focus. You won't be able to see details.

- Try the following order for observing:

    1. The whole form and structure of the object or scene. See it from as many directions as possible. Is it solid?
    2. Size and proportion. Is it larger than your hand? Bigger than a house?
    3. Other parts or sections. How large are they in comparison to the whole? (proportion). Are there openings?
    4. Texture or surface details. How is it created—mostly with lines, dots, or changes in values or colors?
    5. Overall color(s) and value(s).

Figure 11.1.

It takes practice to become a good observer. But, it is worth the effort. Seeing to know, or visual analysis, is a skill that can help you not only in art, but also in many other school subjects and daily activities. So start observing! You will be amazed at what you can see.

SEEING TO CREATE

Besides seeing to know about the physical environment, artists also need to know how to see to *create*. Creative seeing uses not only the eyes, but the imagination, as well.

Like muscles in the body, your imagination must be used to keep it flexible and in top shape. It is one of your most valuable possessions. Respect it, exercise it, and it will serve you well throughout your life no matter what work or interests you follow. Everyone needs an imagination, whether he or she becomes an artist, a scientist, or a first-rate auto mechanic.

Figure 11.2.

Creative seeing means looking at the world in fresh, new ways—ways that allow the impossible to be possible. Seeing to create means combining observation skills with imagination.

For example, look at the image in Figure 11.2. Can you tell what it is a photograph of? If you said waterdrops, you are correct. You were *seeing* to *know*. Now, try seeing the same photograph creatively. What else do you notice about the waterdrops? If you plan to use these drops in an artwork, what else could they be?

Before you decide, turn the photograph upside down. Look at it from as many directions as possible. Could they be bumps on an alligator's hide? Living quarters on an alien planet? Try creative seeing with the other

Figure 11.3.

Figure 11.4. John James Audubon. *Norway Rat.* 1843. Watercolor and pencil, 24½ " x 32⅝ ". Collection, Pierpont Morgan Library, New York. 1976. 12:1.

objects in Figure 11.3. You will be surprised at how good you are at seeing to create. The following questions can be helpful in guiding creative seeing. As you look at a familiar object or scene, try asking yourself:

- How will it look from high above? Or from far below?
- Does it remind you of something else? Some other event? If so, were you happy or sad?
- How would it look 100 times the size it is now?
- If it started changing, what would it become?
- What if it were a different color?
- When observing a natural object, imagine how it would look if it were made by humans?
- How would it look if seen through the end of a cardboard tube? Through tracing paper? Through sunglasses?
- How would it look if seen from more than one angle at one time?
- How would it look if it moved? Fell apart?

HOW ARTISTS SEE

Most artists use both kinds of seeing when they create a work of art. A good example is the beautiful drawing (Figure 11.4) by famous American artist and naturalist, John James Audubon [AH•do•bon].

A **naturalist** [NAT•chur•ul•ist] is someone who studies nature or the natural environment and its inhabitants. Both **botanists** [BOT•ah•nests], who study plants, and **zoologists** [zoe•ALL•a•jests], who study animals, are **naturalists**. For naturalists, good observation skills are essential.

Audubon observed the animals he drew with skill and care. The rats shown in Figure 11.4 seem so real we might expect them to scurry off the page. Using a combination of watercolor and pencil, Audubon drew the proportions of their bodies, heads, and tails very accurately. He also included the smallest details—darting eyes, twitching whiskers, and soft fur.

To be able to draw animals that look this lifelike would be impossible without first developing the skills to see for knowledge and understanding. But, creative seeing is used here also.

Have you noticed how part of the background seems to be missing? The two largest rats appear to be crawling down a surface. A surface that Audubon didn't draw! If the artist didn't draw it, how do you see it?

Do you remember reading about implied or suggested lines? They are lines that the eye creates between objects or along edges. Audubon has made use of our eyes' need to complete things.

By drawing half the body of the rat farthest away, and placing the larger rats in a position that suggests they are standing on a sloped surface, Audubon makes us "see" the sloped surface. His drawing of *Norway Rat* becomes more than a picture of some rodents. This drawing is also about space. It shows how space can be created by position and suggestion. The artist requires you to see creatively, to fill in the missing parts, and to complete the whole. It is a very clever and creative example of seeing to know and seeing to create.

Similar to the animal study by Audubon, is a drawing by contemporary artist, Wayne Thiebaud [TY • bowd] shown in Figure 11.5.

Again, the knowledge and understanding of the form and details of an animal can only come from careful, visual analysis. You can almost see the rabbit's ears twitch and the nose quiver!

But it is the way Thiebaud has used creative seeing that makes this drawing so interesting. Notice, for example, where the rabbit is placed. The tip of one ear almost touches the top of the paper. This divides the background into shapes, making it more a part of the drawing than just background. What other part of the drawing comes close to an edge? Does it come as close as the ear? This careful arrangement of rabbit and space, tells us that the artist is using the rabbit's shape as a design element.

Do you remember how focal point or emphasis works in a visual composition? It is the part of the work that catches your attention first. It can also be a part the artist wants you to pay particular attention to. Can you find the focal point or point of emphasis in this drawing? Is it in the center of the picture plane? How has the artist called attention to it? Is there more than one focal point in this work? If the color of the rabbit's ear first caught your attention, you have found the focal point of the drawing. Thiebaud has exaggerated the pink of the rabbit's ear to create a focal point. He has seen and used the rabbit's form and details creatively.

Thiebaud has seen this ordinary rabbit in a new way, creating a work of art. What other ways has his creative seeing changed the rabbit? Are you able to see the basic shapes that make up the rabbit's body more easily in this drawing or in the one by Dürer in Figure 6.4?

Figure 11.5. Wayne Thiebaud. *Rabbit.* 1966. Pastel, 15″ x 20″. Collection of E.A. Bergman. Photo courtesy of Alan Stone Gallery.

Artists like Audubon and Thiebaud not only make hundreds of observations from life, but they also keep visual records or sketches of what they see. A **sketch** is usually a very simple drawing of a scene, an object, or an idea. Many times, artists make sketches in preparation for a more complete work, such as a painting or sculpture, in another medium. These sketches are sometimes called **working drawings** (Figure 11.6). In other words, the artist *works* from them to create a more complete and finished work of art.

Sketching what you see is a very good habit to develop. Even a good memory cannot always recall every detail of what you have observed. Many artists, many naturalists, and other scientists rely on sketching to record their observations. More personal and immediate than a photograph, a simple sketch, requires little equipment and space. A small, blank-paged, spiral-bound notebook, 5″x 7″ or larger, works well. You can then use a pencil to record what you see. The following chapters on subjects and ideas for artworks will give you suggestions on how to record the basic shapes or forms of what you see. Try keeping your observations in a small sketchbook. The more you practice, the better you will become. You don't need to worry about creating great drawings. These working sketches are for your use. You can even write comments next to them, if that helps you.

Record important details or creative ideas in your sketchbook. Leonardo Da Vinci, as artist and scientist, was a great maker of sketches. He filled dozens of notebooks with drawings and comments, such as those in Figure 11.7.

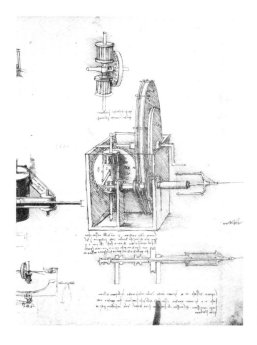

Figure 11.7. Leonardo da Vinci. Page from sketchbook. Textile machine.

Figure 11.6. Examples of working drawings.

The Naturalist's Eye

John James Audubon spent most of his youth in France. For a short time, he even studied with the famous French painter, Jacques Louis David [zhac loo • EE dah • VEE]. David painted in a very realistic and formal style. He smoothed out every brush stroke and sharpened every edge. Audubon's careful style of drawing and painting shows he learned a good deal from the famous David.

In 1803 Audubon made his first trip to America. It was at this time that the idea for a collection of drawings illustrating all the birds of North America came to him. Quite a task, considering the number of species that must have inhabited the American wilderness at that time.

For a while he supported himself by making pencil and charcoal portraits for $25 each. But Audubon's passion for the wildlife of the American wilderness could not be diverted. From 1826 to 1838, he reproduced 435 magnificent watercolor drawings for an enormous book, titled *Birds of America.* In its original form, this is one of the most valuable books in the world! Even now, one Audubon drawing can sell for thousands of dollars.

Although other naturalists before Audubon made wonderful drawings of the animals of North America, it was Audubon who most perfectly combined the skills of scientist and artist. As both naturalist and artist, Audubon used scientific observation and artistic design to create a magnificent set of watercolors.

His interest and enthusiasm for his subjects was so great that he often described them in almost human terms. Blue jays, for example, were particular favorites, though he found their beauty puzzling. It seems to hide all manner of mischief and wickedness. If you have ever observed blue jays for any length of time, you know what he means!

Portrait of James Audubon. Engraving by John Sartain after painting by F. Cruikshanks. Photo courtesy The New-York Historical Society, New York City.

BORN: 1785
DIED: 1851
BIRTHPLACE: Haiti

Figure 11.8. John James Audubon. *Gyrfalcon.* c.1835-36. Watercolor, 38½″ x 25⅝″. Courtesy of the New York Historical Society, New York City.

Student work.

Student work.

Did you learn

- The definitions of these words and phrases: visual analysis; naturalist; botanist; zoologist; sketch; working drawing?
- Why artists have to be good observers?
- At least five ways to improve your observation?
- How Wayne Thiebaud uses a rabbit as a design element?

Understanding and Evaluation

- Audubon's animal prints are reproduced in many publications. Try to locate and compare his work with that of other artists who draw and paint animals. Look at some **botanical** (plants) drawings as well. What similarities are there? What differences?
- Think of ways to use your other senses to assist your art awareness. For example, make a "smell map." The next time you go for a walk, or visit the mall or a movie theater, pay attention to the different smells you encounter. Try to concentrate just on smells. As the smells change, note them. You have made a smell map of a particular location. Malls are great places for smell maps! How could this smell map be used to add interest or information to a painting or drawing of the same place?

Seeing and Creating

- Select a natural object. Use it for a visual analysis. When you think you are ready, make a very realistic drawing of it. How did careful observation help?
- Look at the object under a magnifying glass. Within a circle drawn on your paper, make a closeup study of the object or the part you can see.
- Make a small sketchbook from folded drawing paper stapled in the center. Make at least one sketch each day for two weeks. Make notes on your drawings.
- Use an animal or natural object in a pastel drawing. Concentrate on the form of the animal or object more than the details. Place it carefully, so that you create a balanced, but interesting, composition. Exaggerate the color of one area for the focal point.

Human beings have always found creative inspiration in the forms, colors, and objects of nature. In fact, the vast majority of art subjects throughout the centuries have been inspired by the natural environment. But, being so close to nature, we sometimes take its variety and beauty for granted. (See Figure 12.1 for an example). When was the last time you stopped to admire a sunset? To appreciate the grace and beauty of your pet cat or dog? Have you looked at your own hand lately? Really looked at it? What an amazing tool it is. Its form alone can express a dozen different emotions (Figure 12.2).

One of the many good things about making art is that it also requires us to look at the world around us more carefully and creatively. In order to use a subject in a work of art, you need to know everything about it. One, quick glance just isn't enough. You must really see it for knowledge and creative inspiration.

Many think that the most difficult subjects for art are human beings. There may be some truth in this. Humans are an incredibly complex form to understand.

Look again at your hand. Its form should be very familiar to you. After all, you have used it for many years! But could you draw it from memory? Do you even know how large it is in comparison with the rest of your body? Most people draw hands too small. In reality, your hand is as long as your face! Place the heel of your palm against your chin. The ends of your fingers should reach to your hairline, or very close to it. Spread your fingers. Doesn't your hand almost cover your face?

Look at your hand while you are holding a pencil. Study it for a few moments. Notice in how many directions the edges and creases of the fingers point. Complicated, yes? Don't worry. There are ways to simplify this and other forms of the human body. You will study more about this later.

Besides being a very complicated form, the human body is also expressive. From our earliest years, we learn how to "read" a person's feelings and emotions from the position of his or her body, and the expressions on his or her features. It is little wonder that artists have always been fascinated with the expressive power of the human form.

Chapter 12
THE LIVING WORLD— PEOPLE

WORDWATCH
natural environment
gesture
caricature
Ashcan School
portrait
stereotype

Figure 12.1.

SEEING AND CREATING THE FIGURE IN MOTION

We move! We walk, run, jump, bend, leap, dance, and spin. The human body is almost always in motion. You may remember in the chapter on the design principles—rhythm and movement—that the artist Boccioni used a human-like form for his representation of motion and the dynamic speed of the future (Figure 9.5). Many artists have looked to the human figure in motion as inspiration for artworks that express a range of feelings. Let's look at a few.

When we think of the human form in motion, we usually imagine it engaged in some kind of sport. For centuries artists have shown the human form throwing, jumping, racing, kicking, and generally having a great time competing in sports. To the ancient Greeks, athletic competition was part of their religion. They invented the Olympic games to honor the gods of Olympus. With sports so much a part of their lives and their religion, it is small wonder that Greek artists used sports as inspiration for some of the greatest works of art of antiquity (Figure 12.3).

The tradition of ancient peoples' interest in the human form in motion in sports continues. Today, with both camera and more traditional art tools, artists are still inspired by the grace and expressive quality of the figure in motion (Figure 12.4).

Figure 12.2.

Figure 12.3. *The Charioteer of Delphi.* Greek sculpture about 470 B.C., Bronze with colored inlay. Collection Delphi Museum. Photo credit: Archiv fur Kunst und Geschichte, Berlin.

Figure 12.4.

Figure 12.5. George Bellows. *Dempsey Through the Ropes.* 1923-24. Lithograph, 17 15/16″ x 16 9/16″. Courtesy Amon Carter Museum, Fort Worth, Texas.

One of the greatest action artists of the 20th century was the American artist George Bellows. Bellows broke with a tradition of art inspired by the quiet beauty of country landscapes and images of smiling, happy people. Instead, he found inspiration in the fast-paced, flashy, and often dangerous world of the big city. Bellows was part of an art movement known as the **Ashcan School.** The subjects of the Ashcan artists were realistic scenes and people in the big cities during the first part of the 20th century. Part of the big-city scene was Bellows's gritty, tough world of professional boxing.

Figure 12.5, titled *Dempsey Through The Ropes,* is one of Bellows's most famous works. The artist has captured one of the most thrilling moments in boxing—the knock down punch.

Notice the position of the standing fighter. Legs are wide apart, torso twisted, arms swinging. We can almost feel the power of the punch just by looking at that dynamic stance.

And what about the falling fighter! His tumbling body and flailing arms are in stark contrast to the confident position of the more successful boxer. Have you noticed the crowd? The positions of the figures focus our attention on the falling fighter.

This artwork is a lithograph. Remember that lithographs, like that in Figure 2.8 by Thomas Hart Benton, are created much like crayon drawings. The artist uses value or shading to give mood and expression to the work. Notice in Bellows's work how the values are in high contrast. There are deep shadows next to bright highlights. This adds both drama and excitement to the scene. Also notice the point of view in this work. As a viewer, where would you be standing if you could enter this picture? Why do you think the artist chose this viewpoint?

As you study Bellows's work, pay close attention not only to the movement and expression of the bodies, but also to the facial expressions. What is the artist saying about this crowd of people?

Let's compare Bellows's work to that of another artist. Look at Figure 12.6 by Jacob Lawrence. It is titled *Munich Olympic Games.*

Figure 12.6. Jacob Lawrence. *Munich Olympic Games.* 1971. Gouache on paper, 35½″ x 27″. The Seattle Art Museum, purchased with funds from PONCHO.

Though very different in mood from Bellows's work, Lawrence's work also uses the dynamic action of the human figure to express movement and rhythm.

Lawrence has not represented the human figure as realistically as Bellows. He has exaggerated and simplified the human form for expression. In other words, he has abstracted it to make us feel more intently the strain and effort of the racing figures. The artist is more concerned with the *shapes* of the figures than in giving them roundness or three-dimensional character.

Look at that stride! With a few simple marks that define the main muscles, the artist tells us everything we need to know about the speed and strength of the runners.

Like Bellows, Jacob Lawrence was also concerned with the expressive power of the human face. Although abstracted, the runners' faces clearly show the strain of their effort. You can almost hear the rushing breath from their open mouths.

The viewpoint Lawrence has chosen is that of looking down on the runners. Why do you think the artist chose this point of view? What part do the white lines play in the work?

Of course, even in sports the human figure is not always in motion. Take a look at Figure 12.7. This is another work by Wayne Thiebaud (remember the rabbit?). Appropriately enough, it is titled *The Football Player.*

No wild movement or energy here! Just a solid shape enclosed in a typical football uniform. But, there is something very powerful about the figure. He seems on the verge of standing up, springing into action at the first call from the coach. Like Lawrence, Thiebaud simplifies the human body into shapes. The use of a heavy outline emphasizes the contour of the shapes.

Unlike the works by Lawrence and Bellows, in this work, we cannot really see the expression on the face of the football player. Why do you think the artist doesn't show more of it? Are there any other parts of this work that seem important? What about the numbers? Why 88? [?]

Figure 12.7. Wayne Thiebaud. *The Football Player.* 1963 Oil on canvas. 72″ x 36″. Virginia Museum of Fine Arts, Richmond. Gift of Sydney and Frances Lewis.

Figure 12.9. Diego Rivera. *Delfina Flores.* 1927. Oil on canvas, 32¼″ x 26″. Marion Koogler McNay Art Museum, San Antonio, Texas. Bequest of Marion Koogler McNay.

A **portrait** is a representation in some art medium of a specific individual. In creating a portrait, the artist is interested not only in the expressive possibilities of the human form, but also in the characteristic features of an individual.

When you look into a mirror, you recognize your own face, because you have a certain shape to your features. Close family members may have similar features, especially if they are identical twins. However, no one is *exactly* like anyone else. Noticing facial differences between individuals is important if you want to create a "likeness" of someone. (Figure 12.8). When these individual characteristics are exaggerated in a portrait, we call it a **caricature.**

You may think that only the great and famous are worthy of having their portraits made by an artist. This is not true. Each person is unique and special. And, although the great and famous have often been the subject of many portraits, ordinary people have also inspired masterpieces of art.

Take, for example, the touching portrait of a little girl by Mexican artist Diego Rivera [dee•A•go ree•VER•rah] in Figure 12.9. Her name and the title of the portrait is *Delfina Flores.*

The artist has simplified the details of dress and background, so that we can concentrate on the features

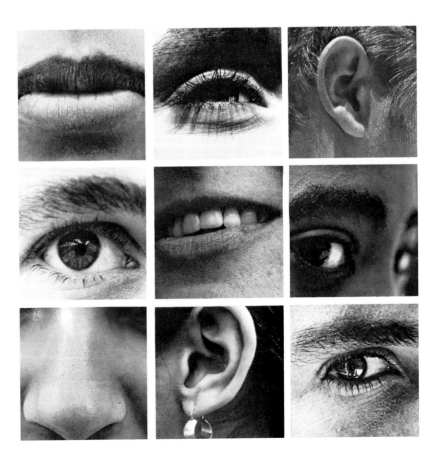

Figure 12.8.

134

and **gestures** of the little girl. A **gesture** is a movement or position of the human form that expresses an emotion or idea. As you examine works that use the human form as subject matter, be aware of gestures. They tell you much about the character of the subject and the artist. In the section on drawing, you will learn how to capture quickly body positions and expression through **gesture drawings.**

When you look at this portrait of Delfina, it is difficult not to feel the shyness and nervousness the artist has captured so wonderfully in the gesture of her hands. They seem to play nervously with a fold of her blouse or the string of red beads. How realistic this gesture is! Have you ever noticed the actions of young children when they are asked to meet someone new, or to pose for a photograph? Diego Rivera must have observed carefully the actions of children to be able to give us this charming and touching portrait of a timid, little girl.

By simplifying the background and the details of the dress, Rivera focuses more of our attention on the expression and gestures of the child. This makes us feel the emotions of the child even more strongly.

Artist Clarence Brisco has created a memorable character study in his portrait of *Ada Simond* (Figure 12.10). Using flowing, curving shapes and lines, Brisco shares with the viewer all the intensity and dignity of a remarkable individual.

Have you noticed how the lines of the hair, the pattern of the dress, and the cloud shapes of the background seem alive with energy? How appropriate this portrait is? The woman portrayed, Ada Simond, was both an activist for human rights and a historian.

So far, we have looked at two-dimensional portraits or paintings. Sculptors also use the human form and features for inspiration. If they are creating a portrait in stone, bronze, or similar material, sculptors usually do not have the benefit of color to help create the likeness of their subjects. Instead, they rely on the form of the features. They must also think about how the person looks from the back and sides as well! Remember, sculpture is three-dimensional. That means you can walk around it and see it from many points of view.

The portrait of *Albert Einstein* (Figure 12.11) by Jacob Epstein [EP•stine] is a fine example of how a skilled sculptor can capture the character of an individual using only the form and position of the features.

Figure 12.10. Clarence A. Brisco. *Ada Simond.* 1987. Oil on canvas, 40″ x 30″. Collection of the artist.

Figure 12.11. Jacob Epstein. *Albert Einstein.* 1933. Tate Gallery, London/Art Resource, New York.

Figure 12.12. Duane Hanson. *Tourists II.* 1988. Polyester and Fiberglass, lifesize. Photo courtesy Duane Hanson.

Figure 12.13. Norman Rockwell. *Breaking Home Ties.* Courtesy: The Norman Rockwell Museum at Stockbridge, MA. Printed by permission of the Norman Rockwell Family Trust. ©1954 the Norman Rockwell Family Trust.

Although one of the greatest scientists of the 20th century, Albert Einstein was also a compassionate and concerned individual. He cared about the fate and condition of the Earth and its people. Epstein has captured that compassion in the eyes and gentle smile of this great genius.

Rather than smooth out the planes and contours of the face, the sculptor leaves it rough. This not only shows us a mature Einstein, but also gives energy and movement to the features. Can you see the creases and bumps made by the sculpting material? It is easy to imagine the artist pressing chunks of clay onto that wide brow and shaggy hair.

This portrait began as a clay sculpture. Clay is considered a **plastic** medium. This means that it can be twisted, pushed, and molded into various forms and textures before it hardens. Although many sculptors work only in clay, some choose to **cast** their work in metal. This is an involved process in which a plaster mold is made of the clay original. Into this mold is then poured a molten metal, such as **bronze**. Bronze is a combination of copper and other metals. You will discover that sculptors use a wide selection of media or materials to create their works. Modern technology has supplied even more.

Artist Duane Hanson uses many modern materials for his sculptures. Figure 12.12 is a good example of his work. Titled *Tourists II*, this work makes many people stop in their tracks when they see it. The couple seem so lifelike that visitors to the exhibit have asked them questions!

Duane Hanson uses a combination of fiberglass and polyester to create these amazing sculptures. He makes casts of his models' entire bodies, then pours liquid fiberglass into the hardened molds. He then paints the figures with great realism and dresses them in real clothes.

Other than the incredible realism of Hanson's work, his sculptures are interesting for another reason. Most of his portraits are **stereotypes**. A stereotype is an image or an idea that a whole group can recognize and agree upon.

Tourists II are stereotypes because they share many of the characteristics we all associate with people who are on vacation or are touring new and different places. The artist is poking gentle fun at the casual dress and numerous cameras that are "typical" of tourists everywhere. Have you noticed the stance of the individuals? The direction of their gaze? Why is this important for a sculpture that features tourists? What other elements of

Figure 12.14

Figure 12.15

Figure 12.16

Figure 12.14. Holbein the Younger. *Henry VIII.*
Photo: Archiv fur Kunst und Geschichte, Berlin.
Figure 12.15. Riguaud. *Louis XIV.* 1701. Oil on canvas,
279cm. x 190cm. Collection, The Louvre, Paris. Photo credit:
Archiv fur Kunst und Geschichte, Berlin.
Figure 12.16. Henry F. Farney. *Peace Be With You.* 1889.
Watercolor and tempera on paper, 20 15/16″ x 13 11/16″. Archer
M. Huntington Art Gallery, The University of Texas at Austin.
Gift of C.R. Smith.

Figure 12.17

Figure 12.18

Figure 12.19

Figure 12.17. Pre-Columbian. *Smiling Girl, holding a basket.* From
Panuco Basin, Northern Veracruz. 600-750 A.D. Fired clay, 7⅝″ x 6⅛″
x 3¾″. Kimbell Art Museum, Fort Worth, Texas.
Figure 12.18. Roy Lichtenstein. *Head-Red and Yellow.* 1962. Oil on
canvas, 48″ x 48″. Albright-Knox Gallery, Buffalo, New York. Gift of
Seymour H. Knox, 1962.
Figure 12.19. Etruscan Wall Painting. *Head of Vella.* Tomb of Orco,
Tarquinia. Photo credit: Scala/Art Resource.

dress seem characteristic or **stereotypical** of people on vacation? How does the sculptor increase our understanding of this work by using real items and clothing?

Artists like Duane Hanson and illustrator Norman Rockwell (Figure 12.13), by using the people we meet everyday as subjects for their art, seem to bring us closer to their subjects. We say to ourselves, "I know someone just like that," or "That reminds me of myself." Figures 12.14 through 12.19 show some examples of the great variety of people that artists, throughout the centuries, have used as subjects for art. Whether famous or unknown, the human form and face remains endlessly fascinating as a subject for visual art.

USING PEOPLE IN YOUR ART

The following diagrams and suggestions will help you use the human figure and face in your own work. It is also important to practice, practice, practice!

- **Where do I find models for figure drawings and portraits?**
  - Your friends and family. You can catch them when they are not rushing around. Observe them watching T.V., reading, or sleeping. If you need action, go to a sports event, the school cafeteria, or the shopping mall. You will see every possible position and expression.

- **How do I draw someone moving about? And what do I use to record their movements?**
  - Use **gesture** drawings or quick sketches like those shown in Figure 12.20. Don't try to record details. Look only for the position of the body or the gesture. These drawings can be made by scribbling. They are working drawings, remember. You are only recording the movement and position of the human form. Make yourself a simple sketchbook by folding in half seven or eight blank sheets of paper. Staple them at the crease. Presto! A sketchbook. Use pencil, or if you really want to learn, crayon. Pencils encourage erasing, not careful seeing. Crayons, on the other hand, force you to look, when you know each mark counts and cannot be erased. They are excellent for gesture drawings.

- **How do I know how large to make the figure?**
  - You are concerned about **proportion** and rightly so. This is one reason gesture drawings are so valuable. They make you look for the overall

Figure 12.20. Gesture drawings capture the movement, position, and proportions of figures, not their details.

Figure 12.21. The above figure is about 7½ heads tall.

position and size of the figure before you get involved in details like hair and eyelashes!

- Figure 12.22 shows the general proportions of human figure. The length of a person's head is a good measurement to use. Hold your pencil at arm's length. Line the point of the pencil with the top of your model's head. Using your thumb as a sliding ruler, place it at the point on the pencil where the chin falls. You now have the length of your model's head. You can determine the height of the figure by measuring the number of heads it takes to complete the figure. Most people are around 7 or 7½ "heads" tall. Learning to measure with your pencil and thumb can be helpful in drawing almost anything.

- **The human figure is so complicated. I just get lost when I try to draw it.**
  - It is easy to get confused and lost when drawing the figure. Try **simplifying** the forms. See if you can convert what you see into simple, geometric shapes (Figure 12.22). This will help you get the correct proportion and position before you begin to look for detail and realism.

- **I love to draw portraits, but I get the nose in the wrong place everytime!**
  - Portraits are fun. We enjoy trying to make our portraits really look like the persons posing for them. But, as with the full figure, proportion and position must come before details and likeness. Figure 12.23 shows the basic positions of the features. Use your pencil and thumb again as a measure. This time, use the length of an eye as the standard of measure. What other distances and sizes can you find that match the length of the eye?
  - Have you noticed
  - the face is oval, not round?
  - the eyes are halfway between the chin and the top of the head?
  - there is one eye's width between the eyes?
  - the ends of the mouth fall in a line with the center of the eyes?

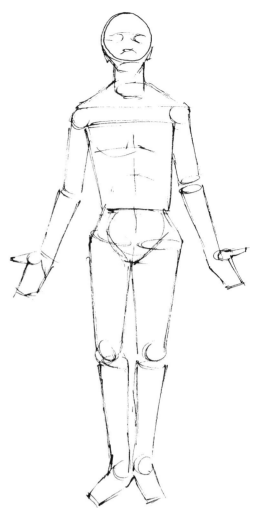

Figure 12.22. The human form can be simplified into basic geometric shapes.

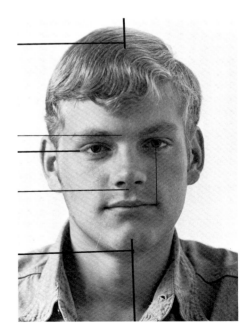

Figure 12.23. Notice the position of the eyes and nose on the face. The ends of the mouth fall in the middle of the eyes. The distance between the eyes is the length of one eye. Try to find other measurements to help place features.

Photograph of Jacob Lawrence. Photo: Davis Freeman. 1985. Courtesy Jacob Lawrence.

BORN: 1917
BIRTHPLACE:
Atlantic City, New Jersey

The Inner Spirit

Some think that overcoming hardships makes artists grow in inner strength and artistic expression. If this is so, it might explain the drive, determination, and talent of Jacob Lawrence.

Growing up during the Great Depression of the 1930s, Jacob Lawrence knew hard times. People were out of jobs, food was scarce, and if you were black like Jacob, you faced another obstacle—racial prejudice. Strangely enough, it was the Depression that gave Jacob Lawrence the chance he needed.

Lawrence attended art classes at the Harlem Community Art Center. This center, and others like it, had been started by the government to give jobs to teachers and to promote the continuation of the arts during these hard times. Lawrence soon distinguished himself as an outstanding student.

Lawrence then moved to Harlem in New York and painted as a professional artist. The Depression, with its many hardships, had promoted an art style called Social Realism. Artists, who called themselves Social Realists, used their work to promote change. They used art to protest the conditions of poverty and discrimination they saw around them. Both Anglo and African American artists were Social Realists during the Depression.

Jacob Lawrence looked at the poor people of Harlem and saw subjects for works of art. He studied the history of African Americans and found epic events for creative expression.

Figure 12.24. Jacob Lawrence. *Other Rooms.* Courtesy Jacob Lawrence. Photo credit: David Freeman, 1985.

Did you learn

- The definitions of these words and phrases: natural environment; Ashcan School; portrait; caricature; gesture drawing; stereotypes; plastic; bronze?
- What the Ashcan artists used as subjects for art?
- The best way to capture the movement of human beings?

Understanding and Evaluating

- Look at other works throughout this book that have people as their main subjects. Compare the style the artists have used to portray these subjects. Which works do you think are the most successful as figure studies? As portraits?
- Look again at the portraits shown in Figures 12.14 through 12.19. Select one you feel is most successful in revealing the true character of the subject. Defend your opinion in a class discussion.
- Some of the individuals in Figures 12.14 through 12.19 were famous, historical characters. Find out more about one of them. Do you think the artist has captured the character and personality? Why, or why not?

Seeing and Creating

- Make some figure drawings from life. Observe people in many different activities. Practice sketching until you can capture basic movements with just a few lines.
- Make a self-portrait in either charcoal, or tempera.
ⓒ [CAUTION: If you are allergic to these materials, use pencil or crayon.]
- Using your self-portrait as a guide, make a construction-paper collage portrait. On the parts of the face that stick out, like your nose, use a lighter color of paper.

Student work.

Student work.

Figure 13.1.

Animals, our fellow living creatures on the planet Earth, have been the subjects of art since prehistoric times. Human beings have admired the beauty and power of animals; we have feared them and we have hidden from their mystery. We have hunted them for food, worshipped them as gods, and loved them as pets. And whether a beloved family pet, or a nightmarish horror from the depths of the sea, animals continue to fascinate and inspire artists. From microscopic blobs to megaweight dinosaurs, animals make wonderful subjects for visual art (Figure 13.1).

SEEING AND CREATING ANIMALS IN ART

Animals, as art subjects, entered the world over 20,000 years ago. Prehistoric humans, who hunted them for food and clothing, believed that by painting animals on cave walls they gained a magical power over them. The unknown artist or artists, who created the lively scenes of running animals pictured in Figure 13.2, showed great knowledge of animal **anatomy,** or the physical structure and working of an animal's body. The animals are drawn with such confidence and sureness that we must believe the artist had studied and drawn them many times before. If you observe, you will see evidence that the artist must have observed the animals closely. Details on the heads and markings on the coats and hides of the animals show that the artist/hunter looked closely to record this information.

Do you remember how Jacob Lawrence simplified and abstracted the runners in *Munich Olympic Games* (Figure 12.6)? By leaving out unnecessary details and lengthening the forms, he enhanced the expressive impact of his artwork. The cave artists may have been doing something similar. Many of the animals were drawn over sections of the cave wall that bulged outward. The prehistoric artist seemed to be trying to give a three-dimensional quality to the two-dimensional drawings.

At our great distance from the **Stone Age** or prehistoric times, it is difficult to know the exact purpose of the cave paintings. Most archeologists believe they were drawn to help stone-age hunters capture the animals they represented. The artists/hunters may have believed the drawings cast a magic spell over the animals. Were the cave artists also inspired by the beauty and movement of the animals they drew? This is a question we cannot answer.

Chapter 13
THE LIVING WORLD— ANIMALS

WORDWATCH
anatomy
Stone Age
woodcuts

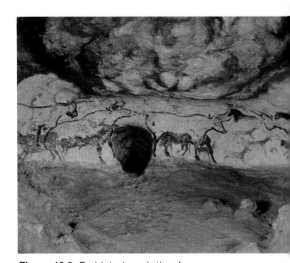

Figure 13.2. Prehistoric painting Lascaux, Dordogne. Photo credit: Archiv fur Kunst und Geschichte, Berlin.

Figure 13.3. Sekkyo. *Bull.* Woodcut, 20″ x 13½″.

Figure 13.4. Sekkyo. *Eagle.* 20″ x 13½″.

We do know that these cave paintings show a wonderful understanding of animal anatomy. They also show great drawing skill, especially in the use of line. Just notice the variety of lines that are used. The lines express so much, with so little. The movement and form of the animals are indicated without help from value or the use of shading. The more you study these ancient works, the more remarkable they become.

Since their discovery in the 1870s, these cave paintings have had a powerful influence on the work of many artists. As you look at the modern artworks reproduced in this book, you will notice similarities between the cave paintings and certain examples of contemporary art.

The artists of both Japan and China have created some of the most beautiful images of animals in all of art. Figure 13.3 is an example of a Japanese woodcut print. **Woodcuts** are made from a block or slab of wood. All wood, not part of the image to be printed, is cut away. Ink is then applied to the raised image, and the woodblock is pressed against paper, creating an impression or print of the image.

In Figure 13.3 the artist has managed to express all the power and spirit of a bull. The artist captures the animal in the action of turning to charge. Even the expression on the bull's face seems to warn that now might not be a good time to approach!

Compare this bull with the one shown in Figure 13.2. In each work, which art element do you think plays the most important part in showing movement? How has the Japanese printmaker called attention to the massive weight and strength of the animal?

Another Japanese woodcut is pictured in Figure 13.4.

Here the artist has chosen an eagle for his subject. Notice how much realistic detail the artist has shown in the feathers and the background tree. Also notice the bark pattern on the tree trunk. It is similar to the shape and texture of the eagle's feathers. This gives greater unity to the visual composition, while adding variety and interest.

Compare this eagle with the one painted by John James Audubon (Figure 13.5). Do you see any similarities? In both works, how much attention is placed on detail?

Some artists are interested in animals as **abstract** forms. In other words, they borrow the shapes, colors, lines, textures, and values of animal subjects, without trying to present a realistic image of the animal. An example of this is a painting by Arthur Dove, titled *Team of Horses,* and shown in Figure 13.6.

American artist Arthur Dove has used a team of horses as the inspiration for his abstract or non-objective painting. He has reduced the horses to basic art elements: color, line, shape, and value. If you study the painting, you can identify shapes and colors that would be found if you were looking out over the backs of a team of horses pulling a wagon. Well, why not just draw the horses realistically? A good question, and one people ask about **abstract art** all the time.

Do you remember that one of the purposes of art is to show us something new about the world? It lets us see something familiar from a new direction or point of view. Art should also make us think and it should make us feel.

Sometimes the best way for an artist to make us see in new ways and to feel a new experience is by abstracting. This may mean simplifying or refining the image to its basics. In a way it is like squeezing the juice from a piece of fruit. The juice is the essence of the fruit, with all the taste and smell that help us identify the fruit as an orange, a grape, or an apple.

Art is not always about visual realism. Art is about expression and communication. Some artists prefer communicating through the essence of objects or feelings than through the realistic form of the objects themselves.

Arthur Dove found elements for creating an interesting visual composition in a team of horses. The curve of the horses' necks, the ragged edge of their bouncing manes, the geometric shapes of the harnesses are all here—but abstracted and refined to their essence. Are there other details of the horses that you think were used to form

Figure 13.5. John James Audubon. *Great American Sea Eagle.* 1877. Hand colored engraving and aquatint, 36⅛" x 21 9/16". Courtesy Amon Carter Museum, Fort Worth, Texas.

Figure 13.6. Arthur G. Dove. *Team of Horses.* 1911-12. Pastel on composition board, 18⅛"x21½". Courtesy Amon Carter Museum, Fort Worth, Texas.

part of the composition? Where did the artist's choice of colors come from? From looking at this work, can you tell whether the artist was interested in the movement of the horses? If so, how have rhythm and movement been shown?

These examples show us that some artists are interested in animals for the variety, beauty, and expressive power that their forms and details can suggest.

Although you may think the lives of animals can have little drama or excitement compared to our own lives, life and death struggles go on every day. As archy, that poet of cockroaches, observes:

> i have just been reading
> an advertisement of a certain
> roach exterminator
> the human race little knows
> all the sadness it causes
> in the insect world. . . .

from Don Marquis:
archy and mehitabel

Artist Melissa Miller, in canvases that swirl with movement and flare with color, has chosen animals as the actors for her visual dramas. And what dramas they are! Take Figure 13.7, for example.

Figure 13.7. Melissa Miller. *Zebras and Hyenas.* 1985. Oil on linen, 72 5/16″x83⅞″. Archer M. Huntington Art Gallery, The University of Texas at Austin, Michener Collection Acquisition Fund, 1985.

146

Zebras and Hyenas shows many of the characteristics of Miller's paintings. The colors are intense, almost painful to the eyes. The flaming landscape and sky heighten the terror of the frantic zebras and the menace of the stalking hyenas. Movement is everywhere. Heads twist; necks arch; legs tangle. The excitement and confusion of the scene is enhanced by the interplay or mingling of colors, patterns, and vigorous brushstrokes. Have you noticed how the garish glow of the sky is reflected on the animals? The whole scene seems to be on fire. Even the cooler colors—green and black—are warmed by that fiery sky.

Take some time to study the composition of this work. Can you identify a focal point or point of emphasis? How are the lines or stripes of the zebras used to make us feel the confusion of the scene? Is there any part of this work where your eyes are allowed to rest? Do you think the artist has taken a side in this conflict? Does she favor one group of animals over the other? Which group? Does she try to make you, the viewer, take a side? How?

Another popular animal subject for art can only live in the zoo of our imaginations. These animals seem to be special favorites of just about everyone, although they have long since left our world. Of course, we are talking about dinosaurs.

You have probably seen hundreds of illustrations of those giants of the distant past. They have never been more popular! They decorate wallpaper, star in movies, and are the cuddly toys of small children. And what amazing beasts they were! They come in an endless variety of forms, textures, and sizes. From specimens the size of rabbits to a walking four-story building! If dinosaurs had not existed, artists would have had to make them up.

Figure 13.8 A shows how a creative gardener/sculptor changed ordinary bushes into dinosaur forms. When any kind of living plant such as a bush, hedge, or tree is cut and shaped into an animal form it is called a topiary [TOE • pee • air • ee]. Like clay, paper maché, wood, or bronze, living plants can become a sculpting medium for three-dimensional art. What kind of sculpting tools would be needed to create topiary dinosaurs? Can you identify the kinds of dinosaurs shown in Figure 13.8 A?

Figure 13.8 B is an illustration or ink drawing of a dinosaur you probably recognize—brontosaurus [bron • toe • SOAR • us]. These creatures were some of the largest animals ever to live on Earth. We know something about

Figure 13.8 A – Topiary Dinosaurs
Photo by John Smithers.

Figure 13.8 B – Brontosaurus. Pen and Ink Drawing

their size and weight from the bones and footprints that have been found. The drawing shows how the brontosaurus left huge footprints in the soft ground of the marshes it called home. Take some time to examine the illustration in more detail.

How has the artist created an illusion of distance? Which part of the dinosaur's body appears closest to you? The tail or the head? Repeated lines are used to create form and value (shading). What parts of the dinosaur's body are in shadow? What parts are drawn with curved lines? Why? What would happen if these curved lines were straight?

You might want to try using ink for drawing dinosaurs yourself. Be sure to include a background or environment for your dinosaur. How can you show the great size of dinosaurs? In the illustration, is the flying creature a bird? [**CAUTION:** India ink is permanent. Wear protective clothing. Use only water-based, non-toxic felt markers as well].

USING ANIMALS IN YOUR OWN ART

Animals can provide an endless source of subjects for your own work. But, as with the human figure, it takes practice.

- **Where can I find animal subjects for art?**

It is true, you probably won't see a herd of elephants wandering around in your backyard! But there may be other animals wandering there. Family pets can make excellent subjects. You can draw them while they sleep or eat. Try to make quick gesture sketches of their movements. As you practice gesture drawings with human and animal subjects, you will become skilled at capturing characteristic movements and positions.

- **Why not just copy from a photograph? Wouldn't it be easier?**

Relying on photographs for art subjects is *not* a good idea. For one thing, photographs don't always show you all you need to know when you draw or paint a subject. Photographic shadows hide shapes and details that are essential for making a good drawing of a subject. They also present you with only one viewpoint. Whenever possible, artists need to be able to examine objects from many viewpoints. Finally, photographs freeze action and movement. Even though you may not be able to capture all the details of an animal's movements by sketching it from life, you can catch movements that cannot be seen in a static photograph. The more you practice, the better you will become. And remember, using animals as subjects in artworks is not merely reproducing their physical details. As an artist, you will be able to say much more about them in creative ways if you study and draw them from life. Try it. It gets easier the more you do it.

When you have an opportunity to visit a zoo, livestock show, or farm, take along your sketchbook. You will find a rich supply of interesting animals to draw.

Don't overlook the less obvious creatures of the animal kingdom—fish and other sealife, insects, and those microblobs we mentioned. Remember, artists look for the new, the unexpected. What about a pencil portrait of a housefly?

- **But, animals are complicated to draw. I always get the head the wrong size!**

Just as with drawing the human figure, animal forms need to be simplified to be captured as art subjects. Figure 13.9 shows an example of how an animal's form can be reduced to simple shapes. Correct proportions are much easier to achieve with this method. You can worry about details like feathers, fur, eyes, and ears later.

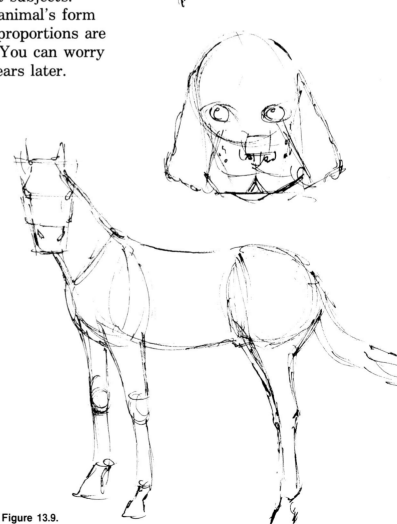

Figure 13.9.

Photo Credit: Bill Kennedy

BORN: 1951
BIRTHPLACE:
Flatonia, Texas

A Smile Is Worth a Thousand Words

Melissa Miller uses the animals, plants, and scenery of Texas in many of her works. And although the animals, her favorite subjects, are painted with a kind of joyful realism, they are strange. Sometimes they smile! This gives them a humorous, cartoon-like appearance. But, more often than not, the mood of the painting is violent and filled with tension. Putting all these elements together in the same work makes us think of a dream or nightmare. There may be more than a touch of Surrealism in Melissa Miller's amazing paintings.

Pack and Possums is characteristic of Miller's painting style and subject matter. Although they are being chased, the hiding possums don't seem too worried. They actually look as if they are smiling!

The brushwork of the grass runs in one direction, while the dog's fur flies in another. This adds to the scene's wild activity and movement.

Melissa Miller has another unique way of composing a picture. She doesn't show us very much space or sky. Our view is directed to the action. In Miller's paintings, we can't stand back out of the way; we have to get involved. This is another reason the little smiles that turn up on the animal's faces are so effective. They seem to sense our presence. It is as if they are saying, "We know you are there, even though you try to hide."

Figure 13.10. Melissa Miller. *Pack and Possums.* 1982. Oil on canvas, 54″x64″. Courtesy Texas Gallery, Houston, Texas. Photo credit: Bill Kennedy.

Did you learn

- The definitions of these words and phrases: anatomy; Stone Age; woodcut?
- Why animals have always been popular art subjects?
- Why Stone-Age humans drew animals?
- How to find live animals for your art subjects?
- Why it is better to draw from life?

Understanding and Evaluating

- Find some examples of animals used in advertising. How are they shown? Are they realistically shown or caricatured?
- Look at Melissa Miller's animal paintings shown in this text. Would you call her style caricature? Realistic? Why?

Student work.

Seeing and Understanding

- Make several gesture sketches of a live animal, such as a family pet or one you might see at the zoo. Use your sketches to make a full-color painting of the animal. Try to add drama to the setting as Melissa Miller does.
- Practice simplifying animal forms into geometric shapes. When you draw from life, pay close attention to the proportion of the head and legs to the body.
- Under the direction of your teacher, make a clay sculpture of an animal. Try to capture the form and details of fur, ears, etc.

Student work.

Figure 14.1.

Deserts, mountain ranges, jungles, coastlines, and swamps are all landscapes. They are all part of the **natural environment**. Fortunately, planet earth is very diverse in the variety of landscapes it contains. By contrast, think about how boring living on the moon would be. Craters, craters everywhere, and not a tree in sight!

Even within the boundaries of the United States, we have every kind of natural scene, from the scorching desert of Death Valley to the towering peaks of the Grand Teton Mountains (Figure 14.1). As human beings, we enjoy this diversity of views. We spend thousands of dollars every year on vacations to see and enjoy these natural wonders; on cameras and film to record what we see. And although human progress and technology has not always treated the natural environment with kindness, we are becoming more aware of the importance of caring for our natural resources. Then, perhaps, we will always be able to enjoy the isolated splendor of Canyon de Chelley as Edward Curtis saw it in 1852 (Figure 14.2).

Most people, if they have any artworks displayed in their homes, will usually have a landscape. There seems to be something very satisfying about looking at natural scenes. Maybe they remind us how much a part of the earth we are, no matter how our lives are directed by technology. But landscapes, as the main subjects of a work of art, do not have a long history. At least, not so long a history when compared to that of the human figure or to animals.

Landscapes, as main subjects of paintings and drawings, became popular during the 17th century. Of course, long before that, artists had painted landscapes, but they were used mainly as background for the real subject or idea of a work. However, from the 17th century to the present day, landscape, as an art subject, has continued to be appreciated. In the next section, you will read about and see the artworks of several artists, past and present, who have made the natural environment the main topic of their creative work. You might want to try your hand at drawing or painting a landscape. Even though you don't live near a "vacation perfect" scene, there are many interesting art ideas to use in your immediate neighborhood or community. You just need to see creatively.

Chapter 14
THE SURROUNDING VIEW— LANDSCAPE, SEASCAPES, AND CITIES

WORDWATCH
aerial perspective
natural environment
human-made environment
typography

Figure 14.2. Edward Curtis. *Canyon De Chelly.* Eight Miles above Mouth. 1852. Lithograph, 7⅛"x4 5/16". Courtesy Amon Carter Museum, Fort Worth, Texas.

Figure 14.3. Jacob van Ruisdael. *Stormy Sea.* c. 1650's. Oil on canvas, 38⅝" x 58¾". Courtesy Kimbell Art Museum, Ft. Worth, Texas.

SEEING AND CREATING LANDSCAPES, SEASCAPES, AND CITIES

Artists have many ways of looking at their surroundings. Some are interested in showing the details of a particular scene so accurately that you could find the spot on which they placed their easel. Others simply wish to use the parts of their landscape—trees, rivers, rocks, hills—to express a feeling or special mood. The location of their scene may be entirely imaginary.

To create mood in a landscape, artists pay close attention to climate changes. Most landscapes include a view of both land and sky. The sky, alone, provides a wonderful subject for art. Its ever-changing colors and cloud shapes can be powerfully expressive tools. Dark, threatening clouds and slashing winds create moods and feelings familiar to us all. In fact, the spooky mood created by the rolling thunder and lightning flashes of an approaching thunderstorm is so well known that it has become a regular backdrop in countless horror and mystery movies. The natural environment is full of drama.

It was probably this drama that first appealed to the great landscape and seascape artist of the 17th century, Jacob van Ruisdael [YOK•ub von ROIS•doll]. Figure 14.3 shows one of his seascapes, titled *Stormy Sea.* It is obvious that the artist is taking great pains to show us how weather and sea can become partners against the feeble efforts of humans to survive. Looking at those towering thunderheads and that writhing sea makes you glad to be on land, safe and dry.

The mood created in this exciting work is enhanced by the use of strong contrasts in color and value. The white foam of the waves is stark against the dark values of the water in the foreground and the brooding clouds in the background. The slash of white waves provides a dramatic backdrop for the struggling boats. The horizon, the line where sky meets earth or sea, is hidden in the gloomy atmosphere of the approaching storm. Can you

?

see any ships out there? Are they doomed?

In this painting, and in others you will see, the artist makes use of **aerial perspective**. Do you recall reading about **linear perspective** in Chapter 7? Linear perspective was a method by which an artist could give an illusion of depth or space to a two-dimensional artwork. The main idea behind linear perspective was that objects appear smaller as they recede into the distance.

Painters, probably beginning with our friend Jan Van Eyck (remember him?), discovered yet another way to create an illusion of space. They discovered that by changing the values of colors—darker close up; lighter and more gray farther away—they could create a convincing illusion of space. If you want to see aerial perspective for yourself, you can look out over a landscape where you can see for some distance. Notice the colors in the most distant objects you see. The colors are very faint, somewhat gray. By contrast, observe the color and value of objects close to you. Notice how intense the colors are. How strong the values are. That is aerial perspective.

There is something else you should notice in the Van Ruisdael painting—scale. Look at the size of the people. Can you find them? Obviously, the artist has little interest in showing us these tiny figures as individuals. We can't even see their faces, much less recognize them. They are dwarfed by the violence of nature. It is paintings like this that really put human beings in their place! In the face of natural forces, we are helpless and insignificant. The theme of human beings at the mercy of nature was popular throughout the 18th and 19th centuries. American landscape artists like Albert Bierstadt [BER • staht] (Figure 14.4) continued the tradition. As you observe landscapes from various centuries, see if you can recognize this theme, and whether it has changed throughout the years. Do humans have more control over

?

nature now?

Along with Van Ruisdael and Bierstadt, American artist Frederick Church was a master of the use of aerial perspective. His wonderful landscapes not only thrill us with their realism, but they capture us with their moods.

Figure 14.4. Albert Bierstadt. *Sunrise, Yosemite Valley.* Oil on canvas, 36⅜"x52⅜". Courtesy Amon Carter Museum, Fort Worth, Texas.

Figure 14.5. Frederick Edwin Church. *Morning in the Tropics.* 1877. Oil on Canvas, 54⅜″ x 84⅛″. National Gallery of Art, Washington, D.C. Gift of the Avalon Foundation.

In Figure 14.5, *Morning in the Tropics*, the creation of atmosphere and setting is so realistic you can almost smell the ripe scent of rich vegetation and feel the humidity and heat of a jungle river. This is art so realistic that it seems to engage all our senses.

Similar in subject, but different in viewpoint, is a work by another American landscape painter, Martin Johnson Heade. *Two Hummingbirds above a White Orchid* (Figure 14.6) shows a jungle scene. We are asked to focus on the beautiful orchid in the foreground and the two hummingbirds in the middle ground. While nature doesn't seem quite so overpowering from this point of view, it does seem mysterious. Strange as some alien blossom from a distant planet, the orchid seems to have as much life and movement as the hummingbirds. And did you notice the background? The distant hills are painted in pale colors and light values. In contrast, the colors and values of the orchid are intensified. Aerial perspective at work again.

The **human-made environment** includes everything we live in or use that was created by human beings. Buildings, automobiles, furniture, washing machines, toasters, televisions, computers—all are part of the human-made environment. Like the natural environment, the human-

Figure 14.6. Martin Johnson Heade. *Two Hummingbirds above a White Orchid.* c. 1870. Oil on canvas, 18⅛″ x10″. Courtesy Amon Carter Museum, Fort Worth, Texas.

Figure 14.7. The differences between natural and human-made objects can be used to create interesting works of art. What would trees look like if they were human-made?

made environment can offer a wide variety of ideas for art.

How do you tell a human-made object from a natural one? Look at the objects in Figure 14.7. Which are natural? Which are human made? Are there certain characteristics that human-made objects share? What do you think they are?

Look again at the objects in Figure 14.7. What do you think they are?

We sometimes overlook the objects of our lives as too common or ordinary to use as inspiration for a work of art. Many artists, however, find the human-made environment rich in creative inspiration and expressive content. As you will see in the following works, artists frequently use the scenes, products, and conditions of modern life to reflect their own feelings about living in contemporary society.

Most of us live in a city, although it may not be as large as Chicago, Los Angeles, or Houston. Regardless of the size, most cities share some common characteristics. For example, architecture.

Architecture is the art form that deals with the design of structures, such as buildings and bridges. Architects, the artists who work in the visual art form of architecture, may also be called upon to help design whole cities. As you look at the architecture of your community, you will notice many different styles. There will be sleek, glass-enclosed boxes that may contain a bank, department store, or office (Figure 14.8). There will be other styles for schools, shopping malls, restaurants, and family homes (Figure 14.9). All these structures were designed by architects.

Figure 14.8. Examples of architecture surround us.

One of the first artists to take advantage of the modern city and its structures as a subject for painting was Fernand Leger [fur • NAND lah • zhay]. Attracted by the geometric precision of skyscrapers, machines, and billboard lettering, he simplified and abstracted them even further (Figure 14.10). He reduced these structures and products of the modern world to art elements: shape, color, line, value, and space. In doing this he became part of an art movement known as Cubism.

Cubists were artists who looked for the basic geometric shapes and forms that make up all objects. They would break up or "cube" an object into a kind of rectangular puzzle. The smooth, glossy surfaces and mathematical exactness of the human-made environment of the city was perfect material for their art. Leger, and the other Cubists worked in the first half of the 20th century.

Figure 14.9. Every community contains a variety of architectural styles for family houses.

Hardly the modern world to us! Yet their way of simplifying shapes and emphasizing the art elements over small details, will have a great influence on art for many years to come.

Figure 14.10, titled *The City*, shows many of the characteristics of Leger's art and Cubism. Notice how you are able to recognize shapes that you might find in the downtown area of any city. There are grid shapes that represent construction cranes, lettering from billboard signs, streets, windows, and bridges. The two figures near the center of the composition seem to be walking downstairs. If you have ever visited a large city with a subway system, you know this is how you get to an underground train platform.

By abstracting buildings, cranes, and other objects, Leger is able to show us how interesting the city is. Art elements are everywhere, and in every possible combination. What a wealth of visual material!

Figure 14.10. Fernand Leger. *The City.* 1919. Oil on canvas, 90¾"x117¼". Philadelphia Museum of Art: A.E. Gallatin Collection.

? Take some time to examine this interesting painting. It is a good one to test your understanding of art elements and design principles. For example, how does Leger create unity in his work? He shows us many different shapes and colors. Is this a symmetrical or asymmetrical composition? How has the artist created space? Is linear perspective used? Overlapping?

Oil Refining (Figure 14.11), by George Grosz [GROSS], is similar in some ways to Leger's painting. The subjects are the human-made structures of an oil refinery. Steel pipes, storage tanks, warehouses, and billowing smoke-stacks are used in this painting as shapes that divide the negative space into yet more shapes.

Unlike the Leger work, Grosz has maintained most of the realistic detail of the refinery. But have you noticed how crowded this painting seems? There doesn't seem to be enough space to contain all those buildings and equipment. This crowding helps convey the complexity and energy of a large refinery or industrial plant. We have no quiet place to rest our eyes. Everywhere we look there are more pipes, more smokestacks, and more confusion.

When you compare this work with the painting by Leger (Figure 14.10), you see that both artists have created busy, crowded visual compositions. If you visit a large industrial plant, you see a good deal of movement, whether by people or machines. Noise is everywhere! If you could turn up the imaginary volume in both the Leger and the Grosz paintings, what sounds would you hear? Can sounds be painted? What color would the sound of a car horn be?

Street signs, billboards, store names, neon signs, and advertisements are also part of the modern, human-made environment. We see so many words printed on and around city buildings that we hardly notice them. Rarely do we take time to notice the type of letters used or the arrangement of the letters. But, some artists find the variety and even the confusion of modern signs and advertising inspiration for their art.

Figure 14.12, titled *Pool, 1973*, is by the American artist Robert Cottingham. Looking at the amazing realism of this painting (yes, this is a painting!), it is difficult to believe that it is not a photograph. This is another example of Photo-realism, where modern, every-day structures or objects are used as subject matter and lettering on signs and advertisements plays an important role.

Robert Cottingham once worked for an advertising agency. Looking at *Pool, 1973*, it is easy to see the influence of his former profession. He uses a variety of lettering styles in the work, but, because we are allowed to see only part of the signs, the letters also act as shapes within the painting. We also find ourselves wanting to complete the unfinished words, as if there

Figure 14.11. George Grosz. *Oil Refining*. Oil on canvas covered board, 30⅛″x22¼″. Dallas Museum of Art, gift of A. Harris and Company in memory of Leon A. Harris, Sr.

Figure 14.12. Robert Cottingham. *Pool, 1973*. Oil on canvas, 78″ x 78″. Virginia Museum of Fine Arts, Richmond. Gift of Sydney and Frances Lewis.

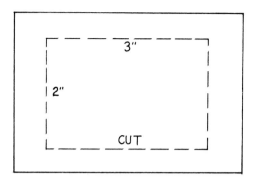

Figure 14.13.

Figure 14.14.

may be some secret meaning in them. Have you noticed how many different styles are used? Some are thick and square; others thin and long. Like everything else in the human-made environment, lettering is designed. The design and arrangement of lettering is called **typography** [tie • PAH • gra • fee].

Let's examine the composition of the Cottingham painting. Like both Leger (Figure 14.10) and Grosz (Figure 14.11), Cottingham has crowded the picture area (picture plane). There are so many shapes, colors, lines, spaces, and textures that our eyes jump from one to the other. The cluttered confusion of much commercial advertising is well illustrated in this painting.

The artist also adds to the complexity of the scene by carefully including every shadow and reflection. Can you make a guess at the time of day this painting depicts? What about the point of view? As the viewer, are you standing in the street looking at this scene? Why, or why not? Where is the focal point of the composition? Is there more than one? Is this arrangement symmetrical or asymmetrical?

USING LANDSCAPES, SEASCAPES, AND CITIES IN YOUR ART

The following suggestions will help you use both natural and human-made environments as art subjects.

- **I don't live in a place that has a beautiful landscape scene. How can I draw or paint a landscape?**
  You don't need a "beautiful" scene like those in postcards. Sometimes unexpected scenes make the most interesting art. For example, a familiar scene can mean more to us than a beautiful one. Even though you may not have a view of mountains, trees, or lakes outside your window, there is probably something there that is familiar and meaningful to you. These feelings are important to express and share through art.

- **There are so many things in view. How do I decide which to draw?**
  A good question. Your eyes let you see more than you can contain within the edges of a piece of paper. One helpful way to shape your view to the shape of your paper is to make a viewfinder (Figure 14.13). When held at arm's length, the open area will "frame" different views for you. If you want to include a certain object in your view, you place it within the frame of the viewfinder.
  Although you cannot hold the viewfinder up while you draw, you can use it long enough to make a light sketch of the main objects in the view you have selected.

A viewfinder can be useful to frame other subjects. It allows you to decide what view makes the best composition.

Figure 14.14 shows two ways a landscape can be planned using foreground, middle ground, and background.

- **I know perspective helps my drawings, but I have trouble seeing how perspective works in a real scene.**

Figure 14.15 shows how the main parts of linear perspective work in a real scene. Can you find the vanishing point? The eye level? Use perspective to help. If you want to draw an interior view, you can still use perspective. Figure 14.16 gives you an idea of how to use linear perspective for interiors.

You can draw more complex objects like cars when you use perspective (Figure 14.17).

- **When I draw signs on buildings, they look funny.**

It is difficult to place letters on a building without using the same rules of perspective you used to draw the building. Figure 14.18 gives you an idea of how to draw letters in perspective. Even if you are designing a poster with lettering, you can create some surprising effects.

Notice the lettering styles used in the signs you see every day. They will give you ideas for your own artworks.

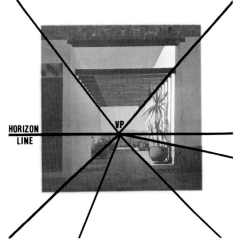

Figure 14.15. A view in one-point perspective.

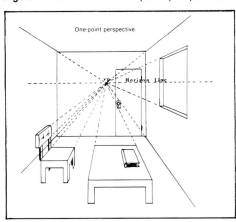

Figure 14.16. The interiors of buildings can also be drawn using the rules of linear perspective.

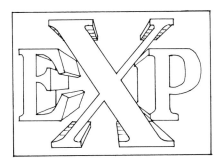 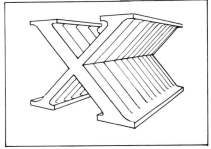

Figure 14.18. Lettering can be enhanced by linear perspective as well. When letters are used on perspective buildings, they must be drawn to the same vanishing point as the building.

Figure 14.17. More complicated forms, can be drawn using the rules of perspective. The forms must first be simplified to a geometric form, such as a cube or rectangle.

Two-point perspective.

Portrait of Frederick Church. 1868. Napoleon Sarony Photographer. Albumen print, 8.9 cm. x 5.9 cm. National Portrait Gallery, Smithsonian Institution.

BORN: 1826
DIED: 1900
BIRTHPLACE:
Hartford, Connecticut

The Endless View

During the middle of the 19th century, American landscape painting and drawing reached a level of excellence that has never been equaled. One of the most gifted painters of this period was Frederick Church.

Church made thousands of landscape sketches and full drawings. He enjoyed working in a variety of drawing media, including pencil, pastel, charcoal, and pen-and-ink. He would change materials when he wanted to achieve a new effect.

Never without a small, handy sketchbook, Church could record the movement of clouds or a flash of sunlight on water with the speed of a camera shutter. He demanded great accuracy from his drawings and as much information as he could get about a particular scene. To achieve this kind of detail, he drew and wrote notes to himself. He noted with great care the exact pink or gold of a sunset. Many of his sketches have more writing than drawing!

The reason for all this exactness was that hundreds of sketches and notes would be needed to complete the detailed landscape paintings for which Church became famous. Both *Morning in the Tropics* and *Icebergs* were probably created from sketches, rather than painted "on location." Both are amazing, not only in their realism, but in the "climate" they create. Church was so skilled at duplicating changes of weather and the effects it had on the landscape, that we can almost feel the temperature of the air.

Figure 14.19. Frederick Edward Church. *The Icebergs.* 1861. Oil on canvas, 64⅜"x112½". Dallas Museum of Art, anonymous gift.

Did you learn

- The definitions of these words and phrases: natural environment; human-made environment; aerial perspective; typography?
- When landscape painting became popular?
- How aerial perspective is created?
- A common characteristic of the human-made environment?
- How the Cubists painted?

Understanding and Evaluation

- Find examples of aerial perspective in other artworks in this book. Is it always a landscape or a seascape? What happens when no aerial perspective is used?
- Apply the four levels of art criticism to Figure 14.6 by Martin Johnson Heade. What do you think the artist is saying in this work?
- Look again at the works by Leger, Grosz, and Cottingham. Do you think they have a positive view of city life? Why, or why not?

Seeing and Understanding

- Using a viewfinder, make a simple pencil sketch of a landscape. Even your own yard will do. No beautiful scenes are necessary. Use your sketch to create a landscape painting. Before transferring your sketch, cover the painting with a background wash of thinned tempera or watercolor. When dry, transfer a light outline of your sketch to the painting. Complete the painting with tempera. Try to set a mood through the particular use of a color scheme.
- Use your viewfinder again. This time take it to a location where there are signs and advertisements. The local grocery store or mall would be good. Find a view with signs crowded together. Make a working sketch with few details. Use your sketch to make a cut-paper collage.

Student work.

Student work.

Chapter 15
THE INNER VIEW— IMAGINATION AND FANTASY

Do you dream as you sleep? According to scientists who study the way people sleep, everyone dreams. We just don't always remember our dreams. Those we do remember are usually filled with actions and scenes that are both strange and mysterious.

In our dreams we are able to do things we could never do in reality. In dreams we can fly, jump unbelievable heights, and run incredible speeds. We sometimes do all these feats in locations as strange as the floor of the ocean or the surface of the moon. Dreams are only one part of the inner world—the world of the imagination. In your imagination there is no place in time or space beyond your reach. Your imagination is one of your richest and most important sources for creative ideas.

Visual art is certainly one of the best ways to express your imagination. While you can share fantastic dreams and ideas with others through words, creating a visual image of your fantasies is so much more exciting.

EXPLORING THE IMAGINATION THROUGH ART

To some degree, all artists use their imaginations. It is difficult to be creative or inventive without exploring the inner landscape of the imagination. But some artists work there all the time! At first glance many of their art-works appear to be composed of normal, everyday subjects. We recognize houses, streets, trees, and watches. But, on closer inspection, we realize that all is not as it seems. The objects and scenes appear dream-like. We have entered the imaginative and fantastic world of the **Surrealists** [sir • REAL • ists].

During the early part of the 20th century, a group of artists decided that they wanted to create art that would express both the moods and feelings of the imaginative world of dreams or the subconscious. These artists called themselves **Surrealists**. The art movement they began is called **Surrealism**. Once you know what to look for it is fairly simple to identify art that is Surrealistic. In most cases it will contain many objects that you can easily recognize. These objects are usually painted in a realistic, photographic manner. This style is important in creating the mood of a dream or fantasy. By letting you recognize the objects, the artist gives you a point of reference—of reality. You think, "Oh yes, I know these things. I see them all the time. I feel comfortable with them." Suddenly, you notice that the familiar objects are not where they should be. They appear to behave as you might see them in a dream or nightmare. Welcome to the world of Surrealism! Let's look at some famous examples.

Spanish artist Salvador Dali [SAL • vah • door DOLL • ee] became the most famous Surrealist in the world. Part of his fame was due to a long life (he lived well into his eighties) and a very eccentric lifestyle. Dali was famous for dressing in gaudy costumes and posing for his photograph at every opportunity. At times his antics and strange behavior were more like that of a rock star than an artist. But, how he could paint!

Figure 15.1 shows one of his most famous works, *The Persistence of Memory*. A master at painting objects in breathtaking detail, this painting shows him at the height of his skill. *The Persistence of Memory* is characteristic of Surrealistic paintings in many respects. We recognize some objects—a watch, a tree branch, and a cliff. But watches don't drape themselves over tree branches nor slither down the sides of tables! Dali has made the ordinary, extraordinary. The real has become "super" real. We seem to be sharing a dream with the artist. And look at that space. There is distance between objects. Dali has been very skillful in using both linear *and* aerial perspective to create an illusion of space. But let's look closer still.

[?] Can you read the time on each of the watches? What about those insects? What are they? Have you decided what kind of object is supporting the wilting timepiece in the middle ground of the painting? What kind of mood does this painting create for you? Does this painting have a focal point? Where is it?

Figure 15.1. Salvador Dali. *The Persistence of Memory.* 1931. Oil on canvas, 9½"x13". Collection, The Museum of Modern Art, New York, given anonymously. Ordinary objects placed in extraordinary locations characterizes much of the work of Surrealists like Dali.

Figure 15.2. M.C. Escher. *Stars.* 1948. 32 cm. x 26 cm. Wood engraving. National Gallery of Art, Washington, D.C. Rosenwald Collection.

The work of Dutch artist M.C. Escher [ES•chur] may be familiar to you already. His amazing images (Figure 15.2) have graced thousands of posters and record albums. Although he has been dead since 1972 and his most famous works were created during the 1940s, he still enjoys great popularity. People are fascinated with his complicated and puzzling images. Escher enjoyed blending the mechanical precision of machines with the mysterious realm of imagination.

Figure 15.3 shows Escher at his most imaginative and trickiest. Titled *Ascending and Descending,* this work creates, a image that is, at first look, perfectly normal. But, in true Surrealist fashion, Escher has visual surprises in store. Everything is fine until you start examining the top floor of this most unusual building. Using his impressive drawing skill and his understanding of the rules of linear perspective, Escher creates a **visual paradox**. This is something that can be created in a drawing or painting, but not constructed or experienced in reality. The figures marching so purposely around the top story of Escher's building are going both up and down at the same time.

Figure 15.4 shows another Escher for your enjoyment. This painting is titled *Mobius Strip.* If you follow the ants carefully, can you tell how they get from one side of the strip to the other?

Both Figure 15.3 and Figure 15.4 seem to be images created from the world of dreams, and ones that exist only there. Strangely enough, the Mobius strip can be made (see On Your Own at the end of this chapter). However, don't be surprised if it turns out to be as full of surprises as its paradoxical twin!

Another famous Surrealist is René Magritte [mah• GREET]. Do you recall what other work by Magritte you have seen in this book?

As full of surprises as his fellow Surrealists, Magritte was also fond of adding humorous twists to his visual fantasies. Figure 15.5, titled *The Empire of Lights,* is an excellent example of visual paradox. Can you find the paradox? Everything looks so normal, so ordinary. What is Surrealistic or dreamlike about this pleasant scene? Hint: Cover the top half of the painting with your hand. What time of day is it? Now, cover the bottom half.

USING YOUR IMAGINATION

As you have already discovered, your imagination can take you anywhere and show you anything. You can time

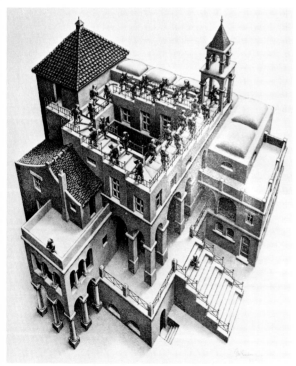

Figure 15.3. M.C. Escher. *Ascending and Descending.* 1960. Lithograph 355 cm. x 285 cm. Collection Haags Gemeentemuseum. ©1990 M.C. Escher Heirs / Cordon Art-Baaarn-Holland.

travel, exceed the speed of light, or create your own world. Visual art lets you share your imagination and dreams with others. But, sometimes the most imaginative and creative of us needs a little help to get started. The following suggestions can help activate your imagination.

Doodling

You sit with the phone at your ear listening to the latest school gossip. A notepad and pencil are close at hand. You begin making circular shapes with the pencil. Some remind you of a cloud you saw the other day. Your circles turn into clouds. Those clouds now remind you of hot air balloons you saw on television the other night. What would it be like to see the top of the highest mountain from a balloon? Your clouds now become balloons. By this time you have talked on the phone beyond your time limit and have covered several sheets of notepaper with **doodles!**

Doodles are like a map of the imagination's wanderings. Most doodles don't serve any purpose other than to occupy our hands as we do something else. However, doodling can be a way to "jump-start" the imagination when it is sluggish. Images drawn when you are relaxed, letting your conscious mind wander, can be very inventive and creative. When we doodle, we are not concerned with making things look correct or with following directions. The imagination is free to explore as the hand records the results of these creative explorations.

So, from now on, take your doodles more seriously! Save them—at least long enough to see if any ideas can be developed from them. When looking for an idea, try doodling. It works.

Decalcomania

Have you ever noticed the swirling patterns made when you stir chocolate syrup into milk or when you mix two colors of paint together? Just as the random shapes of clouds suggest objects to us, so do these swirling patterns. Sometimes, all you need to jog your imagination is to look at the shapes and spaces made by an unusual art process.

Do you remember reading about **decalcomania** (Figure 6.6)? Surrealist painters like Max Ernst used decalcomania to create interesting backgrounds and imaginative landscapes. By pressing crumpled paper or plastic onto the surface of wet paint, they created unusual

Figure 15.4. M.C. Escher. *Mobius Strip.* 1963. Woodcut 453 cm. x 205 cm. Collection Haags Gemeentemuseum ©1990 M.C. Escher Heirs / Cordon Art-Baarn-Holland.

Figure 15.5. Rene Magritte. *The Empire of Lights.* Oil on canvas, 18 1/2" x 24 1/8". Musees Royaux, Brussels.

167

Figure 15.6. Sample of frottage.

marks and shapes. Because these patterns are not planned, but random, they have great variety. If you look at these random shapes, they will suggest animals, people, landscapes, creatures, and places of the imagination. When these shapes are found, you can make them clearer by adding to them or by blocking out parts that are not needed.

Frottage

Frottage [fro•TAHG] is another process that can create fantastic images (Figure 15.6). Even more simple than decalcomania, a frottage print is created by placing a piece of paper over a textured surface, then rubbing over the paper with the side of a crayon. The texture of the object beneath the paper is revealed on the paper. You can predict the way some textures will look. If you rub over a coin, for example, you will get a pretty good image of the coin's detail and its lettering. If, however, you rub over something more complex, like a flattened foil T.V. dinner tray, you will see some amazing textures. Turn the tray beneath the paper after each rubbing. Rub again, and the textures and shapes will become even more interesting. The shapes and spaces of the texture will suggest many new images to you.

MAKING THE ORDINARY, EXTRAORDINARY

Part of developing your own creativity and imaginative power is in being able to see the ordinary in extraordinary ways. It can be as simple as asking, "What if?". Let's try a few what if's.

What if
- the ocean caught fire?
- the landscape was made of vegetables?
- every red thing in the world turned green?
- insects were little machines?
- we had to live underground?

Like the Surrealists, we change everyday objects by putting them in unusual places, or using them in extraordinary ways. This is also called creative **brainstorming**. With brainstorming, everything is possible. No idea, no matter how absurd, is rejected. This is the creative thinking process that many individuals use to develop fresh, new ideas and plans. It can also be an effective way to solve problems.

MEET RENÉ MAGRITTE

Painter of Dreams

It is said that Magritte's first lessons in art came from the local children who played near his house. It is true that he did not begin to study art in a serious way until his family moved to Brussels in 1916.

Like most young, struggling artists at the beginning of their careers, Magritte found himself working at odd jobs. For a while, Magritte worked in a wallpaper factory.

The most important moment in Magritte's art career came when he saw his first Surrealistic painting. The dreamlike mood of the work made a powerful impression on the young man. He eagerly sought out the company of other Surrealistic painters. He wanted to learn all he could about this exciting way to paint. By 1925 he was devoting himself completely to painting.

Even though he had a rather unsuccessful first exhibit, Magritte's fame and popularity spread throughout Europe. He was given a one-man exhibition in New York in 1936. By now he had become one of the masters of the Surrealistic style of painting. Young artists now came to Magritte for advice and inspiration.

Magritte was a good role model for artists who wanted to learn how to create successful Surrealistic paintings. The objects in his works are painted with incredible detail and precision. No brushstrokes are allowed to show. The surface of all the objects must be as hard and smooth as Magritte could make them. This style of painting helped Magritte achieve the mood of mystery and wonder that was at the heart of the Surrealist movement. Placing objects like the big green apple in *The Listening Chamber* (Figure 10.3) in an unusual place, like a very small room, must be done with totally convincing detail. Wild brushwork or unreal colors would spoil the mood of wonder.

Photo of René Magritte. Photographer Duane Michals. 1984. Gelatin-silverpoint. Courtesy Sidney Janis Gallery, N.Y. ©Duane Michals.

BORN: 1898
DIED: 1967
BIRTHPLACE:
Lessines, Belgium

Figure 15.7. René Magritte. *The Surprise Answer.* Oil on canvas, 16″ x 2½″. Musees Royaux, Brussels.

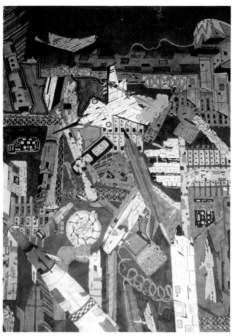

Student work.

Student work.

Did you learn

- The definitions of these words and phrases: Surrealism; visual paradox; frottage; decalcomania; brainstorming?
- At least two characteristics of a Surrealist painting?
- The names of two famous Surrealist painters?
- What makes a visual paradox?

Understanding and Evaluating

- Write a short story to accompany *The Surprise Answer* (Figure 15.7).
- Make a list of five other possible titles for *The Persistence of Memory* (Figure 15.1).
- Compare Figure 15.1 by Dali with Figure 15.7 by Magritte. How are they similar? How are they different?

Seeing and Creating

- Begin a doodle near the top of a sheet of drawing paper. Let your mind wander as your hand moves. Any image, shape, or line that comes into your mind, doodle it! Work for five minutes, then stop. Look at your work from several different directions. When you see something that inspires you, use it. Continue until the whole sheet is filled.
- Make a Mobius strip by cutting a long strip of paper. Hold an end in each hand. Bring them together. Make a circle. Now, take one end and turn it upside down on top of the other end. There should now be a curve in the paper. Glue the ends together in this position. You now have a Mobius strip with one continuous surface. Use it to make some Escher-like drawings using felt markers. Hang it as a mobile, when complete.

In order to share our ideas, feelings, and moods with others through art, we must give them a reality or form. These forms of expression can be a drawing, a painting, a sculpture, or a craft object. In this unit you will learn more about the various forms of visual art and about the materials and tools associated with each. Do you remember that materials such as crayons, chalk pastels, and clay are called art media? (Remember: medium is the singular form). In the following chapters you will read more about a variety of media and about suggestions on how to use them properly and creatively. As in other chapters, you will also have a chance to see how other artists use various media to create.

Some chapters, especially those on drawing and painting, include exercises and helpful hints to build your skills. These are very important. To do some of these exercises you will need your teacher's direction and school art materials; others, you can practice on your own. More creative ideas are found at the end of the chapter in the section called ON YOUR OWN.

If you are really interested in improving your art skills, you need to practice. Few people, if any, are "natural" artists. Good artists work hard at their creativity and their technical skills. For, no matter how wonderful your ideas, you cannot express and share them, unless you are able to understand and use the forms and media of art. After all, no one expects you to play a piece of music perfectly after only one lesson at the piano! Why should you expect to draw or paint like Leonardo after only a few crayon sketches?

Unit V

THE MEANS OF EXPRESSION

Chapter 16

WORKING IN TWO-DIMENSIONS— DRAWING

WORDWATCH
medium
spontaneous
India ink
stippling
crowquill pen
crosshatching

Do you remember the first drawing you ever made? As a very young child, you probably took great delight in tightly gripping a bright crayon or marker and wildly scribbling across a big sheet of paper or even the living-room wall! Everyone likes to draw, no matter what their age. Drawings can be quick, one-minute sketches (Figure 16.1) or realistic, detailed studies (Figure 16.2).

Drawing is by far the most popular art form. Even though they may not consider their sketches to be art, most people feel fairly comfortable taking a pencil or marker and sketching some ideas on paper. Designs for the most complicated tools and machines, elaborate buildings, or automobiles often begin with a simple draw-ing. Some people use drawing to solve not only design problems, but also problems of organization and creative invention. Creative thinking and problem-solving can be greatly helped through drawing.

There are many materials and tools to select for draw-ing (Figure 16.3). Some are practically unchanged since their invention years ago. Others are products of modern technology. Both kinds can be used to express an amazing range of emotions and creative ideas. Let's examine a few of the most popular.

PENCILS

Pencils are good for making both quick sketches and detailed drawings. They are inexpensive, clean, and easy to carry. The ordinary, No. 2 pencil can produce some very nice drawings. However, you may want to try some "real" drawing pencils. *Soft* drawing pencils (6B to 2B) can be found in many art-and-craft stores. Some can even be found at the neighborhood supermarket. These pencils allow you to create a wide range of values in your draw-ings. Because their lead is soft, you can make dark areas

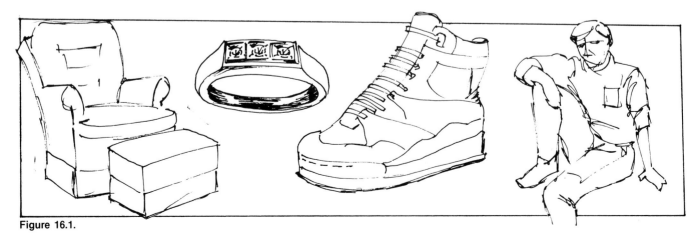

Figure 16.1.

very dark, and barely tint areas you want to be light. Most pencils work on a variety of surfaces.

Figure 16.4 is a pencil drawing made by Friedrich Richard Petri [FREED • drik • PEA • tree] of his friend Jacob Kruechler [CREWSH • lur]. Notice how the artist has captured the position of horse and rider with quick lines. Even though the horse and rider are still, the pencil strokes give motion and energy to the drawing. Both seem to be resting between daily activities. Because pencils are simple drawing tools, easy-to-carry, they are useful in recording the interesting people or scenes we see daily.

Skill-Builders and Helpful Hints:

When making quick sketches or gesture drawings, try holding your drawing tool between your thumb and first finger, as shown in Figure 16.5. Although this position may seem awkward at first, it will eventually become natural and comfortable. Holding any drawing tool in this fashion encourages you to draw with more arm movement, creating bolder, more action-filled drawings. It also prevents you from getting caught up in small details before you have drawn the basic forms of your subject.

- Draw lightly. When beginning a drawing, keep your lines light and sketchy until you have the basic shapes and their proportions the way you want them. If you train your eye to see accurately and your hand to have a light touch, you won't need to erase very much.
- On a sheet of white drawing paper, see how many different kinds of lines you can create. Vary them. not only in width and value (darkness and lightness), but in expression. Try expressing the following feelings with one line each: excited, fearful, shy, nervous, puzzled, curious, and depressed.
- Sharpen your eye by making a blind contour drawing. Using either your hand or a shoe, follow the outline or contour with your eye as you draw it. You are not allowed to look down at your drawing paper! Try not to lift your pencil once you have begun. GO SLOWLY. If your eye gets ahead of your pencil, you will be lost. This exercise takes practice, so don't be upset if your first few attempts look strange! The secret is in your concentration and the coordination between your eye and hand. See the example of a student's contour drawing at the end of the chapter.

Figure 16.2. George Bellows. *Lady Jean.* Black lithographic crayon on white paper, 22"x13½ ". Courtesy of The Fogg Art Museum, Harvard University, Cambridge, Massachusetts. Bequest of Meta and Paul J. Sachs.

Figure 16.3. Drawing Tools.

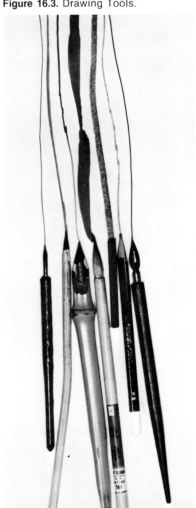

Figure 16.4. F. Richard Petri. *Jacob Kruechler on Horseback.* Undated. Pencil on paper, 6¾"x4½". Texas Memorial Museum, Gift of Alfred Wupperman.

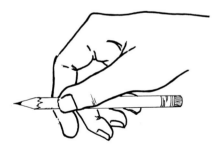

Figure 16.5. The best way to hold a drawing tool, such as a pencil or crayon, when making quick sketches.

Figure 16.7. Practice making several value grids like this one.

- Gesture drawings, like those shown in Figure 16.6, can sharpen your observing eye and drawing hand, as well. Try making some gesture drawings of the people or objects you see around your school or neighborhood. Time yourself. Begin with sketches no more than thirty seconds long. That's right—thirty seconds! No time to worry about eyelashes and the number of buttons on the shirt. Look for basic shapes—how they relate and fit together. Make at least ten, thirty-second gesture drawings. Now, you can take a whole minute! Do ten more, a minute in length. Doesn't a minute seem a long time now?

- On a worksheet prepared by your teacher, or on a piece of white drawing paper, try your hand at shading with a pencil. If you don't have a drawing pencil, you may use a No. 2 pencil. On your drawing paper, draw a grid like the one pictured in Figure 16.7. Beginning with the first block, fill it with the darkest value you can make with your pencil. Fill each of the following boxes with a slightly lighter or higher value, until you reach the final box. This should be left blank. It represents the lightest value you have—the white of the paper.

- Repeat the exercise in another line of boxes without divisions. This time create as smooth a transition or connection between each value as possible. The trick is to keep your pencil strokes very small and smooth. If you are successful, you should not be able to see the edge that separates one value level from another. This takes practice, so don't be discouraged if you don't succeed right away. As you practice, you will notice a great improvement in your drawings.

CRAYONS

"Crayons are for coloring, not drawing!" If you believe this, you are like many people. Crayons, those wonderful

Figure 16.6. Gesture drawings.

174

drawing tools that you enjoyed when you were very young, are frequently overlooked as serious drawing media. After all, who wants to create "art" with a material that some kindergarteners eat! Well, think again. Crayons can be wonderful tools for "serious" art.

For example, look at Joseph Stella's crayon drawing of flowers (Figure 16.8). Notice how delicately he has shown the structure and form of the flowers. Some leaves and parts of the stem are drawn very lightly. Doesn't this make them seem farther away? Remember the wonderful seascape by Van Ruisdael in Chapter 14 (Figure 14.3)? The artist used aerial perspective to make parts of the painting appear far away. Joseph Stella shows that you can do the same thing with a simple drawing of a natural object. He draws lightly with the crayon (lighter values = farther away) when he wants to push something into the background. He presses down with the crayon (darker values = closer) when he wants to bring something forward.

Crayon is probably the most inexpensive color medium. Depending on the size of the set, you can get a wide range of hues, tints, and shades for a very low price. With some sets you even get a sharpener! Crayons are a good substitute for more expensive drawing materials, like oil pastels. Although the wax in crayons makes color mixing and blending a little more difficult, it is still possible with some practice.

Skill-Builders and Helpful Hints:

- From a box of crayons, select the primary colors (remember them?). On a worksheet supplied by your teacher or on a sheet of white drawing paper, try to mix the secondary colors. See how many different shades (mixed with black) and tints (mixed with white) you can create from each primary and secondary color. The secret to mixing crayons is not to build up the colors too quickly. Pressing down too hard will cause the wax to build up. This will prevent you from adding other colors.
- Make a value chart like the one you made in pencil, but use crayons instead. You may want to select a fairly dark color, such as blue or green. What is different about making this value chart with crayons? Is it easier or harder than using pencil?
- To cover large areas of your drawing, you might find it helpful to peel away the paper wrapping on the crayons. This allows you to draw with them on their sides, using the full length of the crayon. Interesting effects in value can be achieved this way (Figure 16.9).

Figure 16.8. Joseph Stella. *Flowers*. Undated. Pencil and crayon, 10⅝"x11". Yale University Art Gallery. From the Estate of Katherine S. Dreier.

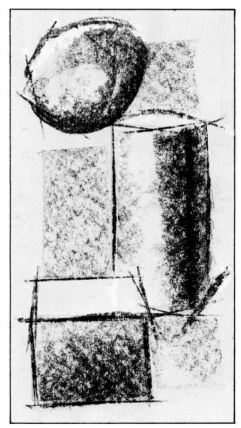

Figure 16.9. When the paper is peeled away from a crayon, the side can create some interesting shading effects.

CHALK PASTELS AND CHARCOAL

Chalk pastels, like crayons, come in box sets containing a variety of colors and values. Although they are called chalk, pastels or artist's chalks are not the same as the chalk used on the board in the classroom. The colors of pastels are much stronger and more vivid. The range of values (tints and shades) is also wider.

Pastels not only give artists many beautiful hues to work with, but they also are fairly easy to use in creating value in drawings. By rubbing over the lines or edges of shapes drawn in pastels, smooth, even values can be created. Large shapes or spaces can be quickly filled with smooth values by rubbing over them with a cloth or paper towel.

Edgar Degas [DAY•gah], a famous French artist of the 19th century, used pastels in many drawings (Figure 16.10). Degas was fascinated with the world of the ballet. Throughout his life, he drew, painted, and even sculpted figures of ballerinas. Surprisingly, he was not always interested in the glamorous poses. He liked to attend ballet rehearsals or practice sessions. Here, he could capture in drawing the confusion and haste of the young dancers preparing for a performance. He would draw them twisting and turning to warm and flex their tired, cold muscles, just as athletes do before a big game. He often drew them in awkward poses, bending over to tie on their delicate, satin ballet shoes.

Pastels gave him the ease and freedom to record quickly these frantic activities. The wide range of pastel colors and values allowed him to show the glamorous side of the ballet—the beautiful sets and costumes. The pastel hues of the dancer's dress in Figure 16.10 make it seem as delicate and light as a cloud.

Charcoal has been a favorite drawing medium for many centuries. In fact, there is some evidence that prehistoric humans may have used burned or charred pieces of wood to draw on the walls of caves.

The drawing charcoal we use today comes in several shapes and degrees of softness. Stick or vine charcoal looks like its name—a thin stick or piece of a vine that has been burned. Compressed charcoal comes in small, block-like sticks. It varies from very soft to very hard.

Charcoal is not very expensive, though it will cost more than a No. 2 pencil. Like chalk pastels, it can be used to create smooth values by rubbing and blending with cloth or paper towel (Figure 16.11). But also like pastels, it can be messy! When drawing with charcoal or pastels, it is

Figure 16.10. Edgar Degas. *Dancer with Fan.* 1879. Pastel on paper, 17⅜"x11⅜". Private collection.

Figure 16.11. Samples of shading with charcoal and chalk pastel.

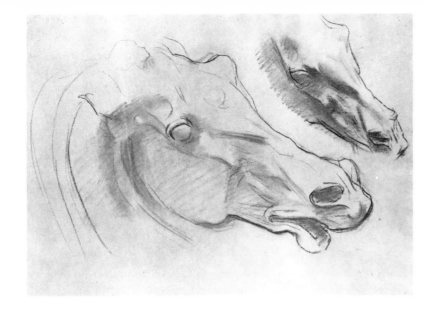

Figure 16.12. John Singer Sargent. *Study of Horses' Heads for Apollo in his Chariot with the Hours.* c. 1910-15. Charcoal 13½" x 9". The Cocoran Gallery of Art, Washington, D.C. Gift of V.S. Ormond and Emily Sargent.

wise not to touch your face, or you may accidently give yourself a moustache!

Ⓒ [CAUTION: Charcoal and chalk pastels both produce a good deal of dust. Some people are allergic to this dust and are uncomfortable working with these materials. If you know you have this problem, tell your teacher. Other drawing materials can be substituted.]

Figure 16.12 is a working drawing by John Singer Sargent. Titled *Study of Horses' Heads*, it shows why charcoal is considered a **spontaneous** [spon • TANE • e • us] drawing medium. In this case, **spontaneous** means that the work appears to have been drawn with speed and energy. It seems fresh and lively. The artist is not concerned with finishing every small detail. Many artists' sketches or working drawings appear spontaneous.

Sargent was probably planning a larger, more detailed drawing or painting using horses as part of the composition. The ease of drawing with charcoal allowed Sargent to capture all the visual information he needed for his larger work.

Skill-Builders and Helpful Hints:

Ⓒ [CAUTION: Some people are allergic to the dust of pastels and charcoal. Wear a protective mask if necessary.]

Practice shading with both pastels and charcoal. Make a value chart for each. Try to blend smoothly between each value change. Is this harder than using pencil? What about crayon?

When working on pastel or charcoal drawings, protect the rest of your drawing from smearing by placing a paper towel under your hand as you work.

Both pastels and charcoal can be used to create smooth backgrounds for drawings made in crayon or pen-and-ink.

Figure 16.13. The crowquill pen is sometimes referred to as a calligraphy pen. It comes in a variety of interchangeable points for varied line widths.

Figure 16.14. Since ink drawings cannot be erased, they are good for training the eye and hand.

This is a good way to use up small, broken pieces of pastels and charcoal.

PEN-AND-INK

Drawing in pen-and-ink can be scary! It is almost impossible to make changes. But drawing with ink can be great practice for sharpening your observation skills and your drawing hand.

Figure 16.13 shows a type of ink pen called a **crowquill** [crow•quill] or **calligraphy** [cah•LIG•rough•e] pen. The ink used with this pen is called **India ink**. India ink is black, but drawing ink also comes in many colors. The crowquill pen is dipped into the ink bottle and then used to draw. When the pen stops drawing, the pen must be dipped once more into the ink. [**CAUTION:** India ink is permanent. That means it will not come out of your clothes.] When using any type of permanent ink, use extreme caution. If possible, wear an old shirt or smock to cover your clothes. [**CAUTION:** Never play around open bottles of ink.]

The name *crowquill* and the way it is used may remind you of the old-fashioned feather quill pens you have seen or read about in history books. The Declaration of Independence was signed with quill pens. The crowquill or calligraphy pens we use today are a modern version of the feather-quill pen. We have still more modern versions of these drawing tools.

Most of you use felt-tip or water-based markers from time to time. These modern versions of crowquill pens are convenient and fairly clean. However, some can be expensive for drawing, especially when they run out of ink and cannot be refilled.

Some felt-tip pens give off dangerous vapors and smells. [**CAUTION:** They should not be used in a closed space.] Other pens and markers are water-based and are not dangerous. Figure 16.14 shows the kind of lines and marks that are possible with different kinds of pens.

Figure 16.15 shows a drawing by Thomas Cole. It is a good example of the variety of lines and textures possible with pen-and-ink. Called the *Gnarled* [narled, don't pronounce the G] *Tree Trunk*, this drawing has lines used for shading. Do you remember what shading with lines is called? (see Chapter 3). What do you notice about the direction of the crosshatched lines? Has the artist been successful in creating an illusion of shading? Of a three-dimensional object?

Shading in ink is very different from shading with other drawing materials. You can't lay the side of a crow-quill or felt-tip pen down and shade the way you can with crayon, pastels, or charcoal. There are two main ways to create value with ink—**crosshatching** and **stippling**. Crosshatching, as you know, is a way to build shading by drawing lines in one direction, then crossing those lines with others (more lines=darker value). **Stippling** is shading or value built with dots or small marks (more dots=darker value). Figure 16.16 shows how changes in value can be created with both crosshatching and stippling.

Skill-Builders and Helpful Hints:

- On a worksheet prepared by your teacher or on a piece of white construction paper, lightly draw in pencil a cube, a cone, a pyramid, a rectangular box, and a sphere. Now, imagine light coming from one direction. Using either pen and India ink or felt-tip pen, shade the opposite side using crosshatching. On some of the objects it will be necessary to *curve* the hatch lines. Why? Which forms need curved lines? What would happen if you used straight lines on these objects? Do your objects look three-dimensional?
- Repeat the exercise using stippling. How is it different from crosshatching? Do the forms look three-dimensional?
- Study a ball or sphere (a white one if possible) under a spotlight. Notice how the light reflection and shadows fall on the surfaces. Are they located where you thought they would be? Make an ink drawing of the sphere using either crosshatching or stippling for shading.

Figure 16.15. Thomas Cole. *Gnarled Tree Trunk.* 1826. Pen and brown ink over pencil, 14⅞″ x 10¹¹/₁₆″. Founders Society Purchase, William H. Murphy Fund. ©Detroit Institute of Art.

Figure 16.16. Examples of shading with ink.

179

Portrait of George Bellows.
Self-portrait c. 1917.
Conte crayon on paper, 12 1/16″ x 8 1/16″.
National Portrait Gallery, Smithsonian
Insitution.

BORN: 1882
DIED: 1925
BIRTHPLACE:

Columbus, Ohio

Figure 16.17. George Bellows. *Dance in a
Madhouse.* 1907. Black crayon, charcoal, pen
and ink on wove paper, 48 cm. x 62.5 cm.
Charles H. and Mary F.S. Worcester
Collection. © 1990 The Arts Institute of
Chicago. All Rights Reserved.

The Truthful Eye

George Bellows's art career began the day he arrived in New York City from Columbus, Ohio. The year was 1904. It was an exciting time to be a young, talented artist in New York.

Before Bellows arrived, an interesting group of artists had banded together in a kind of "art club." There were eight original members, so they called themselves "The Eight." These young men had certain things in common, First, they had all been students at the National Academy of Art in Philadelphia. Second, they had all worked as illustrators for various magazines and newspapers. This work took them into the gritty, tough world of big-city life. They shared the belief that the real subjects of the city—rough people, working in rough places—should be the subjects of their art.

Of course, this was not what they had learned at the Academy. There they had drawn and painted in the "academic" style. It was very traditional. Subject matter for artworks had to be elegant and refined, not gaudy or vulgar. Rebelling against the academic method of art, "The Eight" caused quite a stir. The original eight members included some of the finest American artists of their time. It was into this exciting and rebellious climate that George Bellows stepped.

Bellows had little trouble finding a place for himself in the New York art world. He not only had the ability to draw with great realism, but he could also capture the moment with his amazingly accurate eye and rapid hand.

Like Frederick Church before him, Bellows was skilled in drawing in a variety of media. Figure 16.17 titled *Dance in a Madhouse,* is very different from his portrait of *Lady Jean* (Figure 16.2). To record the frenzy of a madhouse dance, he used three different media: crayon, charcoal, and ink. It is difficult to mix media together successfully, unless, of course, you are a George Bellows! Thick lines, thin lines, deep shadow, glaring light—all add to the confusion and wild movement. His choice of subject—the inmates of a mental institution—shows how he too had accepted the style of The Eight.

Did you learn

- The definitions of these words and phrases: medium; crowquill pen; spontaneous drawing; India ink; stippling; crosshatching?
- Two ways to sharpen your eye for observation and drawing?
- That aerial perspective can be used in drawings, as well as in paintings?
- A good substitute for oil pastels?

Understanding and Evaluation

- Make a survey of the drawings you have seen in this book. Notice which drawing medium was chosen for each (it is always listed in the credit line beneath the work). Are certain drawing media selected for portraits? For landscapes? For animals?
- Compare George Bellows's painting in Chapter 12 (Figure 12.5) with the drawings in this chapter. Pretend you don't know they were made by the same artist. What similarities of style are there? For example, how is line drawn?

Seeing and Creating

- Make a landscape drawing in pencil. Complete details of texture and line with India ink. Finally, use an ink wash to add more value and mood to your drawing. Mix a small amount of water with ink in a small jar.
- ⓒ Apply with brush. [**CAUTION:** India ink will stain. Wear a smock or old shirt.]
- Make a stipple drawing of a human-made object. Select something that is fairly large. Small items are hard to draw and shade in stipple.
- Use crayons to make a large drawing of a still life made up of toys or some other brightly colored objects. Leave some paper showing between objects. Press down with crayons. Cover with a wash of ink. Crayon will resist most of the ink.

Student work.

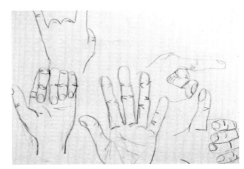
Student work.

Chapter 17

WORKING IN TWO DIMENSIONS— PAINTING, PRINTMAKING, AND COLLAGE

WORDWATCH
pigment
edition
brayer
paint medium
printing plate
collage
opaque
monoprinting
transparent
stencil
Impressionism

As you look at the works of art in this book, you may notice that many are paintings. Painting, as an art form, has a long history—at least 25,000 years, maybe longer! Remember the cave paintings from Lascaux? People have long felt the need to decorate both themselves and their surroundings with color. After all, painting is all about color.

Unlike the color media of crayon and pastel, paint must be in a liquid state to be used. It can then be applied with a brush (Figure 17.1). There are two main parts of this liquid color—**pigment** and **paint medium**.

Pigment is made up of particles of ground color. These particles are mixed to make red, green, blue, or any other color of paint. Many years ago, before pigments were manufactured in laboratories, they were created by grinding up semi-precious stones! Talk about valuable paintings!

The liquid solution that holds the pigments together is called the **medium**. It may also be called the *binder*. Many centuries ago, artists had to find pigments, grind them up, and mix them with some liquid to hold them together. One of the favorite mediums was egg! Later, artists like Jan Van Eyck started using linseed oil to hold the pigments. Oil painting was born!

There are many kinds of paint—oil, tempera, acrylic, and watercolor. When applied, they can appear in two ways—**opaque** [o•PAKE] or **transparent**. Oil, tempera, and acrylic are mainly used for an opaque application (Figure 17.2). This means that little or no paper is allowed to show under the paint. You can't see through it. Watercolor, on the other hand, is considered a transparent paint. When applied with water, it allows the paper, or other marks on the paper, to show through. You can see through watercolor (Figure 17.3).

Figure 17.1. Paint brushes come in a variety of types and sizes.

Figure 17.2. In a thick consistency, both liquid acrylic and tempera paint are opaque (no paper shows through).

Figure 17.3. Watercolor is a transparent painting medium. When enough water is added to acrylic and tempera, they can also appear transparent.

Twilight Games (Figure 17.4) by artist Alma Gunter, is an example of paint that is applied opaquely. The areas of color are very solid. But, notice the curtains in the window! The artist allows us to look into the house by making the curtains somewhat transparent. This pleasant work is done in acrylic paint. Acrylic paint is the newest type of paint available. Can you guess by its name what the binder is? If you guess plastic, you are correct. Acrylic paint is very tough and strong like the plastic from which it is made. It also allows an artist to apply opaquely or transparently, as in Alma Gunter's painting.

Ⓒ Though acrylic paint has many advantages, it is, unfortunately, expensive. [**CAUTION:** It also will not come out of clothes.] When using acrylic paint, you should always cover your clothes with an old shirt or smock.

A good, cheaper substitute for acrylic is liquid tempera. It can also be thinned to use in a more transparent way. However, it is not as successful as watercolor. Tempera, acrylic, and watercolor can all be thinned with water. Brushes used with any of these paints should be washed

Ⓒ carefully. [**CAUTION:** Brushes left to dry in acrylic paint cannot be cleaned.]

Although painting has been a popular means of creative expression for many centuries, something special happened to painting in the last part of the 19th century. Around 1872, a group of artists, mainly French, decided that true color and light could not be accurately painted, if subjects were always seen inside dimly-lit rooms. Artists needed to get outdoors to paint the colors of the world reflected by the dazzle and glare of sunlight. They wanted to paint an impression of what you see when you look at things in natural light. The art movement they founded became known as Impressionism.

One of the greatest Impressionists was French painter Claude Monet [clawd mow • NAY]. Figure 17.5 is one of his most famous paintings. It is a painting of the great Gothic cathedral of Rouen [ru • on]. The artist shows us the dazzle and play of light on the ancient stone by applying paint in short strokes. He uses the brushwork to break up the surface into small bits of color. You almost need to squint your eyes to look at it. Do you recall any other paintings that remind you of this way of painting? Which ones? How are they similar? Would this way of painting be possible in tempera paint? Acrylic? What about watercolor?

WATERCOLOR

Watercolor paint can come in small blocks of pigment in sets of several colors, or in tubes. By adding water,

Figure 17.4. Alma Gunter. *Twilight Games.* 1978. Acrylic 14″ x 18″. Collection of Sally Griffiths.

Figure 17.5. Claude Monet. *Rouen Cathedral.* 1894. Oil on canvas, 39½″x26″. National Gallery of Art, Washington, D.C., Chester Dale Collection.

the artist can make clear, bright colors. The more water added, the more transparent the paint.

Watercolor is a difficult painting medium to master. Practice and patience are important in learning to use watercolors well. You have already met one of the greatest watercolor artists of all time—John Singer Sargent.

Figure 17.6 shows he was also a master at watercolor. *Muddy Alligators* is a fitting name for these fat, lazy, wallowing beasts! Sunlight and shadows play across their bumpy hides. Sargent has painted them in their natural surroundings. Tree trunks are reflected in the still, muddy water of the swamp these creatures call home.

[?] Can you find places where the color seems to run and smear? Much of the vegetation in the background has been applied with big loose strokes on wet paper.

This is one of the special advantages of watercolor. If the painting paper is wet first, the colors will run, creating interesting shapes. Sargent has also used a more realistic painting style in this work. Can you find those places? Why do you think he used a loose painting style for the background and a tighter style for the alligators? Can you tell how he created the texture of their hides? Look at the shadowed areas on the alligators. What colors do you see?

Skill-Builders and Helpful Hints:

- Review the color-mixing exercise in Chapter 3. Under the direction of your teacher at school, or on your own at home, try applying tempera paint on a piece of construction paper in a variety of ways. Try putting it on thickly with short, quick strokes. Mix several tints of one color. (Review tints in Chapter 3, if necessary). Apply the tints with short brushstrokes. Can you create an effect similar to the work by Monet (Figure 17.5)? Now, try smearing them on the paper with a piece of cardboard. Smear two or more colors together using the cardboard. Wouldn't this be a good way to create an interesting background for a landscape? Use the edge of the cardboard. Can you make images with the edge?

PRINTMAKING

Have you ever covered your hand with paint or chalk and pressed it against a piece of paper or some other surface? If the answer is "yes," then you have been a printmaker.

In art there are many methods for creating a print. Most prints are made by placing paper, cloth, or some other material against a prepared surface. This prepared surface is called the **printing plate**. Some printing plates are prepared by cutting lines or groves into them with special tools. In this way a drawing can be transferred to a printing surface made of wood, linoleum, or metal. ©[CAUTION: Tools and gouges used to cut printing plates can be dangerous. Always cut away from your body.]

After cutting, the plate can be covered with printing ink and pressed against paper or cloth to produce a print. Prints made this way are called *woodcuts, linoleum cuts, etchings,* or *engravings.* Many copies of a drawing can be made from them. As the artist makes each print, it is given a number in the order in which it was printed. For example, the first made is numbered one. An entire set of prints based on one drawing is called an *edition.*

In Chapter 2 you saw a *lithograph* by Edvard Munch (Figure 2.6). Do you remember how it was created? Thomas Hart Benton also made lithographs (Figure 3.8). Lithographs use very large, heavy stones as the drawing surface for the prints. These stones and the press that holds them are too expensive for most individuals. Fortunately, there are easier ways to print.

Found Object and Vegetable Prints

You can make a print from anything. The next time you clean out a drawer or the garage, look for printing ©"junk"—wood scraps, broken tools, or pieces of plastic. Coated with water-based paint, they can create unique textures and images when pressed against paper or cloth. You can also use vegetables to create prints. Cabbages or onions, cut in half, coated with ink or paint, and printed, make wonderful texture prints.

Figure 17.7. Michael Penning. *Chicken Pot Pie.* 1978. Monoprint, 14¾" x 14¾". Courtesy of Garner and Smith Gallery.

Figure 17.8. Robert Indiana. *The American Eat.* 1962. Frottage 25″ x 19″. Courtesy Virginia Lust Gallery. Photo: James Dee.

Figure 17.9. Stencil prints are good examples of how negative and positive shapes can be used in a composition.

Monoprints

Printmaking is *duplication*. This simply means that an original is copied numerous times. In art there are many different ways to duplicate or print an image.

While most printing methods produce more than one copy of a drawing, there is one method which creates only one original print. This printing method is called **monoprinting**. Do you remember what "**mono**" meant in monochromatic? Well, it means the same in monoprint—one.

In monoprinting, a drawing is created on a smooth surface, such as a piece of glass or plastic that has been evenly coated with a thin layer of printing ink or paint. By placing a sheet of paper over the surface, the drawing can be transferred to the paper. Since most of the ink or paint is transferred each time, a new drawing must be made before every print.

Figure 17.7 is an example of a monoprint made by artist Michael Penning, Can you see where he has scratched letters into the wet ink? Notice how much the print looks like a drawing or painting. The subject is funny, but familiar. You might think about eating chicken pot pies, but have you ever thought about printing one? If the words were not included, would you be able to recognize the subject? Why, or why not? What other foods could be used as art subjects? Do you remember the name of the artist that used hamburgers as models?

Frottage Prints

Another simple, but interesting, way to make a print is by **frottage**. Frottage is a print made by rubbing. Paper is placed on top of a textured surface. The paper is then rubbed with a drawing tool like a crayon. Details of the texture of the object will be picked up on the paper. Any surface that has texture can be used to make a frottage print.

Figure 17.8 is an example of a frottage print made by American artist Robert Indiana. What do you think he used to make this print? Can you see the strokes made by the crayon? Where did the title for this print come from? Robert Indiana uses words and letters in both his drawings and paintings. Compare this work with the print by Penning (Figure 17.7). How do words add to these works?

Stencil Prints

Have you ever cut a shape out of paper or cardboard and used it to draw around? If so, you were making another type of print—a stencil. The shape you cut is a positive stencil, but what about the space left in the paper? You can use it also. It is the negative. Stencils allow one image to be repeated until it becomes a **pattern**. You often find decorative patterns in wallpaper and fabrics. Many of these are made with stencils. Figure 17.9 shows a pattern made with stencils.

Skill-Builders and Helpful Hints:

* When making a monoprint, always apply the water-based printing ink in a thin, smooth coat using a **brayer**. This printing tool is a rubber-like cylinder attached to a handle. A small amount of ink is squeezed from the tube at the top of your printing plate. The brayer is used to roll the ink over the surface. When the printing area is well-covered and the surface looks smooth like "velvet," you are ready to draw.
* Water-based inks dry fast! Make your drawing as quickly as possible. Sometimes, dampening the printing paper with a sponge or paper towel will help. Lay or hang your print in a safe place to dry. Don't forget to give it a title and to add your name.

COLLAGE

Collage is an art form in which materials, even objects, are attached to another surface. You may have made photographic collages by cutting pictures from magazines and gluing them to paper or cardboard like artist Romare Bearden does (Figure 17.10). Colored tissue paper is frequently used in collages.

Artist Kelly Fearing is known for the beauty of his collages. In Figure 17.11 you see a fine example. Beautiful materials (silk ties) have been cut into strips so that the edges will ravel into fringe. A delicate drawing in colored pencil has been added. How has the artist created unity between the collage part and the drawing part? What other fabrics would make interesting material for a collage? Sometimes Kelly Fearing uses precious and semi-precious stones in his collages. Their jeweled surfaces and colors bring even more beauty to these art-works, not to mention, adding to their value!

Figure 17.10. Romare Bearden. *Autumn.* 1987. Collage, 36″x24″. Photo courtesy: ACA Galleries. Estate of Romare Bearden.

Figure 17.11. Kelly Fearing. *Recapitulation on a Fish Motif 4: Opalescent Green, Blue, Blue Green, and Blue-Purple.* 1977. Collage with prismacolor pencil drawing, 17¼″x11½″. Private collection.

Photogravure, 20.1 cm. x 15.7 cm. National Portrait Gallery, Smithsonian Institution. Artist: Langdon Coburn, 1907.

BORN: 1856
DIED: 1925
BIRTHPLACE:
Florence, Italy

Figure 17.12. John Singer Sargent. *The Daughters of Edward Darley Boit.* Oil on canvas, 87" x 87". Collection, Museum of Fine Arts, Boston. Gift of Mary Louisa Boit, Florence D. Boit, Jane H. Boit and Julia O. Boit, in memory of their father.

A Society Artist

Although many artists, like The Eight, were rebelling against the Academy tradition, some were not. John Singer Sargent managed to stay within the tradition of the Academy and still create wonderful, lively art.

Sargent's American parents were living in Florence, Italy, at the time of his birth. As a young man, Sargent showed an early ability in drawing and was sent to study art in Paris. The European Academies of art were even more strict and traditional than the American ones. This didn't bother Sargent. He wanted to learn as much about art as possible.

After moving to England, his ability as a portrait painter soon caught the eye of rich, beautiful people. Suddenly, everyone had to have their portrait painted by the charming Mr. Sargent.

Finally, in 1876 he paid his first visit to America. The wealthy people of this country wanted to be painted by the famous John Singer Sargent, just as had the English. What was so special about his portraits?

For one thing, they were large! He usually painted his subjects far larger than life. He also made them look so rich and beautiful. The dresses, jewels, expensive carpets and furniture were all beautifully painted. What sets Sargent apart was his remarkable ability with paint. Though his paintings appear very realistic and detailed, they aren't. If you look closely you can see great slabs of color applied with bold, swift strokes. Yet, Sargent was so sure of his ability to handle a brush loaded with paint, he could almost throw it on the canvas. Each brush stroke was perfect.

In addition, to his large-scale society portraits, Sargent was a master in drawing and in watercolor. *Muddy Alligators* shows that he handled watercolor as skillfully as oil paint. While most artists never achieve fame and wealth during their lifetime (think of poor Van Gogh), Sargent managed to do both. His life was filled with popularity, achievement, and success.

Did you learn

- The definitions of these words and phrases: pigment; paint medium; opaque; transparent; Impressionism; printing plate; edition; monoprint; stencil; brayer; collage?
- The two parts needed to make paint?
- The names of two kinds of opaque paint?
- Where the Impressionists wanted to paint?
- Four methods of printing?

Understanding and Evaluation

- Make a list of reasons you would or would not call Degas an Impressionist. Defend your opinion in a class discussion.
- Compare Sargent's style of portrait painting (Figure 17.12) with that of Brisco's (Figure 12.10). What are the differences? Similarities?

Seeing and Creating

- Under the direction of your teacher, make several monoprints. Use landscape as the subject matter.
- Make an Impressionist-style painting in an opaque painting medium. Use a landscape as subject matter.
- Make a watercolor study of some plants. Dampen your paper first. Use the bleeding of the watercolor to suggest the plant forms.

Student work.

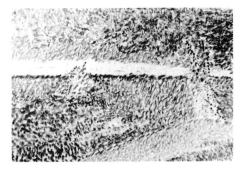

Student work.

Student work.

Chapter 18

WORKING IN THREE DIMENSIONS— SCULPTURE AND CERAMICS

WORDWATCH
sculpture-in-the-round
relief
carving
modeling
armature
terra cotta
ceramic
greenware
bisqueware
plastic state
leather hard
slip casting
throwing wheel
glazing

SCULPTURE

Sculpture is a special art form. It uses three dimensions, where painting and drawing use only two. You can walk around sculpture. When permitted, you can touch all its surfaces, from back to front. Sculpture is as real as you are. And just like you, it uses the space around it.

When you lift an arm, you push that part of your body out into the surrounding space. Parts of sculptures do the same thing. You have looked at and read about a number of sculptures in this book already. Can you recall any of them? Look at Figures 1.10, 5.11, and 5.12. They all use surrounding space as part of their compositions.

Most of the sculptures you will see are of two main kinds. There are sculptures you can walk all the way around and see from every side. These are **sculptures-in-the-round**. There are also sculptures called **reliefs**. These are similar to a very thick collage. The back of the relief sculpture is flat like a painting, images are only shown on the front. When the sculptor makes these shapes stand far out in front, they are said to be in high relief. If they stand out just a little, they are called low relief. Figure 1.9, the back of the gold throne of Pharoah Tutankhamon, shows a sculpture of the king and queen in low relief.

There are many materials or media that can be used to make sculpture. Stone, clay, metal, plaster, paper, cardboard, wire, wood, and paper maché are just a few that sculptors use to express ideas in three-dimensions. Some modern sculptors have even started using the earth itself as part of their work. One very famous modern sculpture that does this is shown in Figure 18.1. It is *The Vietnam Veterans Memorial* in Washington, D.C.

Huge stone slabs, constructed of black granite, polished to a mirror surface, are placed in a kind of open trench. The backs of the granite slabs are placed against one wall of the trench. In other words, the earth has been used to surround part of the sculpture. It has become part of the work of art.

This simple, impressive work has become one of the most visited and honored monuments in a city of monuments. Can you name any other important sculptures in Washington, D.C.?

The sculptor of this work is a Chinese-American woman named Maya Ying Lin [MY•yah yeeng len]. She was only twenty-one years old! Wanting to call attention to the

Figure 18.1. Maya Ying Lin. *Vietnam Veterans Memorial.* Washington, D.C. Photo courtesy: National Park Service.

individual soldiers who gave their lives in the Vietnam War, Maya Ying Lin carved the names of each soldier killed on the surface of her work. This is very different from the way most war memorials have been made in the past. They usually showed some figures of soldiers representing those who died. *The Vietnam Veterans Memorial* lists every name of those who died.

The material from which this monument is made— black granite—will last forever. Granite is one of the hardest rocks known. Many government buildings and monuments are made of granite. We know it lasts a long time, because the ancient Egyptians used granite for many of their sculptures and buildings. Some of these are as unmarked by the passage of time, as if they had been made yesterday.

Because most stone lasts a long time, it has always been a favorite material for sculptors. But stone, whether granite or marble, must be **carved**. The images the sculptor wants to show are revealed in the block of stone by slowly chipping away the pieces that are not needed. ⓒ This takes time, strength, and special tools. [**CAUTION:** Carving of any kind must be done with extreme care. Goggles must always be worn to protect the eyes.]

Fortunately, there are materials that are much safer and easier to work. Try wire, for example.

WIRE

You have already become familiar with the sculpture of Alexander Calder (Figure 5.12). Another one by Calder, Figure 18.2, titled *Sow*, is made by bending wire. When details are needed, the wire is bent to make them, without being cut apart or added to. This humorous sculpture is very similar to a type of drawing. Can you remember what it is called?

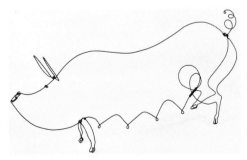

Figure 18.2. Alexander Calder. *Sow.* 1928. Wire construction, 7½″x17″x3″. Collection, The Museum of Modern Art, New York. Gift of the Artist.

Figure 18.3. Eduardo Chillida. *Abesti Gogora I.* 1960-61. Oak, 5'h.x11'l.x5'4½"w. The Museum of Fine Arts, Houston. Museum purchase.

Figure 18.4. Red Grooms. *Matisse in a Garden.* 1973. Strathmore 100% rag watercolor paper, plexi bonnet, 43½"H x 36¼"D. Virginia Museum of Fine Arts, Richmond. Gift of Sydney and Francis Lewis.

MOBILES

Calder was also famous for his sculpture that moved. Do you remember what moving sculpture is called? Look again at Figure 5.12. Wire has been used in this work to outline the shapes and to support the moving pieces of the sculpture. However, in order for mobiles to move, they must be carefully balanced.

WOOD AND FOUND MATERIALS

Wood is a popular material for sculpture. It is fairly inexpensive and not too difficult to sculpt. Wood sculpture can be created through **carving** like stone, or **assembling**. When you **assemble** something, you put it together. In assembled wood sculpture, the pieces of wood can be attached by gluing or nailing. You can make simple wood sculptures in this way.

Figure 18.3 is a huge, assembled wood sculpture by Edward Chilida [chill•EE•dah]. Giant pieces of rough wood are arranged together to create a sculpture that uses the surrounding space as part of its composition. Can you find those areas? Do you think these pieces were found as they are, or did the artist shape them by carving?

Since almost any material can be used for sculpture, some artists have created works out of **found objects**. Car bumpers, soda straws, bottle caps, toothpaste boxes, and plastic bags can all be used for found-object sculpture. Some cannot be glued together, so creative ways must be found to connect them. What other materials can you think of that would make interesting sculptures? Perhaps as we recycle more materials to prevent pollution of our planet, we can create new media for works of art!

PAPER

Artist Red Grooms also enjoys creating art with humor. Take, for example, his paper sculpture of artist Matisse. Do you remember his work? If not, look again at Figure 4.5.

This sculpture is called *Matisse in a Garden.* (Figure 18.4). The aging artist is shown sitting in the garden he loved so much. This sculpture is made entirely of paper! Did you ever think of paper as a sculpture medium? It can be. Surprisingly, sculpting with paper is not as easy as you might think. Planning carefully beforehand is very important. Once paper is glued in place, it is difficult to change.

192

PAPER MACHÉ

Can you think of another kind of sculpture that uses paper? You might have made sculpture from this material before. If you thought paper maché [ma•SHAY], you are right. In this case, paper strips are dipped in a glue-like mixture and applied to an **armature**, a simple structure or base on which sculpting materials can be placed. Armatures for paper maché can be made of wadded paper, wire, or balloons. Figure 18.5 shows a variety of armatures that can be used for paper maché.

CLAY

Clay is one of the most ancient and universal sculpture mediums. Figures and containers (ceramics) made of clay are part of the cultural and historical heritage of almost every civilization. Clay, unlike stone or wood, is worked by **modeling**. [CAUTION: Some people are allergic to clay dust. These individuals may need to wear masks while working with clay.]

The sculptor **models** the wet clay by adding pieces on—*addition*, or by pinching chunks off—*subtraction*. Do you recall the portrait of Albert Einstein by Jacob Epstein (Figure 12.11)? Before casting the work in bronze, a model was first sculpted in clay. This served as the mold for the liquid metal. In this sculpture, both types of modeling were used. Can you tell where the sculptor used addition? Subtraction?

Figure 18.6 shows a wonderful animal sculpture by Charles Umlauf [UMM•lof]. *Wild Boar* is worked in a kind of clay called **terra cotta** [pronounced just as it reads!]. This clay is reddish brown in color. You may have already had a chance to use this clay, since it is commonly used in school art classes.

Umlauf's *Wild Boar* shows what a perfect sculpting material clay can be for animals. The sculptor is able to show us in this work not only the form of the animal's body, but also many of the details. Clay is excellent for modeling and holding textures like fur, hair, and feathers. If you look closely at the back, you can see where the sculptor used a tool like a fork or comb to create the hair of the boar.

A wild boar is an excellent choice of an animal to sculpt from clay. Boars or wild pigs are short and compact. They have thick necks and chunky legs. Clay, although flexible, is not very strong when wet. It will not support very much weight. What animals might not be good subjects for clay? Why?

It is likely that Umlauf used an armature to support the clay when wet. This armature, like those for paper

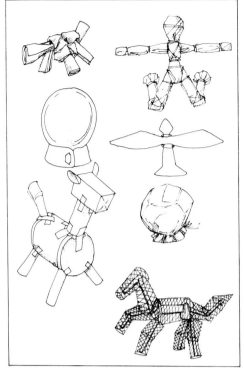

Figure 18.5. There are a number of ways to provide support for wet layers of paper maché.

Figure 18.6. Charles Umlauf. *Wild Boar.* 1979. Clay model for bronze casting, 18″x30″. Collection of the artist.

193

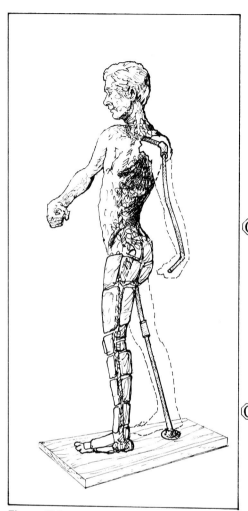

Figure 18.7.

maché, allows damp sculpting materials to be applied. Clay armatures are frequently made of wood and wire. If you look closely under the wild boar, you can see something that looks like a fifth leg. This is the stand of the armature. It holds the weight of the sculpture, Figure 18.7 shows how armatures are used in clay sculpture.

PLASTER

Do you remember *Dual Hamburgers* by Claes Oldenburg (Figure 10.10)? They were made of plaster. Plaster, ©sometimes known as Plaster of Paris, is inexpensive and can be bought in many hardware stores. It is mixed with water to form a liquid, which is then poured into a mold. When the plaster hardens, it can be carved, painted, or decorated in any number of ways. [CAUTION: Some people are allergic to plaster dust. They should avoid the material or use a mask.]

Plaster, although very messy, is an interesting material to use for sculpture. Poured into simple half-pint milk cartons and allowed to harden, it can be carved like ©stone. [CAUTION: Any carving tools should be used with extreme caution and only under the direction of a teacher. Masks and protective goggles are essential. Liquid plaster should never be poured down a sink.]

Skill-Builders and Helpful Hints:

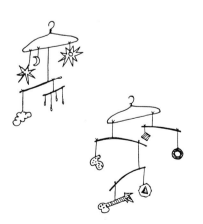

- Many kinds of wire can be used for sculpture. Even clothes hangers can be bent and formed. The test of a good wire for sculpting is whether it is thin enough to bend, but strong enough to support its own weight. With the wire you are testing, make a circle about the size of your head. Hold it at the base where the two pieces meet. If the circle stays upright, the wire is probably strong enough. A base for wire sculpture can be made from pieces of scrap wood.

- If you want to construct a wire mobile, try using an arrangement similar to the one at the left.

- Wood scraps and other cast-off materials make inexpensive media for sculpture. Some will need to be connected with methods other than nailing and gluing. String, yarn, and thin wire might be useful.

- Many kinds of paper work well for paper sculpture, but construction paper seems to have just the right thickness. Although not as flexible as clay for creating texture, paper can be used in more ways than only by cutting and folding.
- Glue is not the only way to attach pieces of paper. Scissor cuts can be made in two pieces of paper. Each cut is then slipped into the other cut.
- Ⓒ [**CAUTION:** Any sharp tools like scissors and compasses should be used with care.]
- Newspaper strips for paper maché should not be wider than one-half inch. If they are any wider, they will make bumps along rounded forms. They should never be cut with scissors. This makes a sharp edge that will show under paint. Always tear the strips. With some testing, you can find the grain of the newspaper. This is the direction that the paper will tear in neat strips!
- When working with clay, try not to get it too wet. As it dries while you are sculpting, dampen your hands to keep it moist.
- Thick clay forms (over three inches) should be hollowed out, if possible. Be sure to check with your teacher about the best way to do this. Failure to hollow them may cause pieces to break when they are fired in a kiln (See section on ceramics).
- Ⓒ [**CAUTION:** Liquid plaster should never be poured down a sink. If your hands become covered with liquid plaster, do not wash them in the sink. First wipe them with paper towels.]

CERAMICS

Ceramics, or the making of clay containers, possibly has a longer history than sculpture. Small, simple pots and drinking vessels have been found at archeological sites throughout the world. In fact, the existence of pottery in so many ancient cultures has helped archeologists date these civilizations. It seems that each age wanted its own style of pottery. As years passed, styles changed. Archeologists and art historians can now match styles with certain periods. Figure 18.8 shows the elegance with which the ancient Greeks fashioned pottery or ceramics. This pot, called an **amphora** [am•FOR•ah], may have been used to hold water or wine.

Think for a minute about the plate you ate from this morning? Do you remember its shape, color, or decoration? Was it **ceramic**?

Figure 18.8. Greek: Europe. Southern Greece. Black-figured panel amphora. Last quarter 6th century B.C. Ceramic, Dallas Museum of Art, Munger Fund.

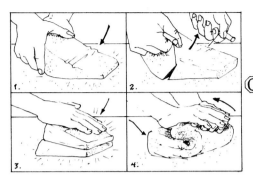

Figure 18.9.

Ceramic containers, whether plates, bowls, or other shapes, share some common characteristics. They are usually made from a type of clay, such as the terra cotta you have just read about. In order to be usable as containers, they are fired in a **kiln**. A **kiln** is a type of oven made just for firing clay. It is not like the oven in your kitchen. This one reaches temperatures of over 2000 degrees Farenheit! [**CAUTION:** A ceramic kiln is very dangerous. Never touch or open a working or hot kiln.]

Unfired clay is called **greenware**. The first firing in the kiln makes the clay very hard, but not waterproof. Ceramic pieces that have been fired once are called **bisqueware** [BISK • ware].

Types of Ceramic Construction

There are many ways to make a clay container by hand. Some you may already know. The basic methods for hand-building with clay are **pinch, coil,** and **slab.** Each uses clay in a different way to construct the form. These three methods need few tools and no special equipment for building. Therefore, they are known as *hand-building* methods.

Before using clay to build anything, there are a few things you should know. Clay is known as a **plastic** medium because you can bend it and push it around. It stays in the **plastic state** only when moist or damp. As soon as it dries, it hardens.

Clay, even the packaged kind you use at school, contains air bubbles. These bubbles, almost too small to see, must be worked out of the clay before making anything! If not, they may cause your beautiful container to explode in the kiln! This would be a disaster, and it might also wreck the work of others. To avoid this, the clay is **wedged** before use.

Wedging is the way air bubbles are removed. Figure 18.9 shows one way to wedge clay. The clay is pressed and worked until all air bubbles are removed. Your teacher will give you instructions on various ways to wedge clay. If you have ever watched anyone make bread, you have seen them knead dough. This is similar to wedging.

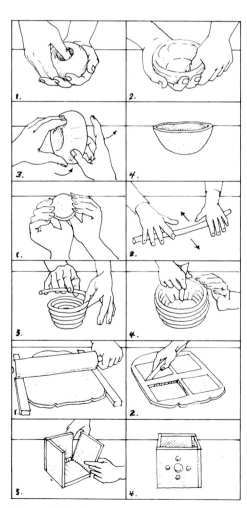

Figure 18.10. Ceramic containers can be made by three simple methods: pinch, coil, and slab.

Pinch Pots

One of the easiest ways to make a clay container is by the **pinch method**. A ball of damp clay, the size to fit comfortably in your two hands, is opened by pushing your thumb in the middle. Don't push too far; your pot needs a bottom! The ball is then turned slowly with the thumb inside, with the other fingers pinching or pressing the clay. Figure 18.10 shows the pinching method.

Coil Pots

Coil pots can be made much larger than pinch pots. "Snakes," or ropes of clay, about one-half-inch thick are rolled beneath the hands and a hard surface. On a disk of clay, the coils are built one on top of the other, until the desired height is reached. Figure 18.10 shows coil building. The coils must be pressed together, at least on one surface, to stay attached after drying. Otherwise you may have a large number of clay bracelets!

Slab Pots

Just as the name suggests, **slab** pots are made from slabs or flattened sections of clay. These sections can be rolled smooth with a rolling pin, bottle, or heavy cardboard tube. Figure 18.10 shows the construction of slab pots. After the slabs are rolled and cut to the desired size, they must be allowed to dry a little. Otherwise when set on their edges, they will bend over. The desired stage of dryness is called the **leather-hard** stage. The name is a good one, since the clay must be firm to the touch, but still flexible. Just as with coil pots, the edges of the slabs must be pressed together.

Between the slabs, it is sometimes necessary to use a kind of clay glue called **slip**. **Slip** is made by mixing a large amount of water with a little dried clay. You want the slip to look and feel like mud gravy! If it is too thin, it won't hold the slabs together (Figure 18.11). Slip can also be used, when necessary, to hold coils together.

Think again about that plate you ate from this morning. Do you think one of the above methods was used to make it? Probably not. Most commercial ceramics, like our dishes, are made by either **slip casting** or **wheel throwing**.

Slip casting is a method in which large numbers of ceramic pieces can be made exactly the same. Each plate looks like every other plate. To get this kind of matching. plaster molds are made and slip is poured into them. They are then fired in a kiln, like other ceramics.

Wheel-thrown ceramics are made on a **throwing wheel**. If your art class has a wheel, your teacher might teach you how to **throw** pots. No, that doesn't mean "throw" them against the wall! **Throwing** refers to the method of constructing ceramics on a wheel.

Wheel throwing takes much practice and a surprising amount of strength. Ceramists who wheel throw always make it look so easy. It isn't! How can you tell if your breakfast plate was wheel thrown? One way is to hold it level with your eyes. If the edge seems uneven, it might have been thrown by a "potter" or ceramist on a wheel.

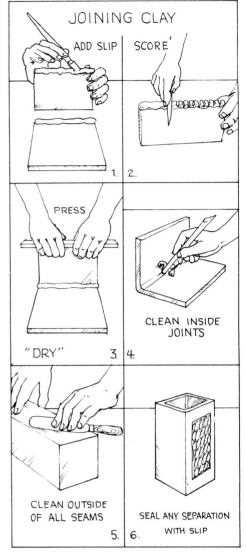

Figure 18.11.

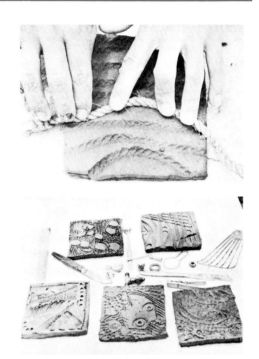

The special quality and beauty of hand-made objects, like ceramics and other crafts you will be learning about, come partly from their imperfections. Works made with the human touch are of far more value than those made by machines. You should always value your own art and that of others for the unique, human qualities it contains, even though it may not be as perfect as a store-bought version.

Figure 18.12. Texture is easy to create in damp clay. It gives interest and expression to ceramic containers.

Texturing and Decorating

Figure 18.12 shows the many different ways clay can be textured. Texture in clay serves the same purpose it did in drawing and painting. Texture adds interest and variety to artworks.

There are a wide selection of simple tools that can be used to texture clay. Forks, combs, paper clips, many kitchen tools, and wooden sticks can all be used. Most can be used in more than one way. For example, a paper clip can be pressed into damp clay or scratched into fairly dry clay.

Other ways to decorate ceramic containers include painting and **glazing**. Painting can be done with both tempera and acrylic paint. Glazing must be done with direction from your teacher and with the use of the kiln.

When ceramic pieces are **glazed**, they are covered with a special coating that makes them waterproof. Although ceramic glaze looks like a dull paint when you use it in its liquid form, it is composed of tiny grains of glass. When the glazed piece is fired in a kiln, these grains melt and form a hard, colorful coating. This also makes the work waterproof. [CAUTION: Glazing should be done only with your teacher's direction. Some glazes contain lead and must be avoided.]

Skill-Builders and Helpful Hints:

- Don't worry about smoothing clay pieces until after you have the form the way you want it. Hold it at eye level to determine if one side is lower or higher than the other.
- Place slip on both surfaces to be joined. When adding handles, spouts, or heavy decorations, it is sometimes wise to use slip and a small coil of clay to seal the seams.
- If you have more work to do on your piece at the end of a class, be sure to cover it with damp paper towels or rags. Plastic can then be placed over the rags. This should keep your work in a moist condition. Don't put very wet rags on your clay! Squeeze them out well, before applying them over the container.

Monuments of Honor

At age twenty-two, Chinese-American Maya Ying Lin is one of the youngest and most successful sculptor/ architects in America today. While still a student at Yale University, Maya, along with the rest of her class, was asked to design a memorial for the dead and missing veterans of the Vietnam War.

Competition for a design had begun in 1979, when a fund was established to raise money for a memorial to be built in Washington, D.C. There were two requirements for the monument. First, all the names of the dead or missing American soldiers had to be placed on the monument. This could have presented a problem since there were 57,939 names to be listed. Second, since the monument would be placed in view of both the Lincoln Memorial and the Washington Monument, the monument would have to look right alongside these other famous works.

Maya, along with 1,400 other artists, submitted her design, and she won! You can imagine the excitement this must have caused this talented young woman. But as with most good things, there was a negative side as well. As soon as Maya's design was accepted and shown in the press, protests began.

Many people felt her design, with its stark, black granite slabs, was too depressing. They wanted a more traditional war monument, where figures of soldiers are shown standing bravely together. But, Maya's original design was finally built (Figure 18.1).

This monument is now one of the main attractions of Washington. It attracts thousands of visitors daily. Most come to remember a loved one or to honor the brave, American people who gave their lives in Vietnam.

Recently Maya Ying Lin received another important sculpture commission. She has designed and built a memorial to the Civil Rights movement. Like the Vietnam Memorial, this one also uses black granite, etched with names. This time the names remember those who gave their lives in the struggle for equal rights. A continuous stream of water covers the names etched in granite. This symbolizes the flow of change and the power of an idea whose time has come.

Photograph of Maya Ying Lin.
Photo credit: Conde Nast

BORN: 1968
BIRTHPLACE:
ATHENS, OHIO

Figure 18.13. Maya Ying Lin. *Civil Rights Memorial.* Photo ©Maya Lin 1989.

Student work.

Student work.

Did you learn

- The definitions of these words and phrases: sculpture in the round; relief; carving; assembling; modeling; armature; terra cotta; ceramics; greenware; bisque-ware; plastic state; wedging; leather hard; throwing wheel; glazing?
- Three methods of making sculpture?
- Four sculpture materials?
- The difference between modeling and carving?
- Three stages of clay?
- Three ceramic building methods?

Understanding and Evaluating

- Compare three sculptures shown in the text. Describe, in short paragraphs, how each uses space.
- Find photographs of one or two national or state monuments. Apply the four levels of art criticism to them. Is the Washington Monument a sculpture or piece of architecture? Have reason for your opinion. Can it be both? Why or why not? Compare it to Saarinen's *Gateway Arch* (Figure 5.10).

Seeing and Creating

- Design on paper a monument honoring some national event. Arrange your design so that at least part of it uses the surrounding landscape. On the back, list the kinds of materials to be used. Consider the symbolism of your work. What does it mean?
- Make a wire sculpture of an animal. Choose an animal that has a very distinct shape.
- Under the direction of your teacher, make an animal container using two of the hand-building methods discussed. The shape of the pot should reflect the form or texture of the chosen animal.

Since prehistoric times, human beings have invented, designed, and produced objects to make life safer, easier, and more satisfying. With few exceptions, these objects were made by hand. They were not originally intended as works of art, but were made to be used for everyday activities or special ceremonial ones.

In early times, no one thought of art as one thing and crafts as another. Today, however, we think of **crafts** as art objects having a **functional**, or useful, purpose, as well as an aesthetic one. For example, a woven blanket can serve as a cover for warmth as well as an art object. The jewelry you wear, the plates you eat from, the furniture you use, when handmade are considered **crafts**. Notice "handmade" has been added to the definition. In today's world most of the objects we use are made by machines. Handmade objects, when well-designed and constructed with good craftsmanship, are special and highly valued.

FIBERS

Figure 19.2 is known as the *Bayeaux* [BAY•you] *Tapestry*. A **tapestry** is a piece of woven or decorated fabric. This particular tapestry, over 230 feet long, records a famous event in English history. The victory of William the Conqueror at the Battle of Hastings. The fabric is of finely woven linen with figures and lettering embroidered on it. It must have taken many hands and hours (years?) of work to complete such a task. The fact that such an important event was recorded on fabric shows that crafts, such as weaving and stitchery (embroidery), were considered important works of art. The function or use of this fabric was probably more as a document of history than a piece of material to use for warmth or clothing. It hung in a place of honor on the wall of a great hall.

Stitchery or embroidery is a way to decorate a piece of cloth. A piece of material is selected for the background. Colored threads or yarns are then stitched into the fabric to create designs or pictures. Many consider the fabric craft of stitchery as "painting with thread." Although you are unlikely to want to begin a stitchery as long as the *Bayeaux Tapestry*, you might want to try your hand at creating smaller versions of 'thread painting." Many clothes seen and worn today are highly decorated with stitching and pieces of colored fabric. Applying other pieces of fabric to a piece of material is called **appliqué** [AP•lah•kay]. Figure 19.3 shows an example of appliqué

Chapter 19
CRAFTS

Figure 19.1. Craft items tend to be functional, as well as beautiful.

201

created by the Indians of Panama. It is called a **mola**. Layers of fabric are stacked one on top of the other. Shapes are cut from each layer so that the material underneath can show through. The edges of each shape are then hemmed neatly. The subject matter of molas can include animals, plants, people, or even words.

If you want to try your hand at creative stitchery or appliqué, Figure 19.4 shows you some basic embroidery stitches. Beyond that all you need is some cloth, a needle, and some thread or yarn. Of course, you also need a creative idea. Fabric designs, such as stitchery and appliqué, give you an opportunity to wear your art!

WEAVING

The craft of weaving is thousands of years old. Fine woven fabrics have been found in the tombs of ancient Egyptian kings and Chinese emperors.

At some point in history, human beings decided that they needed cloth for clothing. Up until that point, the skins and furs of animals had been enough to meet their needs. Making cloth in quantities large enough to cover an average-sized individual meant inventing a tool or machine that could hold some threads straight, while others were being worked or woven through them. This invention became known as the **loom**.

Looms are simply wooden structures designed to hold some threads straight. These threads are known as **warp** threads. The person working the loom or the **weaver**, passes other threads through the warp threads. These passing threads are called the **weft**. When a loom is first set up for weaving, it is being **warped**.

Of course, not all looms have to be made of wood. You might have made simple weavings using a cardboard loom, or even one made of straws. In fact, some very interesting weavings can be created on looms fashioned from a tree branch. The warp threads are wrapped around two limbs of the branch, and the weft threads are woven between.

Figure 19.5 shows some basic weaving techniques. As the weft threads are woven through, they can be pushed down on the row beneath by something called a **beater**. This is a comb-like tool whose teeth can pass between the warp threads and push the weft down. A comb or plastic fork works well as a substitute. Another handy weaving tool is a **shuttle**. This holds the yarn as it is passed between the warp threads. A piece of cardboard with notches cut in the ends will hold enough yarn to weave several inches.

Although most people think of yarns or threads as weft materials, many other items can be used. Strips of

Figure 19.3. The indians of Panama are noted for their molas or appliquéd cloths. Each layer of material is cut and hemmed to reveal the next layer.

paper, cloth, and plastic can also be woven. Shells, beads, and even small stones can be added for variety. And what about long pieces of natural grass, hay, or sticks? Do you own any piece of clothing that has been hand-woven? From the examples of weaving you have seen, how does it differ from machine-made fabrics? Why is weaving considered a craft?

MACRAMÉ AND KNOTTING

Another very ancient craft is that of knot tying or **macramé** [MA•cra•may]. It is said that the craft was invented by sailors who had to fill long, boring hours on watch with some activity. Knowing how to tie a variety of knots for use on board ship, and having plenty of rope to use, these bored sailors began to knot with design and creativity. Again, as with so many ancient crafts, the needed materials are very simple and inexpensive. For macramé, all you need is thin rope or cord. If you are going to create an elaborate project, you may want to anchor your first cords on a piece of cardboard or cork with straight pins. (Figure 19.6). Knotting can be used to finish and enhance weavings and other stitchery projects.

BATIK

Batik [bat•TEEK] is a very old process of decorating fabric. The origins of the process are lost, but is still widely used in Indonesia and Java. Many contemporary artists use the process of batik to create beautiful fabric for use in clothing or to admire as a wall hanging.

The process of batik isn't difficult, but it does involve several steps and some planning. The main thing to keep in mind is that in areas of the design where a light color is wanted, this color must be dyed first. It can then be covered with melted wax, protecting it from the other dye colors.

The first step in batiking, as with any creative project, is to come up with a good idea. Though batik is, in many ways, similar to drawing, it seems to work best when the basic design is simple. That is, when small details are left out. Once a design has been developed, it is transferred to a piece of light-colored cloth. Pure cotton fabric works best, since it will accept most dyes smoothly. The design can be transferred with a light-colored chalk.

In step two, areas of the design selected for the first dyeing are left open to receive the first dye color (light). Other areas, where a different color is needed, are covered and protected with heated wax. [**CAUTION:** The batik process should only be done under teacher supervision. Heated wax can cause severe burns.]

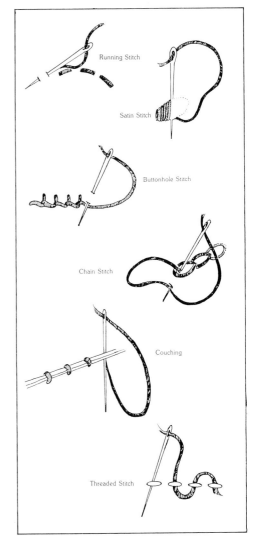

Figure 19.4. Sample stitches of basic embroidery stitches.

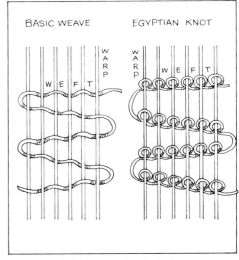

Figure 19.5. Basic weaving techniques.

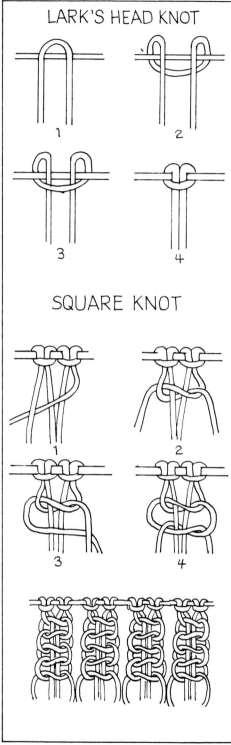

LARK'S HEAD KNOT

1

2

3

4

SQUARE KNOT

1

2

3

4

Figure 19.6. Even simple rope and yarn can be made into a creative sculpture through the knotting technique of macramé.

The wax acts as a resist to the dye, preventing it from penetrating. At any stage, the cooled wax can be wrinkled and cracked to allow following dye colors to penetrate the cracks. This produces the characteristic look of batik as seen in Figure 19.7. When all dyeing is complete, the wax is removed by ironing.

Figure 19.7 shows the work of fabric-design artist Alvin Nickel. Nickel has traveled to many different parts of the world studying the designs and techniques of fabric decoration. The process of batik is a special favorite of his. Although organic or free-form shapes are frequently used in traditional batik, Nickel chooses complex geometric patterns. Many of these patterns have their origin in the art of Africa and Indonesia.

For each color and value you see in this beautiful design, a separate dye had to be mixed and used. These can sometimes reach into the hundreds! Painting with hot wax can be tricky. If you use a brush, the wax cools almost before you can apply it to the cloth. This makes a wide, thick line, or a shape with rough edges. The sharp, controlled lines and edges seen in Nickel's work can only be achieved with a **tjanting** tool [JANT•ing]; (don't pronounce the "t"). Shaped like a small bowl at the end of a paint-brush handle, the hot wax is held in the bowl and allowed to leak out through a narrow spout. This spout, similar to a pen point, controls the flow and direction of the wax. Batik is an interesting and very beautiful craft to learn, but it does take patience and practice to master it.

SOFT SCULPTURE

Soft sculpture seems almost a contradiction in terms. Most sculpture is made of hard materials like stone, bronze, or wood. But, you have already encountered an example of soft sculpture. Do you remember where? Look back at Figure 10.11. This work by Claes Oldenburg is a good example of the fun and humor that has made soft sculpture a popular art form. The reason for including soft sculpture here, rather than in the section on sculpture, is that most soft-sculpture artists work with fabric and other clothlike materials. It can be thought of as sculpture, craft, and fabric design all in one! Think about objects to create as soft sculpture. You will come up with many creative ideas. A subject that would ordinarily be sculpted in clay or paper maché becomes extraordinary when stitched together with fabric and thread!

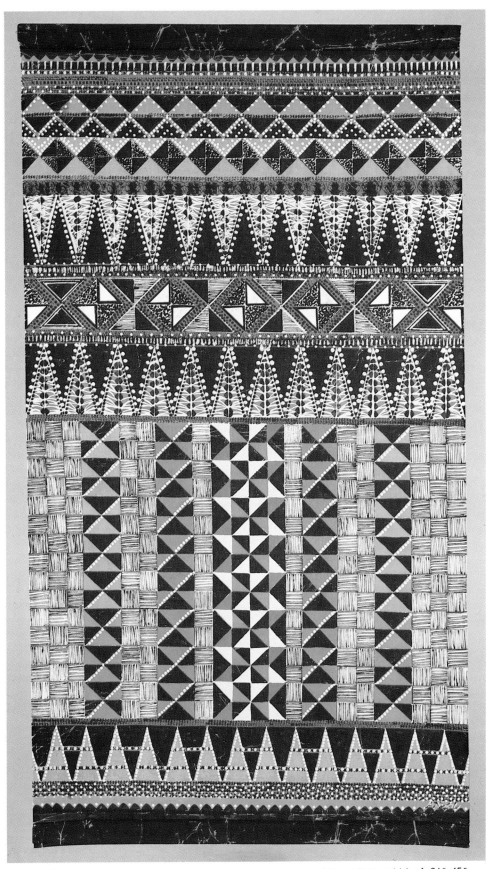

Figure 19.7. Al Nickel. *Batik Prada Tumpal II.* Batik on cotton with applied gold leaf, 81″x45″. Collection of the artist.

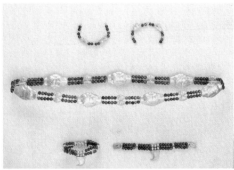

Figure 19.8. Examples of Jewelry. Egyptian Costume and Toilet Jewelry XII Dynasty. c. 1897-1797 B.C. Leopard-head girdle, claw anklets and lion bracelets. The Metropolitan Museum of Art, Rogers Fund and Henry Walters Gift, 1916. All rights reserved. (16.1.6, .7, .14-15).

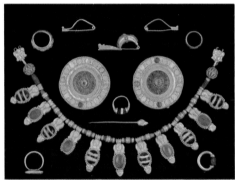

Etruscan. Metalwork Gold. VI and V Century. B.C. Jewelry group, 14 13/16"l. The Metropolitan Museum of Art, Harris Brisbane Dick Fund, 1940.

left. German. Metalwork Gold. XVI Century. 4½"h. The Metropolitan Museum of Art, Bequest of Michael Friedsam, 1931. right. Italian. Metalwork Gold. 1536. 4¼" h. The Metropolitan Museum of Art. Gift of J. Pierpont Morgan, 1917.

Skill-Builders and Helpful Hints:

- When designing with stitchery, try to select your threads and yarns for their textures, as well as for their colors. A wide variety of textures is as effective in fabric as it is in drawing, painting, or sculpture.
- Yarn comes in packages called **skeins** [skain]. Skeins vary in the amount of yarn they contain, so read labels carefully.
- Cut plastic bread bags and other colorful plastic bags into 1″ or ½″ strips. Use these for weaving.
- When changing yarn in the middle of a weaving, try not to tie a knot. Backweave the new yarn beneath the weaving for an inch or two. This will make a neater connection.
- Collect a variety of fabrics for use in appliqué. Try combining appliqué and stitchery in one work. Use stitches like crosshatch lines in a drawing.
- Most fabrics will ravel when cut. To prevent this, hem or tape the raw edges. Sometimes raveling can be used as part of your fabric design. Some fabrics can be raveled to make decorative fringe.
- Add beads, shells, and other small items to macramé or weavings.
- Soft sculpture can be stuffed with worn pantyhose or the lint from a clothes dryer! It is clean and very soft.
- Batiks can be mounted on posterboard or wood for display.

JEWELRY

Figure 19.8 shows examples of jewelry from many time periods. Human beings have always enjoyed creating beautiful objects in precious metals and stones to wear for pleasure and status. Some jewelry was of such value and symbolic importance that it was passed down as a symbol of divine kingship. Think of the one item that reminds you of a king or queen. You will probably think of a crown.

Although using gold, silver and precious stones may be beyond your reach, there are a number of ways to create simple, attractive jewelry. First, what materials can be used for jewelry? Well, just about anything. Pieces of cardboard, plastic, buttons, beads, cloth, shells, rocks, and wire are all used in jewelry making. A good source for jewelry materials is pieces of old junk jewelry. These old pieces can be reassembled into new works.

Many of the craft processes mentioned in this and other chapters can be used in jewelry making. You may have already learned how to make clay pendants and beads (Figure 19.9). Paper and paper maché are good media to use also. They are very cheap and lightweight. The weight of a piece of wearable art, like jewelry, is important. The most beautiful jewelry cannot serve its purpose—to be worn—if it is so heavy the wearer can't move!

What other considerations are important when you design jewelry? A necklace is a form of jewelry. How many others can you name? Look up the word **tiara** [tee•AH•rah]. If you were going to make a tiara, what materials might be best?

One of the main concerns in jewelry construction is how to join the parts you have selected and fashioned. If you are using paper, cardboard, or other lightweight materials, you can usually rely on white glue. Others, like plastic, wood, or thin metal, may need to be attached by other methods. For example, tiny holes can be punched or drilled into plastic, wood, or metal so that thin wire or thread can be used to attach one piece to another. Figure 19.10 shows several ways to connect jewelry parts.

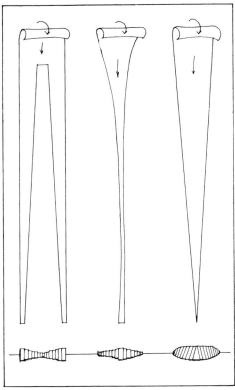

Figure 19.9. Beads of various types are some of the easiest jewelry items to make. They can be strung on thread, string, wire or leather shoe laces.

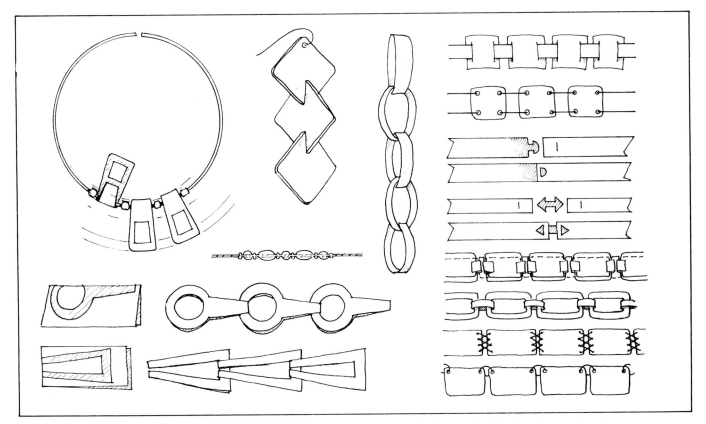

Figure 19.10. In addition to white glue, thin wire, small nails, and screws can also be used to join jewelry parts together.

BORN: 1926
BIRTHPLACE:
Oshkosh, Wisconsin

To Delight the Eye

While designing on fabric requires using the same art elements and design principles as in any other work of art, there are also special concerns. For one thing, fabric is often used for clothing. If paint is applied directly to the surface for decoration, it might peel off or stiffen the material. For this reason, fabric is usually decorated with colored dye. The people of Indonesia, through many centuries, have perfected the art and craft of batik. Artist Alvin Nickel has spent a good portion of his life studying and mastering this beautiful, complex process.

After graduating from the Art Institute of Chicago, Alvin Nickel worked at a number of jobs that involved both designing and teaching. He has been a professor of art and art education at The University of Texas at Austin since 1960.

Although batik design was well-known in this country, Nickel realized that if he were to master the authentic process he needed to go where batik originated—to Indonesia.

If you look on a map and locate Indonesia, you will see that it is really a large group of islands. The capitol of Indonesia is Djakarta [jah•CAR•tah]; (do not pronounce the "D"), which is located on the island of Java.

Nickel traveled throughout Indonesia studying the process of batik with native artists. He was able to collect many fine examples of batik, as well. Some of his adventures in remote native villages were exciting. No matter how remote or primitive, Nickel found the people of Indonesia to be warm, friendly, and generous. Knowing his interest in everything that has to do with batik, friends gave Nickel handmade tools. One of these tjanting tools was used to decorate the batik pictured in Figure 19.7.

Figure 19.11 shows another Nickel batik that uses objects, such as colorful umbrellas and fans found in the Indonesian culture.

Figure 19.11. Al Nickel. *Bali Moon: Auspicious Accoutrements.* Dye discharge, metallic pigments with applied gold leaf on cotton, 84″x55″. Collection of the artist.

Did you learn

- The definitions of these words and phrases: functional; crafts; appliqué; stitchery; loom; beater; shuttle; warp; weft; macramé; batik; tjanting tool; soft sculpture?
- The names of five crafts?
- Another name for stitchery?
- The colors that must be dyed first in batik?
- A special tool used in batik?

Understanding and Evaluating

- Apply the four levels of art criticism to a craft work shown in this chapter. Write out your observations and opinion.
- You have been asked to judge a craft show. Make a list of things you will look for in selecting the best work from these areas: batik, weaving, and stitchery.
- Find out more about the Bayeaux Tapestry. Did you know Halley's comet's return is recorded in this tapestry?

Student work.

Seeing and Creating

- With a small viewfinder, isolate a small portion of a color photograph from a magazine. Draw its basic outline onto a piece of cotton or burlap. Translate the photograph in stitchery or appliqué.
  On a large sheet of paper, draw the outline of a jacket on both sides of the paper—one side for the front; one side for the back. Draw in crayon or marker a design for both sides. Use a theme, such as the four seasons, the future, or the animal kingdom.
- Warp weaving threads onto an unusual loom such as a tree branch or bicycle wheel. Add beads and other items for texture and variety.

Figure 20.1. Gibbs Milliken. *Blue Wall with Trumpet Vine.* As rich in color and value as a painting, this beautiful photograph clearly illustrates the artistry of a talented photographer.

Although most artists continue to use traditional art materials and techniques to express their ideas, modern technology offers many unique and exciting opportunities for creating new art forms. Photography, film and video production, computer graphics, and animation offer new challenges for artists today.

PHOTOGRAPHY

In our daily lives, we are bombarded with huge numbers of photographic images. It is difficult to imagine a world without the photograph to inform and entertain us. Photographs are valuable sources of ideas and information about the world. In many cases, they provide our only reference for how something looks. For example, few people travel to the moon. Yet, photographs of the moon's surface can be used to inspire and direct us in representing, through art, how such a place might look.

Like paint, clay, and stone, photography offers artists another creative tool through which to communicate their unique views of the world.

Photography, as a technical process, is only about 150 years old. In the early years, photographs were used primarily to record, that is to make a visual record of an event. It was only later that the creative and expressive possibilities of photography were realized.

Photography becomes an art form when an ordinary subject, viewed through the eye of the photographer, is transformed into something new. Like any artist, the photographer must *select* and *compose* in order to change a common subject into something special. The camera isolates and frames, helping the viewer to select and compose. A fine photographer is as aware of art elements and design principles as any other artist.

The quality of a photograph also depends on the reproduction or **printing** of the **negative**. The **negative** is the image on the film as it comes from the camera. **Printing** is the series of steps that must be followed to **develop** or reveal the image. The photographer uses **cropping**—enlarging a central image or reducing the surrounding space—to focus attention. **Enlarging** is used to expand the whole photographic image. **Exposing** is used by the photographer to control the amount of light entering the camera lens. All these methods are used to create photographic art.

Figure 20.1 is an example of how photography becomes more than "picture-taking" in the hands of a skilled

Chapter 20
PHOTOGRAPHY, FILM, AND COMPUTER ART

WORDWATCH
printing
negative
develop
cropping
exposing
enlarging
animation
zeotrope
software
hardware
holograms

photographer/artist. Photographer Gibbs Milliken has used color and shape to compose a work that adds mood, feeling, and mystery to ordinary objects. This photograph has the rich range of values and textures that might be found in a painting. Notice how the colors of the flowers are complimented by the multicolored wall. What a fortunate combination for the observant photographer to capture. Have you ever taken a photograph that you thought was more than just a picture of something? A photograph that was art?

Figure 20.2 shows the work of another artist/photographer, Erwin E. Smith.

Figure 20.2. *Erwin E. Smith.* LS Ranch, Texas, 1908. The Erwin E. Smith Collection of the Library of Congress on deposit at the Amon Carter Museum.

SUNPRINTS

You really don't need a camera to make a photographic print. You can use **blueprint** photographic paper sold at most photographic supply stores. Various objects are placed on the blue side of the paper. It is then covered with cardboard and carried into a sunny place. The paper and arranged objects are exposed to the sun for one minute and then recovered. Under the supervision of your teacher, you can develop your prints by submerging them in a hydrogen peroxide bath. Hydrogen peroxide is sold at most pharmacies. It is ordinarily used to clean wounds or sterilize a potentially infected area. Imagine, it develops photographs also!

Sunprints are like any other visual composition that you design. You need to be aware of the art elements and design principles to create a successful composition. (Figure 20.3).

MAKING A PINHOLE CAMERA

If you think photography is an expensive art form, you are right. Some photographers invest thousands of dollars in cameras and equipment. Of course, you may already own a camera, which means that you can compose and create your own art images. If you don't have a

Figure 20.3. Sunprint.

camera, there is a very inexpensive way to make one. It is called a pinhole camera (Figure 20.4).

The materials for this camera are simple and inexpensive. The main cost is for the **orthochromatic** film. This film can be purchased at photo-supply stores. You want it to be in black and white. You will also need:

- cylindrical cereal box with lid (oatmeal type)
- aluminum foil
- small piece of poster board
- masking tape
- four inches of black-and-white **orthochromatic** film
- scissors
- black tempera paint and a brush

1. Paint the inside of the cereal box with black tempera paint. Allow to dry completely.
2. Cut a one-inch-square opening in the center of the attached box end.
3. Tape a piece of foil over the opening and punch a tiny hole in the center of the foil.
4. Cut a flap from a small piece of poster board to cover the opening completely. This will become the camera shutter. Attach the flap with a masking-tape hinge, so that it can be opened and closed quickly. You may need to secure the flap closed until you are ready to use it.
5. In the center of the opposite end (the end with the removable top), tape four inches of film.

© [CAUTION: The above procedure must be executed in a dark room or in an area lit only by a red incandescent lamp.]

To take a photograph with your camera, simply lift the flap for a second or two and you have a picture! You then need to have the film developed.

SLIDES

Slides are another form of photographic imagery. You can make and project some fascinating images by sandwiching pieces of feathers, string, cut transparent acetate, or tissue paper between sheets of clear contact paper (Figure 20.5). Your contact sheets should be cut to fit within the boundary of a **slide binder**. These can be found anywhere cameras and slide projectors are sold. When projected, your personal slides can suggest ideas for drawings, paintings, or other expressive forms. They can also serve as mini-drawings and paintings on their own. Just remember, the more transparent the materials, the better.

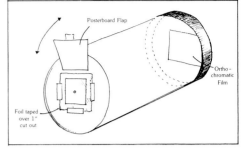

Figure 20.4. A very simple camera can be made from cylindrical box, such as an oatmeal container.

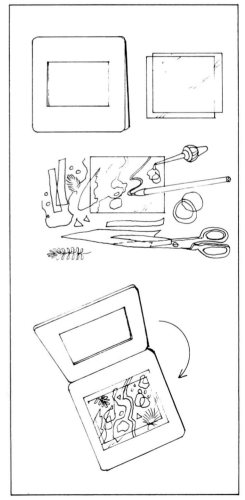

Figure 20.5. While transparent materials work best, a variety of items can be placed between pieces of acetate or clear contact paper to create a texture slide that can be projected.

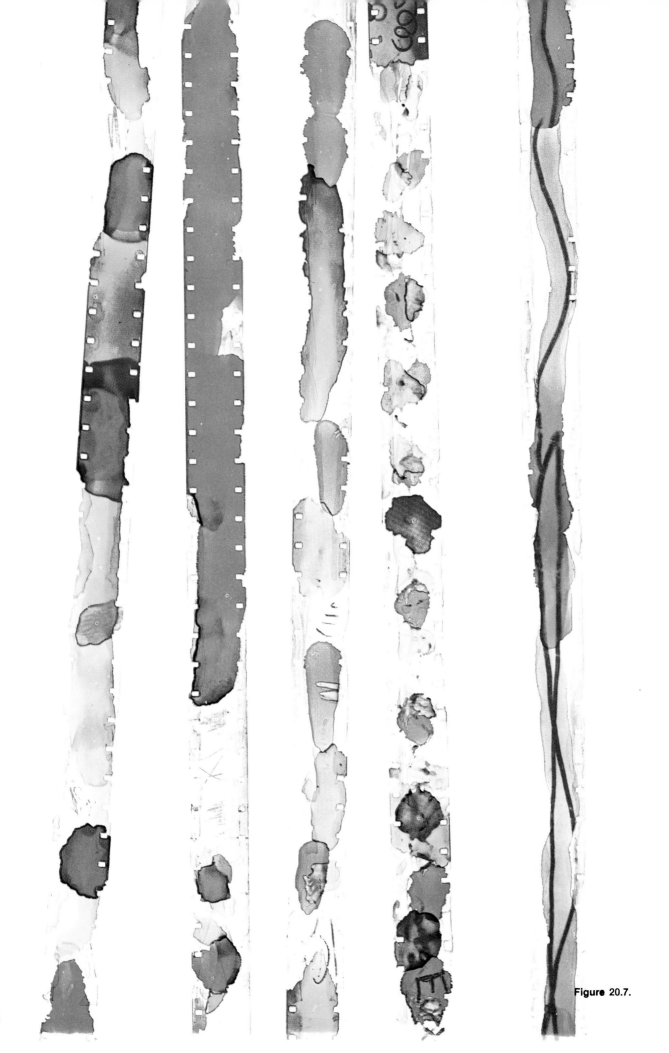

Figure 20.7.

Movies are probably the single most popular form of group entertainment in the world. Since their invention in the 1880s, films or motion pictures have had a tremendous influence on our lives. The art of the motion picture touches us in special ways by adding motion and sound to photographed images. In this way, they come closer than any other expressive form to convincing us of the truth and reality of the images they show.

While the creation of most visual art involves one artist, the production of a major film requires the creative contributions of many people. Directors, actors, cameramen, set designers, and costumers all take part. Of course, to use film as a creative tool does not necessarily mean that you need a budget of millions and a cast of thousands! Many students, with the simplest of movie cameras and equipment, are finding that film is just the right tool for their creative ideas.

Until a few years ago, movies were the only way to capture the world in motion. However, television, plus the invention of videotape, cameras, and recorders, give artists other tools for making images move. In fact, today many schools and individuals own video cameras and equipment.

ANIMATION

A favorite form of filmmaking for many students is **animation** [an•i•MAY•shun]. **Animation** is a film technique in which drawings are given the illusion of motion by being repeated and shown through a projector. An older version of the modern film camera was once a favorite children's toy called the **zoetrope** [ZO•eh•trope] (Figure 20.6).

Another simple kind of animation is possible. Figure 20.7 shows clear strips of 16-mm film that have been cleared by developing or bleaching. [CAUTION: Bleach fumes are dangerous. Bleach should only be used under a teacher's supervision.]

Shapes and lines can be drawn directly onto the film with transparent markers. [CAUTION: Permanent markers and colored inks can stain clothes and emit dangerous fumes. Use only in well-ventilated areas.] It is important to remember that for a film image to be seen by the eye, it must be repeated at least twenty-four times! This makes it difficult to "draw" a story using this technique. Shapes, colors, and lines work best.

Figure 20.7. Clear film can be marked and colored in a number of ways to create a simple motion picture. It is fun to add a sound track also. Any kind of music seems to work.

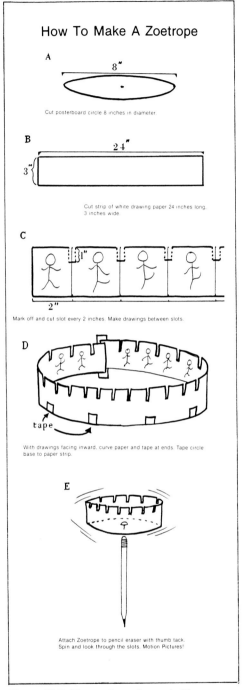

How To Make A Zoetrope

A — 8″ — Cut posterboard circle 8 inches in diameter.

B — 24″ — 3″ — Cut strip of white drawing paper 24 inches long, 3 inches wide.

C — 1″ — 2″ — Mark off and cut slot every 2 inches. Make drawings between slots.

D — tape — With drawings facing inward, curve paper and tape at ends. Tape circle base to paper strip.

E — Attach Zoetrope to pencil eraser with thumb tack. Spin and look through the slots. Motion Pictures!

Figure 20.6. The zoetrope is a primitive version of today's modern motion pictures. Larger versions can be made by drawing the images on cash register tape.

Figure 20.8. Like any other art tool, the computer is only as creative as the artist who uses it. Computers don't make art; people do.

COMPUTER ART

What does the future hold for art equipment, materials, and techniques? It is difficult to tell. New processes and tools for art expression are developed at an astounding rate each year. Indeed, artists of the future may use equipment never before dreamed of as art tools. Remember, artists are inventors. They have a way of imagining and discovering new materials to express their ideas.

A perfect example is one of the newest and most exciting art forms—computer graphics (Figure 20.8). Of course, the computer does not create the art, the artist does. The computer is just another tool, like brushes, pencils, or stone chisels. Who would have dreamed that computers, designed to organize and retrieve large amounts of information, would become "paint brushes"?

Artists, using computers, can produce a still image like a drawing or painting, or animate it like a movie. By now, you have probably seen many examples in films and television commercials using computer animation. Television commercials use it for selling everything from jeans to hamburgers. If you are a fan of today's science fiction and fantasy movies, you have no doubt been dazzled by "special effects" created by computers. In fact, some visions of the future are possible only through computer animation.

If you have a personal computer, you have probably already tried your hand at one of the many art or "paint" programs available for your computer. Everyday, more complex and elaborate computer **software** for graphics or drawing are developed. **Software** are programs that are run on a computer. The computer itself is **hardware**.

What does the distant future hold for art? No one knows. But, if the past is any indication, it should be filled with amazing things. Already artists are starting to think about the expressive potential of lasers and **holographs** (photographic images with the illusion of three-dimensions). The future for visual artists is challenging and full of promise. And, while technology will continue to provide exciting and stimulating tools and materials for creating art, the most important element will remain the artist. Art is made **for** people, **by** people. The adventure continues!

Photographing the West

In some people's opinion, Erwin E. Smith was a lucky little boy. He grew up at a time when the West of myth and legend was still around to be seen and recorded. At the beginning of the 20th century, you could still find real cowboys, cattle drives, and chuck wagons. Cattle were herded from horseback, not in a pickup truck! Most of the wild places of the West were still pretty wild. And young boys could dream of living the life of a cowboy.

Erwin Smith enjoyed everything about the cowboy life. He often worked on his uncle's L.C.S. Ranch, and several other ranches in the area. But, a love for the cowboy life, didn't prevent him from being interested in art. His mother was a fine painter and encouraged his interest. However, when he received his first camera, he knew he had found his life's work.

Smith taught himself photography. He even learned to develop his own pictures. And it wasn't hard to decide what to photograph. The western landscape and the lifestyle of the cowboy became his main subjects.

Over the years Smith made hundreds of photographs. They provide an invaluable record of a period in American history and a lifestyle that no longer exists. What great western artists like Frederic Remington and Charles Russell did with paint and sculpture, Erwin Smith did with photography.

To acknowledge his art and contribution to American history, the Eastman Kodak Company collected many of his photographs into a traveling exhibition which toured the United States. His photographic plates are now part of the Library of Congress Photographic Collection in Washington, D.C. You can also see one hundred of Smith's photographs at the Texas Memorial Museum in Austin. Quite an accomplishment for a cowboy with a camera!

Amon Carter Museum, Fort Worth, Texas.

BORN: 1886
DIED: 1947
BIRTHPLACE:
Honey Grove, Texas

Figure 20.9. *Erwin E. Smith.* JA Ranch, Texas. 1907. The Erwin E. Smith Collection of the Library of Congress on deposit at the Amon Carter Museum.

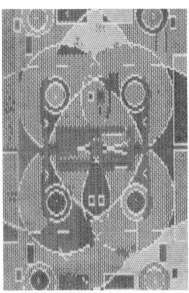

Student work.

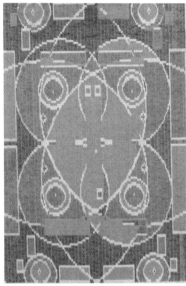

Student work.

Did you learn

- The definitions of these words and phrases: printing; negative; develop; cropping; exposing; enlarging; animation; zoetrope; software; hardware; holograms?
- Three things that a photographer can do to change a photograph?
- How to make a sunprint?
- How to build a pinhole camera?
- How to make a zoetrope?

Understanding and Evaluation

- Collect a number of photographs from several different magazines. Apply the four levels of art criticism to one. How does it compare with a painting? See if you can tell whether the photographer used developing, enlarging, or cropping to achieve the results.
- As you watch television, keep a record of the number of commercials featuring foods that are shown during a two-hour period. What time of the day are most food commercials shown?

Seeing and Creating

- Under the direction of your teacher, make a sunprint. Use a variety of objects. Arrange them in a composition that is balanced asymmetrically. [**CAUTION:** Be careful around any chemicals, such as the hydrogen peroxide, needed to develop the blueprint paper. Be sure there is adequate ventilation.]
- Either with a camera of your own, or a pinhole camera you have made, take some portrait photographs of family and friends. Try to compose your photographs, not just snap a picture. Think about the art elements and design principles when composing your picture.
- Make a set of slides for projecting. When your slide is projected, make a sketch of the composition. Use it for a drawing or a painting. If your slide is arranged carefully according to the principles of design, your drawing and painting will be also.

- **Aerial perspective**—a painting technique devised to create an illusion of depth and distance by *dulling* the intensity of color, and *reducing* contrast between values.
- **Abstract**—an artwork without a realistic presentation of subject matter.
- **Addition**—a method of creating texture and decoration in clay by the addition of other pieces of clay to the surface.
- **Aesthetics**—the study of what is beautiful and why.
- **Allegory**—a symbolic story or fable.
- **Analogous**—color scheme which employs a related group or family or colors.
- **Analysis**—the second level of art criticism. Offers information on how a work is put together or composed using the art elements and design principles.
- **Anatomy**—the study of the physical structure of animals.
- **Animation**—the process of drawing repeated images with small variations to create an illusion of motion. Each drawing is photographed onto film or video tape and shown through a projector or video tape recorder. When shown, the drawings appear to move.
- **Applique**—the fastening or attaching of one fabric onto another.
- **Architect**—a designer of buildings.
- **Architecture**—the art or science of designing buildings.
- **Armature**—a framework of wire or wood used inside a sculpture to support it until the outer covering hardens or becomes firm.
- **Art criticism**—the evaluation of a work of art.
- **Ashcan School**—an art movement established during the first decade of the 20th century. The artworks were characterized by realistic depictions of scenes from everyday life.
- **Assembling**—putting something together. A sculpture process in which objects or materials are attached to form a whole.
- **Association**—a connection between ideas.
- **Asymmetrical balance**—compositional balance achieved with the use of unequal components or elements. No central axis is used.
- **Axis**—the central line or area dividing a symmetrically balanced composition.
- **Background**—the area on a picture plane that is at the top or furthest from the viewer.
- **Batik**—the technique of creating patterns on cloth by applying hot wax to areas of cloth and dying the cloth where there is no wax. Batik is a resist technique.
- **Beater**—the part on a loom which brings one row of weaving down onto the previous row. On simple looms, a comb-like beater is used for the purpose.
- **Bisqueware**—clay fired in a kiln.
- **Botanist**—individual who studies plant life.
- **Brainstorming**—a way to enhance creative thinking. During a brainstorming session, all ideas, no matter how outlandish, are accepted and evaluated for later use.
- **Brayer**—small rubber roller for applying printing ink to a plate.
- **Bronze**—a metal alloy consisting of tin and copper.
- **Caricature**—an exaggerated image; usually a portrait.
- **Carving**—a process used for sculpting. Material is cut away in order to reveal forms.
- **Ceramics**—the art of making objects of clay. Most often used to refer to pottery rather than sculpture.
- **Collage**—visual composition made by attaching materials directly to a surface. Cloth, paper, cardboard, and real objects may all be used.
- **Color scheme**—special arrangement of colors used by artists.
- **Complementary**—color scheme in which a color complement—red/green; blue/orange; yellow/violet—predominates.
- **Constellation**—an arrangement of stars suggesting the outline of figures and animals.
- **Contrast**—the difference in value (light and dark); color (bright and dull, warm and cool); texture (rough and smooth); etc.
- **Converge**—to come together.
- **Crafts**—objects designed and made to be functional or useful, as well as aesthetically pleasing. Weaving, stitchery, and jewelry—are all crafts.
- **Cropping**—focusing on an image by reducing surrounding imagery. Cutting away surplus material.
- **Crosshatching**—a drawing technique in which value is created with line. Repeated lines are drawn in one direction, then crossed by other lines to darken the value of the area.
- **Crowquill pen**—a pen consisting of a staff and a nib or point. To use, these pens are dipped into a bottle of ink.
- **Decalcomania**—a painting technique invented by artist Max Ernst. Materials, such as plastic or paper, are pressed into wet paint and pulled away to leave a texture.
- **Description**—the first level of art criticism. Includes information, such as who painted the work; what's in it; etc.
- **Develop**—a process for revealing the photographed images on negative film.
- **Diagonal line**—lines that are neither horizontal nor vertical.
- **Edition**—a complete set of prints from one printing.

GLOSSARY

- **Emphasis**—giving special attention to an area in a visual composition. Sometimes referred to as the point of emphasis or focal point.
- **Enlarging**—making something larger. Small photographic prints or slides can be enlarged to poster size if desired.
- **Evaluation**—level four of art criticism. This level asks for an opinion or judgment on the quality of the work.
- **Exposing**—revealing a negative film to a light source. As a camera shutter is opened, light exposes the film, recording the desired image.
- **Facade**—the front of a building.
- **Fauve**—art movement during the early part of the 20th century. Works are characterized by bold, expressive color.
- **Focal point**—another name for point of emphasis. The area of a visual composition that is dominant or that attracts the most attention.
- **Foreground**—the area on a picture plane that is at the bottom and closest to the viewer.
- **Form**—the three-dimensional representation of a shape.
- **Freeform**—referring to shapes and forms that do not conform to specifically defined contours. Freeform shapes and forms are frequently organic in nature or character.
- **Frottage**—a printing or drawing technique in which the texture of an object is transferred to drawing paper by rubbing a crayon or other drawing tool over paper placed on top of the texture.
- **Functional**—made to be used. Craft objects are functional, as well as aesthetic in purpose.
- **Futurism**—an art movement around the turn of the century. The artists of this movement were interested in the future as represented by fast modes of transportation and machines.
- **Futurists**—a group of artists around the turn of the 20th century who tried to illustrate motion and speed in their artworks.
- **Geometric**—having straight lines and precise angles. Includes shapes such as rectangles, squares, triangles, and circles. Also includes forms such as cubes, spheres, and cones.
- **Gesture drawing**—a quick sketch used to capture the movement or position of a figure.
- **Glazing**—covering a ceramic sculpture or container with a glass-like surface. Ceramic glazes are made up of ground particles of glass melted in a kiln.
- **Greenware**—clay objects which have been air-dried, but have not yet been fired in a kiln.
- **Hardware**—all equipment associated with a computer—the keyboard, monitor, disk drives, printer, etc.
- **Hologram**—photographic process which creates the illusion of three-dimensions.

- **Horizon/eye level**—in linear perspective, horizontal line representing the eye-level viewpoint of the viewer.
- **Horizontal lines**—lines which lie parallel to the natural horizon.
- **Hue**—the name of a color such as red, blue, green, etc.
- **Human-made environment**—all objects, structures, and surroundings made by human beings. Everything not part of the natural environment.
- **Implied lines**—lines found in natural and human-made environments and created by edges, cracks, and other images that suggest lines to the human eye.
- **Impression**—a method of creating texture in clay by pressing a tool or object onto the surface of damp clay.
- **Impressionism**—art movement from the late 19th century. Began in France with the work of Claude Monet. Characterized by paint applied in small dabs or strokes of color.
- **India ink**—a black, permanent ink used for drawing and writing. India ink can be applied with either a crowquill pen or a brush.
- **Intensity**—the brightness or dullness of a color.
- **Intermediate colors**—colors made by mixing a secondary and a primary color together—blue-green, yellow-orange, etc.
- **Interpretation**—level three of art criticism, gives an opinion of what the meaning of the art work is.
- **Kinetic art**—works of art that move, either through the use of motors, or natural forces, such as air or water.
- **Leather hard**—condition of unfired clay when most of the moisture has left. At this stage, clay cannot be modeled, but can be carved and burnished (polished).
- **Linear perspective**—a system for creating the illusion of three-dimensional space on a two-dimensional surface.
- **Loom**—frame which holds the warp threads taut for weaving.
- **Macramé**—the technique of knotting.
- **Medium**—a material used for art, such as pencil, crayon, ink, paint, etc.; the plural form is media.
- **Middle Ages**—a historical period (5th-15th century, A.D.), during which many great cathedrals were built, such as Chartres.
- **Middle ground**—the area on a picture plane lying between the foreground and background.
- **Mobile**—a form of sculpture in which elements are suspended for movement.
- **Modeling**—shaping some plastic medium, such as clay, to create a form.
- **Modulate**—to create a smooth transition between values.

- **Monochromatic**—a color scheme in which one color predominates.
- **Monoprint**—a printing technique in which only one copy of a print is made.
- **Movement**—a design principle illustrating motion or the illusion of motion created in a visual composition.
- **Natural environment**—all objects and surroundings are not human-made.
- **Naturalist**—someone who studies nature or natural things, such as animals (zoologist), or plants (botanist).
- **Negative**—photographic film images before development.
- **Negative space**—the area surrounding positive objects or shapes.
- **One-point perspective**—the use of one vanishing point to create a perspective view, in which structures show one surface as a rectangle or square.
- **Opaque**—cannot be seen through; when paint is applied opaquely it covers the painting surface completely and hides all that is beneath.
- **Op art**—art movement from the mid-1960s; artworks characterized by use of optical tricks and illusions.
- **Organic**—having the character of a living or natural shape or form.
- **Paint medium**—liquid solution that holds pigment.
- **Parallel lines**—lines equal distance apart along their entire length.
- **Photo-realism**—a style of painting and drawing in which the realism of a photograph is the primary goal.
- **Picture plane**—a two-dimensional surface used for painting, drawing, printing, or collage.
- **Pigment**—the particles of color contained in a paint medium.
- **Plastic**—in a flexible state, such as that of damp clay.
- **Plastic state**—a stage in which clay is damp enough to be modeled and formed.
- **Point of view**—the position from which a viewer observes a scene.
- **Portrait**—image of a person.
- **Proportion**—having to do with the relationship between parts of a whole.
- **Primary colors**—those colors which cannot be mixed: red, blue, yellow.
- **Printing**—transferring a photographic image to paper.
- **Printing plate**—surface onto which a drawing is made in preparation for printing; materials such as wood, linoleum, and plaster form plates used for inscribing with sharp tools.
- **Relief**—a sculpture or carving in which figures stand out from a flat surface.

- **Renaissance**—a historical period (1400-1600 A.D.) during which there was a great awakening of interest and knowledge about art and science.
- **Repetition**—the use of repeating elements in a visual composition.
- **Scale**—a size comparison made against a common standard, for example, human-size scale.
- **Sculpture in the round**—sculpture created to be seen from all sides.
- **Secondary colors**—colors or hues made from mixing two primary colors together; green, orange, or violet.
- **Shade**—value made by mixing black with a color.
- **Shape**—a two-dimensional area of space enclosed with a line or made with color or texture.
- **Shuttle**—a wooden or cardboard piece around which thread or yarn is wrapped to pass between the warp threads of a weaving; holds the weft thread or yarn.
- **Silhouette**—the profile or outline of a shape.
- **Simulated**—not real or artificially created; an illusion.
- **Sketch**—a drawing, usually a working or preliminary drawing, rather than a detailed work.
- **Software**—the programs that run computers and allow interaction with computers.
- **Spontaneous drawing**—a drawing that is made on the spot; presented in a fresh, quick style.
- **Stencil**—a silhouette or profile of an object cut from paper or cardboard used as a pattern for printing.
- **Stereotype**—image or idea that a group can recognize and agree upon.
- **Stippling**—a drawing technique in which value is created by dots; the more dots used, the darker the value.
- **Stitchery**—sewing or decorating with needle-and-thread or yarn.
- **Stone Age**—a historical period characterized by the use of tools made of stone.
- **Surrealism**—art movement that used the subconscious and the world of dreams as inspiration for art. Surrealism means "super real."
- **Symbol**—an image that represents or stands for something else.
- **Symmetrical balance**—compositional balance achieved by placing equal elements on either side of a central axis.
- **Tactile**—having to do with the sense of touch.
- **Terra Cotta**—a reddish-brown clay used for sculpture and ceramics.
- **Texture**—surface quality or character.
- **Three-dimensional**—having height, width, and depth.
- **Throwing wheel**—piece of equipment for shaping a pot; consists of a seat, motor, and rotating wheel;

the force of the turning clay adds to the shaping of the pot.

- **Tint**—value made by mixing white with a color.
- **Tjanting tool**—tool used for applying hot wax to cloth for batik.
- **Transparent**—can be seen through; transparent paint, such as watercolor, does not completely hide what is underneath.
- **Two-point perspective**—the use of two vanishing points to create a perspective view in which structures are seen from corners.
- **Typography**—the art of designing and arranging type or lettering.
- **Unity**—a feeling of wholeness or oneness in a visual composition; elements appear to belong together.
- **Utilitarian**—designed for practical uses; that which is primarily functional.
- **Value**—the degree of light or dark in an area or color.
- **Vanishing point**—a point representing the center of vision of the viewer in a linear perspective drawing.
- **Variety**—the use of many different elements to add interest to a visual composition.
- **Vertical lines**—lines which are upright and at a right angle to the horizon line.
- **Visual analysis**—a method of examining an object or scene to learn more about its structure and details.
- **Visual paradox**—an image that defies common sense and the laws of nature.
- **Visual rhythm**—the use of visual elements to establish a beat or repetition in an art composition.
- **Warm and cool colors**—categories of colors.
- **Warp thread**—the vertical thread held taut by the loom.
- **Wedging**—process of kneading clay to remove air bubbles.
- **Weft thread**—the horizontal thread woven between the warp threads.
- **Woodcut**—a type of print made by cutting lines or grooves into a wood block; ink covers the uncut portions of the block and the lines are left free of ink; when printed, the lines appear white.
- **Working drawing**—a quick sketch done to be used as reference for a later work.
- **Zoetrope**—instrument for creating the illusion of motion through animation.
- **Zoologist**—individual who studies animal life.

INDEX OF SUBJECTS

INDEX

INDEX OF ARTISTS